Gerald Herbert Portal

The british mission to Uganda in 1893

With the diary of the late Captain Raymond Portal and an introduction by Lord Cromer

Gerald Herbert Portal

The british mission to Uganda in 1893
With the diary of the late Captain Raymond Portal and an introduction by Lord Cromer

ISBN/EAN: 9783743365230

Manufactured in Europe, USA, Canada, Australia, Japa

Cover: Foto ©ninafisch / pixelio.de

Manufactured and distributed by brebook publishing software (www.brebook.com)

Gerald Herbert Portal

The british mission to Uganda in 1893

THE
BRITISH MISSION TO UGANDA
IN 1893

BY THE LATE
SIR GERALD PORTAL, K.C.M.G., C.B.
THE BRITISH COMMISSIONER

EDITED WITH A MEMOIR
BY
RENNELL RODD, C.M.G.

WITH THE DIARY OF THE LATE CAPTAIN RAYMOND PORTAL
AND AN INTRODUCTION BY LORD CROMER, G.C.M.G.

ILLUSTRATED FROM PHOTOGRAPHS BY COLONEL RHODES

LONDON
EDWARD ARNOLD, 37 BEDFORD STREET, W.C.
Publisher to the India Office
1894

EDITOR'S PREFACE

SOME six months ago, as the good ship *Sindh* of the Messageries Maritimes was crossing the line on her homeward voyage, bringing Sir Gerald Portal, Colonel Rhodes, and myself back from Zanzibar, the papers from which the following pages have been compiled were first placed in my hands for perusal. I could but little anticipate, as I read them then, that it would ever fall to my lot to prepare them for the press, or that the valued friend who seemed so full of life and vigour, so eagerly looking forward after a protracted absence to home and all that it means to those whose lot is cast among alien faces and in distant lands, had written the last word of the record he had modestly and unassumingly compiled. The sheets of the first eight chapters had been roughly drafted in the intervals of arduous work, of weary marches and watchings by the bed of sick companions, and more than half the story was still to be written. It was his request that I should read through the chapters which he had prepared, and make such suggestions as might occur to me with regard to their style and matter. I have little doubt that the verdict which I then expressed as to their keen and living interest will be fully endorsed by all who read them, and that the regret which they will feel at the abrupt conclusion of the written narrative will approve the advice which I offered, that he should complete the book and give it to the public.

The tragic ending of a life so bright in promise, so rich in actual achievement, has left such intentions unfulfilled. And now, in addition to the fact that the information contained in his manuscripts and notes possesses a vital and most present value, the deep personal interest aroused by his almost romantic personality and the pathos of his untimely death, has impressed on those into whose hands these papers have passed the sense of a duty to his memory, and a response to the universal sympathy displayed, which may best be fulfilled by publishing them even in their incomplete form.

At the request of friends and relations I have undertaken the task of preparing them for the press, somewhat reluctantly indeed, not because I could hesitate to do all in my power to honour the memory of such a friend, but rather because, in the first place, I did not feel myself competent to deal with matter largely outside the range of my own personal experience; and, secondly, because when the request was made, so great a portion of my time was claimed by the public service that I knew it was scarcely possible for me to do justice to any additional work. The companion, however, of his eventful journey home, Colonel Rhodes, had once more left England on a long voyage beyond easy reach of communication, and his return was very uncertain. At the same time it was felt that the publication should not be delayed, and that in this hurrying age of ever-changing interests and distractions the present moment was the appropriate one.

It was generally agreed that it would be beyond the powers of any editor to fill up the gaps in the narrative so as to render the book a full and complete history of Uganda and of the British Mission, such as Sir Gerald Portal had intended it to be, and that all that could now be attempted was rather to make the notes and papers which he left into a personal record and memorial, from which might be gathered something of the nature and character of the man whose loss has been so sincerely deplored.

These papers consist, in the first place, of eight written chapters, left, as I have already intimated, in the rough-and-ready manner of their original conception, which would no doubt before publication have received a finishing touch from one whose feeling for literary style was considerable; secondly, of a pencilled Diary carefully kept in a pocket-book from day to day;

and, finally, of a certain number of letters. In dealing with these materials I have left the written chapters almost untouched, correcting only here and there a hasty phrase, supplying a deficient or eliminating a superfluous word. It was characteristic of his method that he wrote both his public and his private correspondence with but little correction, deliberately and clearly, with considerable force and felicity of expression. Beyond these few additions or erasures, therefore, and the need of an occasional footnote, these chapters have called for little editing.

The Diary, on the other hand, written solely as personal memoranda, and the letters intended only for the eyes of near relations and friends, contain many matters of a purely private character which claim a reverent reticence. In dealing with the latter, I have quoted long extracts from them for the most part, withholding only those portions of an intimate correspondence which seemed too sacred to print. From the former I have extracted all the passages which appear to me essential as illustrating the incidents of travel, the progress of the Mission, the aspect of the country, and the character of the writer himself, beginning from the period where the written narrative breaks off up to the return to Kikuyu, the half-way station on the journey home. A few connecting links have been supplied, a word for clearness' sake inserted here and there, or a note where occasion arose. With regard to the latter portion of the Diary, which deals with the march from Kikuyu to the Tana river, and the journey down the river to the coast, it appeared to me that as much of the route lay through untried country, and as the history of that journey would never be written now, even at the risk of the pages growing monotonous, the daily entries should be given in full as material for future reference. The hard struggle of each day's progress fills its appointed place in the pages of the pocket-book, to the exclusion of all outside thoughts or personal reflections. The last section contains, therefore, a simple transcript from the note-book, while no better summary could be made of all these experiences than that which he has drawn up himself in the comprehensive letter with which it concludes. Such criticisms as are there made on the cartography of previous explorers it seemed to me should not be omitted in the interests of the advance of geographical knowledge, and I feel assured that neither Captain Dundas nor Mr. Hobley will resent the suggestion of rectifications to be made in their valuable maps and records. On the other hand, it has been a matter of much regret that we have been unable to communicate with Colonel Rhodes in order to obtain possession of a map which he is known to have made to illustrate this portion of the journey. If I have not erased the mention of my own name here and there in the Diary or letters, it is because that mention is connected, in my own mind at any rate, with that kindly solicitude of the writer for the health and welfare of others which these private memoranda reveal, for which I often have had cause to be grateful to him.

It was Sir Gerald's intention to have prefaced his book with an introductory chapter on Zanzibar, the famous metropolis of East Africa, now flourishing as a British Protectorate. For various and sufficient reasons I have not attempted to supply the missing chapter, but some account of his work there will be found in the accompanying Memoir.

This record would not be complete without more ample allusion to the name and services of Captain Raymond Portal, Sir Gerald's elder brother, whose death from malarial fever in Kampala cast a gloom on the latter months of the Mission. The Diary, which he also kept since the first day of departure, has been placed in my hands, and after reading it I did not hesitate to include it in the book. It is like himself, fresh, manly, and full of a simple humour, and it will at any rate have a very genuine interest for the friends whom his frank and chivalrous personality inspired with a genuine devotion; for seldom has a man died more beloved or more regretted by his associates than Raymond Portal.

In conclusion, it is my duty to state that, having

obtained permission to edit these papers, I am bound to disclaim as an official all responsibility for opinions expressed in them. The time at my disposal before the date announced for their publication has been very brief, and fully occupied with other important work. It has, however, been a labour of love, though, indeed, a very sad one, for recent circumstances had, after long separations, brought the brothers and myself very near together once more, and the death of those two friends, under conditions so intensely tragic, is touched for me with a pathos which words of mine could but ill express.

RENNELL RODD.

INTRODUCTION

By Lord Cromer, G.C.M.G.

In performing the sorrowful task of writing an introduction to Sir Gerald's Portal's Diary, I am under one considerable disadvantage, and that is that I have never seen the Diary itself. As the work is being published in London, and as I am writing at Cairo, I have necessarily been unable to read the manuscript.

But if I know nothing of the Diary, I knew a great deal of the man who wrote it. He was, in fact, one of my dearest friends.

Sir Gerald—or, to use the name by which he was known to those who were intimate with him—Gerry Portal was one of the best specimens of that class of Englishmen, pre-eminently healthy in mind and body, who, to the great benefit of their country, issue forth year by year from our public schools. He was a fervent Etonian. He may be said to have passed through his short but honourable career singing *Floreat Etona*.

My first acquaintance with Portal dates from September 1883, when I was appointed to be English Consul-General in Egypt. Portal, who had entered into the Diplomatic Service four years previously, was at that time one of the staff of the British Agency at Cairo. With two short interruptions— the first in 1887, when he went on a special mission to Abyssinia, and the second in 1888, when he took temporary charge of the Zanzibar Agency—he remained on my staff till the spring of 1891, a period of nearly eight years.

During all those years—some of them years of much trouble and anxiety—Gerry Portal was not only of great assistance to me in my work, which was at times very heavy, but was also the life and soul of our "family" party at the Cairo Agency. Handsome, plucky, chivalrous, genial, equally at home in the chancery, the drawing-room, or the polo-field, this spirited young Englishman possessed every quality calculated to endear him to those with whom he was brought in contact.

Before Portal had served under me for long, I discerned that he was destined for more than a social success in life. In the autumn of 1887 his opportunity came. I was requested by Lord Salisbury to recommend some one to go on a special mission to Abyssinia. It was at the time somewhat difficult to foretell what would be the precise nature of the difficulties which the English envoy would have to encounter. It appeared to me, however, that the main qualifications likely to be required were iron nerves, a cool head, and bodily strength capable of enduring fatigue. If to these I could add sound common-sense and no inconsiderable degree of diplomatic skill, I thought that I should find an ideal man to answer Lord Salisbury's purposes. All these qualities I found combined in Gerry Portal. I had, therefore, no hesitation in recommending him to Lord Salisbury. My recommendation was accepted.

The adventures of the whole party have been told by Portal himself in his book, *My Mission to Abyssinia*, with the becoming modesty which distinguished him, and which led him to underrate alike the dangers to which he was exposed and the skill which he displayed in meeting them. He describes how the whole party nearly died of thirst, and although their adventures did not end with this narrow escape, it will not be necessary for me to follow up in detail the events which subsequently occurred. But I may mention that I well remember the anxiety which began to grow upon me as week after week passed without any news from Portal. Knowing the disturbed and excited state of Abyssinia at the time, I became alarmed for his safety. I was just beginning to make arrangements with a leading Austrian merchant at Cairo, who had commercial relations with the interior of Abyssinia, with a view to obtaining information as to what had occurred, when, to my great relief, I received a telegram from Massowah on the morning of Christmas Day, informing me that Portal and his party had arrived safely at the Italian outposts. That telegram turned the Christmas Day of 1887 at the Cairo Agency from one of sharp anxiety into one of gladness.

b

The courage and judgment displayed by Portal in his Abyssinian work clearly marked him out for promotion at no distant date. After having on several occasions been placed in temporary charge of the Cairo Agency, he was appointed, in 1891, to be Agent and Consul-General at Zanzibar at a time of much difficulty in connection with Zanzibar affairs. The manner in which he conducted his work at this responsible post fully justified the choice which had been made. Eventually he went on the Uganda Mission, with results which are now known to the world. The deadly African climate proved fatal to his gallant brother, who accompanied him, and ultimately to himself, for I conceive that his constitution was undermined by fever and by the fatigues which he underwent in his Uganda journey.

I have no hesitation in saying that Gerry Portal's premature death was a heavy loss to the Sovereign and to the nation whom he had served so well. The Ministers under whom he had held appointment—Lord Salisbury and Lord Rosebery—have borne emphatic testimony to the esteem in which they regarded him and to his value as a public servant. England, albeit prolific in men of courage and ability, can ill afford to lose before their time those of her sons who resemble Gerry Portal. I cannot doubt that a useful and even brilliant career lay before him. More especially was he born to be an Oriental diplomatist and administrator. Besides those high and attractive qualities to which I have already alluded, he possessed others of great value—excellent manners, tact, moral courage, a firm will, great capacity for promptitude and decision in action, and that keen and ready perception of the realities of Eastern life and politics which appears to come to some almost instinctively, whilst it is not acquired by others after years of residence in the East. Thus mentally and morally endowed, my strong conviction is that, had he lived, he would have left no inconsiderable mark on the history of his country. He died at the moment when his high qualities, which were well known to his intimate friends, were just beginning to be appreciated by a wider circle of his countrymen.

I do not dare to constitute myself the interpreter of the feelings entertained by those who were nearest and dearest to Gerry Portal. To these I can but tender an expression of respectful and heartfelt sympathy with their sorrow. And as concerns the many others who, like myself, regarded Gerry Portal with feelings which may more correctly be described as those of affection rather than of friendship, I can but use the commonplace, but in this instance, very true phrase, that he will ever live in our memory. Within my own recollection few more sad events have happened than the untimely death of this fine young Englishman at a moment when to all appearances the prospect of a long, happy, and useful life lay before him. Speaking for myself alone, I may add that I took a special pride in helping to train Gerry Portal, that I regarded him as one who might not improbably be my successor in Egypt, and that both Lady Cromer and myself entertained towards him feelings of almost parental affection. His unexpected death in the prime of life dashed suddenly to the ground all the hopes which I had founded on his future.

CROMER.

CAIRO, 4th May 1894.

CONTENTS

	PAGE
INTRODUCTION BY LORD CROMER, G.C.M.G.	xiii
MEMOIR OF THE LATE SIR GERALD PORTAL	xxv

PART I

CHAPTER I

My appointment as H.M. Commissioner to Uganda—The staff of the Mission—Equipment of the caravan—The main body despatched to Kikuyu—A farewell state-visit to the Sultan of Zanzibar—We start upon our journey on the 1st of January 1893 . . . 5

CHAPTER II

We arrive at Port Reitz—By the "Central African Railway" to our encampment at Mazeras—An awkward squad—The first day's march 24

CHAPTER III

The day's programme—Crossing the great Taro Plain—The first station of the East Africa Company—A splendid view of Mount Kilimanjaro—Bad news from Kikuyu—A flourishing Industrial Mission 39

CHAPTER IV

The scene of a Masai raid—Our first rhinoceros—Arrival at Machakos—Victualling the caravan—On the war-path—I bag a lion—The Wa-kamba tribe and warriors—The Wa-Kikuyu . 63

CHAPTER V

A state of siege at Kikuyu—An ivory caravan—We push on for Uganda—The game-abounding prairies of Lake Naivasha—First introduction to Masai warriors—The Masai tribe—The Salt Lake of Elmenteita—Hartebeest and antelope—An African forest . . . 86

CHAPTER VI

West of the watershed—Extinction of the buffalo and eland—The Wanderobbo tribe—The fertile Kavirondo district—Mtanda—We cross the Nile and camp in Uganda—The Ripon Falls—Amidst civilisation and rifles—We enter the Fort of Kampala on the 17th of March . . . 117

CHAPTER VII

A short survey of the conditions of the country—The districts suitable for European settlement—Facilities for traffic—Suggestions for improving the road—Proposed regulations for caravans and formation of stations . . . 151

CHAPTER VIII

The kingdom of Uganda; its climate and population—The King and Council—Provincial governors—Oppressive taxation—Intelligence and religion of the peasantry . . . 179

PART II

CHAPTER I

At Kampala—Visit to King Mwanga—Arrangements for a division of territories between the Protestant and Catholic Missions—The slave question—The queen-mother—From Kampala to the Ntebe Hills—Kaima's case—Illness of Captain Portal . . . 205

CHAPTER II

Captain Portal's illness—He returns to Kampala; is joined by his brother—His death and funeral—Sir Gerald Portal's expedition starts from Kampala for Kikuyu . . . 236

CHAPTER III

The return journey—Difficulties of the march during the rainy season—Trouble in Uganda—Illness of Colonel Rhodes—Selim Bey is handed over to the Commissioner—Arrival at Kikuyu—Death of Selim Bey 246

CHAPTER IV

The Tana route to Uganda—Crossing the Malanga river—Difficulties on the route—The Grand Falls—Along the Tana river to Ndura—From Ndura to Witu—Zanzibar 267

PART III

DIARY OF CAPTAIN RAYMOND PORTAL, WITH AN INTRODUCTION   319

EPILOGUE   349

LIST OF ILLUSTRATIONS

	PAGE
Portrait of Sir Gerald Portal, from a drawing by the Marchioness of Granby	Frontispiece
Tippoo Tib	xxxiv
Ripon Falls. From a sketch by C. Whymper	4
Sudi Bin Suleiman, Native Headman of the Mission Caravan	40
My Tent	41
Group from a Caravan preparing to start with Ivory	87
Group at Kikuyu	91
Masai Warriors in their War-Paint	99
Masai Women at Lake Naivasha	102
A 90-lb. Tusk bought in Kabras	125
Crossing the Nzoia River	129
The Nile below the Ripon Falls	135
Embarking to cross the Nile	137
The Nile after leaving Lake Victoria	140
Bridging a Swamp in Uganda	143
A Group of Uganda Natives	198
Port Alice	204
Mwanga, King of Uganda	210
Bishop Tucker outside his Church at Namirembe	211
Group at Kampala; 20th March	212
The King's Drums	213
Apollo, Katikiro of Uganda	216
Lowering the Company's Flag and preparing to hoist the Union Jack at the Fort at Kampala	218
Soudanese Troops at Kampala—Bayonet Drill	221
Baby Elephant, brought into the Fort at Kampala, being fed on milk	223
A War Canoe	224
Tomb of Mtesa, late King of Uganda	228
The Queen-Mother (Namasole)	229

	PAGE
Dr. Moffat and Dead Hippopotamus, near Port Alice	231
Port Alice	233
Captain Raymond Portal's Grave	240
Natives with Hippopotamus (Victoria Nyanza)	251
A Creeper Bridge near Mumia's	261
Bridge over the Malanga River	272
Swahili Bridge over the Malanga River	276
The Seven Forks, Tana River	280
Canoes on the Beledzoni Canal	300
The Tana River: the Grand Falls	308
Portrait of Captain Raymond Portal	To face page 319
Map	At end

˳ All the Illustrations, with the exception of the Portraits of Sir Gerald Portal and Captain Raymond Portal, are from photographs taken during the expedition by Colonel F. Rhodes, who kindly placed them at the disposal of Sir Gerald Portal for the purposes of this work.

MEMOIR

SIR GERALD HERBERT PORTAL was the second son of Mr. Melville Portal of Laverstoke, and of Lady Charlotte Elliot, daughter of the second Earl of Minto. He was born on the 13th of March 1858, and had therefore not completed his 36th year when a life so remarkable not only for its promise, but also for its actual achievement, came to its untimely close. The handsome face and knightly bearing of the two brothers, Raymond and Gerald Portal, were typical of their family's origin in that southern school of chivalry, where French and English vied in feats of arms under the banners of King John and the Black Prince, in the days when lances were broken in the tilt-yards of Aquitaine. Either of the two brothers, indeed, might well have seemed to recall in form and features the goodly presence of that Raymond de Portal who rode with Bertrand du Guesclin to avenge the death of the Queen of Castile in 1336, and of whose martial deeds the troubadours made songs.

He was educated at Eton in the house of Mr. Marindin, with a number of brilliant young contemporaries, who have already distinguished themselves in various branches of the public service. It is interesting to remark, that already in these youthful days those who watched his early development had discerned many of the characteristics which were especially noticeable in his after life : a courage, namely, in carrying through to the end whatever he had set himself to do, a gift for organisation, a power of influencing others, and of winning the best sort of popularity, together with a rapid perception of a favourable opportunity and a capacity for bestowing all his pains on the work in hand. To quote a concrete instance: there occurred in those days an opportunity for lower boys who displayed any aptitude for bowling to obtain, rather as a task than as the amusement of playtime, instruction in "Upper club" during the vacant hours on the afternoons of whole-school days. Of this somewhat irksome privilege Gerald Portal at once availed himself with a perseverance which no doubt assisted in enabling him later on to realise his first great ambition, namely, to represent his school in the cricket-field, as he did in 1886 and 1887.

He achieved a good position in the school, but was there only credited with fair and not remarkable abilities. His tact, however, and his power of winning confidence were displayed in his excellent management as captain of his house, where also, after gaining experience in the School Debating Society, he was mainly instrumental in starting a local Debating Club—then a somewhat novel institution—which maintained a vigorous life as long as the house lasted. At these debates, curiously enough, were first noticed the eloquence and the command of general knowledge of a younger member of the house, who has now succeeded him as Her Majesty's representative at Zanzibar. He also acted as editor of the *Eton Chronicle* and as Master of the Beagles, and thus his school career may fairly be said to have exemplified once more the truth of the often-quoted opinion, that the qualities which distinguish Englishmen in after life are formed in large measure on the playing-fields. He became a keen sportsman, a fearless rider, something more than an amateur in the understanding of horses, and, it is scarcely necessary to add, proficient in all those exercises in which Englishmen excel.[1]

After leaving school he had intended to matriculate at Oxford, but for some inexplicable reason he failed to satisfy the college examiners, and thus afforded a remarkable instance in support of the theory that examinations are not a final test of ability. This accident was the more curious, since he became, at any rate in later years, a man of wide reading, with considerable literary taste and discrimination.

Abandoning, therefore, the prospect of a university career, he entered the diplomatic service after a due course of studies, and having spent the usual period of training in the Foreign Office, was in 1880 appointed an attaché to the Embassy in Rome, when

---

[1] The Editor is indebted to Mr. Mariadin for the facts concerning Sir Gerald Portal's school career.

Sir Augustus Paget was Her Majesty's representative in that capital.

Two years later he was transferred to Cairo, just at that period of crisis in Egyptian history which culminated in the bombardment of Alexandria, at which he was present. Here in the able school of Sir Evelyn Baring (Lord Cromer) he gained that insight into Oriental life which was afterwards to serve him in such good stead, and no pains were spared by his chief to develop the qualities which he had detected in so apt a pupil. This, indeed, was the turning-point in his life, and those who knew him before, as well as after, a few years' residence in Egypt, could not fail to be struck by the change which had come over him with the responsibilities of a position in which he was annually called upon during the absence of his chief to take charge of the Agency. Some five years after his first arrival in Cairo, he was entrusted with the perilous mission to King John of Abyssinia, the object of which was to pave the way for a peaceful solution of the difficulty with Italy, arising from the disastrous episode of Dogali. The story of that most difficult and eventful journey has been written by himself in the simple and unassuming narrative of *My Mission to Abyssinia*, originally printed for private circulation among friends, and subsequently published by Mr. Edward Arnold.

Without entering into the circumstances which led to the Italian occupation of Massowah, it may suffice to state here that it had very quickly led to disputes with the Abyssinian monarch, who not only resisted the levying of taxes at that port on goods coming into his country, but strenuously denied the right of the Italians to be there at all. Although the coast and its parts had been occupied for some 300 years by Turkey, and had finally been transferred to the Khedive of Egypt, the sleeping traditional claims of the Abyssinians, ousted only by the power of the sword, had never been forgotten, and when the successes of the Mahdi brought about the retirement of the Egyptian garrisons from the Soudan forts and the coastal possessions, they beheld with sullen resentment a new power, hitherto unknown in these regions, stepping in to take possession of what they considered their legitimate reversion. This feeling of resentment and the irritation caused by customs disputes, had reached a dangerous point when Rasalula, governor of the frontier province of Hamazen, returning from his Pyrrhic victory over the Mahdi's forces at Kassala, found the Italians in possession of Sahati, a strategical position some ten miles inland from Monkullu. He assaulted the Italian works without success, but on the day following the engagement he was able to intercept with 10,000 Abyssinians a small force of under 500 men, marching to relieve the garrison of Sahati, in a narrow plain commanded on every side by rocky hills which covered the ambuscaded attack, and they were massacred almost to a man. This disastrous episode was naturally followed by a national cry for vengeance, and preparations for an expedition on a large scale were pushed forward in Italy, while in Abyssinia all available forces were collected, and savage patriotism was stimulated to make ready for a desperate resistance.

As time, however, went on, the magnitude of the task which lay before Italy in embarking on a war of reprisals began to make itself felt, and the prospect of extended operations against a far from contemptible foe in the heart of so savage and inhospitable a country appeared calculated to cramp her free action in Europe, so that calmer counsels began to prevail. It was not, however, until nine months had elapsed after the disaster at Dogali that England was invited to use her considerable influence with the object of averting the imminent war. The whole of Abyssinia was meantime in an ever-increasing ferment, the passions of the undisciplined soldiery were thoroughly inflamed, and every province was a moving camp.

It was into this hotbed of fanaticism that Gerald Portal was instructed to proceed and endeavour to impress upon the king the advisability of a pacification within the short space of five weeks, beyond which, for climatic and other reasons, the Italian Government could not delay warlike operations should the effort be of none effect. In this brief space of time he had secretly to equip and organise his caravan, to reach Massowah, and to make his way to the king's headquarters, wherever they might prove to be. He was accompanied in this expedition by Mr., now Captain, Beech, of the Egyptian army, and by his English servant Hutchisson, who later also followed him to Uganda.

At the outset, on their departure from the Italian headquarters, the party were led by treacherous guides a two-days' march away from water, and there abandoned, to find that all the supplies brought with them had been drained or spilled from the bottles, and they were thus forced to return, under the rays of a pitiless sun, by a path they were not sure of being able to retrace, speechless with thirst, with blackened tongues and lips, to the original point of departure, the interpreter brought from Egypt falling a victim to his sufferings. New guides and porters were hastily collected, and a second start was made. Twice they were detained as prisoners, and throughout they carried their lives in their hands; but in spite of constant opposition and repeated menace, the determination of their leader carried them through. It would occupy too much space here to follow their progress through all the perils and adventures which beset them until the final accomplishment of the mission, or to show how, if it had no other results, it at least served the purpose of gaining time until the march of events in the Soudan created a diversion, and drew the attention of the Abyssinians to another quarter, where the death of King John at the battle of Metemmeh and subsequent internal dissensions finally averted the breaking out of hostilities on the Italian side. The thrilling story is told at length in the volume which has been referred to, and it will here suffice to quote his own words from the preface:—" Few men, even among African travellers, have stood face to face with death so often in the course of a few months,—from want of water, from the decrees of the highest authorities in the land, and at the hands of unscrupulous and over-zealous chiefs, —and have lived, absolutely unhurt, to tell the tale." For his services on this occasion he was rewarded with the C.B.

In 1889 he was selected to take temporary charge of the Agency at Zanzibar, and during his six months' tenure of office there won such golden opinions that in March 1891 he was definitely appointed to succeed Sir Charles Euan Smith at that post. In the meantime he had married Lady Alice Josephine Bertie, daughter of the seventh Earl of Abingdon, who did not hesitate to accompany him to his new destination, where her name will long be remembered for many acts of kindness, and will always be associated with the tropical garden which under her exclusive care rapidly grew up round the residence of Her Majesty's Agent.

Zanzibar had now become a British Protectorate, but as yet it was so little more than in name. The task before him was to make that Protectorate effective, and out of the chaos of an uncontrolled Arab despotism to develop a system of orderly government, to turn the resources of the islands to account for the benefit of the inhabitants, and to reform a thousand abuses. For the work in hand his Egyptian training had especially qualified him. Many of the difficulties to be faced were merely repetitions on a smaller scale of those with which he had grown familiar in Egypt, and a few words

TIPPOO TIB.
From a Photograph by Colonel Rhodes, taken in Zanzibar.

about the conditions prevailing in this metropolis of Eastern Africa will suffice to show how great those difficulties have been.

It is perhaps scarcely necessary, in view of the many books of travel in which our latest Protectorate in Eastern Africa has been described, to enter here upon its antecedent history. It will be remembered that, since the time of its conquest by the Arabs of Muscat, Zanzibar formed an appanage of that sultanate until the death of Sultan Said, when, disputes having arisen among his heirs, the throne of Zanzibar was separated in 1856 from that of Muscat, with the concurrence of the powers chiefly interested, and given to Majid, the son of Said. Majid was succeeded by his son Barghash, a ruler of enlightened views, who visited England, and brought back with him to his African dominions a quantity of European plant and machinery, who acquired steamers to facilitate trade communications, and who greatly extended the dominions, commerce, and influence of Zanzibar, while he throughout maintained the most cordial relations with Great Britain, and relied in all his acts on the friendly counsels of Her Majesty's representative, Sir John Kirk. His force of undisciplined irregulars was placed under the orders of another Englishman, Lieutenant Mathews of H.M.S. *London*, now Sir Lloyd Mathews, K.C.M.G.; and it has been the influence of these two men, their power of sympathy with both native and Arab, and their constant upright and just dealing over a long course of years, which has made the establishment of the British Protectorate a comparatively easy task.

Sultan Barghash derived a very large revenue from the duties which were levied at the coast on all goods coming down from the interior to his ports, and the power of his name was respected in the interior up to the central lakes. But his possessions were ill defined and his sovereignty not uncontested. At the settlement, therefore, which took place at the Conference of Berlin in 1885, the dominions of Zanzibar on the mainland were specified and recognised as extending to a limit of ten miles inland, along the eastern coast between the river Tana to the north and the boundary of Portuguese East Africa to the south. The islands of Lamu, Manda, and Patta were also recognised as belonging to Zanzibar, together with the northern port of Kismayu and those on the Benadir coast, each including a small radius of surrounding territory. Then followed the keenly-contested race of the European powers for the partition and occupation of Africa, and in return for a sum of £200,000, Germany acquired the Zanzibar territories between the Umba river to the north of Zanzibar Island and the Portuguese boundary. The coastal region between the Umba and the Tana was leased to the Imperial British East Africa Company, together with the islands north of the latter river and the Kismayu district, but in these regions the sovereignty of the Sultan was still acknowledged, whereas the cession to Germany was absolute. The actual territories administered directly by the sultanate were, therefore, confined to the two islands of Pemba and Zanzibar, and the ports on the Benadir coast, but these last were also shortly destined to be ceded under lease to Italy. Meanwhile Sultan Barghash had died, and had been succeeded by his brother, Seyyid Khalifa, who reigned but a short time, and was again in turn succeeded by a still younger brother, Seyyid Ali, who occupied the throne at the time of Gerald Portal's second arrival in Zanzibar.

The islands of Pemba and Zanzibar are portions of the same coral reef running nearly parallel with the African coast, from which the latter is separated at the nearest point by a channel not twenty miles in width. They nowhere rise to a height of more than 400 feet above the sea, and are of extreme fertility, producing some four-fifths of all the cloves that are consumed, with magnificent mango groves and cocoanut palm-trees, and it is anticipated that many valuable sorts of spices will here find a congenial soil. The islands are covered with small villages or nests of native huts, but the only town of any importance is Zanzibar itself, the population of which it is difficult to estimate correctly, but which probably contains upwards of 35,000 souls, while the population of the islands is supposed now not much to exceed 150,000, of whom a very large proportion are domestic slaves. The rest are either Arabs, the original population of Swahilis, or British Indians, which last probably number upwards of 6000, and are all to be found in the city occupied as petty traders, merchants, and clerks. A considerable area is occupied in Zanzibar by the palace and its dependencies, by the spacious stone-built houses of the Arabs, of the European and trading community, the missions and the consulates, but a far larger circuit is covered by the wattle and mud huts of the native population with their palm-leaf thatch, the scene of constant conflagrations. The native population, and especially the slaves, are a light-hearted, merry folk, who find life easy enough in a climate which minimises wants, but the unruly elements are present also in the shape of half-caste Arabs, who flock to the island in their dhows at certain seasons, and a number of semi-savage irregulars whom former sultans have introduced into the island, so that the policing of so large a centre with its narrow, labyrinthine streets, blind alleys, and ruinous houses is no light task to take in hand.

Together with his appointment as Agent and Consul-General at Zanzibar, Gerald Portal was also nominated Commissioner for the British sphere on the mainland, including the coastal region and the *hinterland* occupied under charter by the I.B.E.A. Company, where the restless and hostile district of Witu to the north of the Tana, and Kismayu, surrounded by a belt of fanatical Somali tribes, gave cause for constant anxiety.

The position of Zanzibar was a very difficult one, and required the most delicate handling. In the first place, as has already been stated, the Protectorate was so far rather a name than a fact; the Arabs were ready enough to accept the advantages of protection, but had slight appreciation of its reciprocal obligations, and the Sultan was but little disposed to cede any of his personal prerogative, or to yield into other hands any portion of his unlimited control over the revenues. Secondly, domestic slavery still continues among the populations under Mohammedan law, and though many decrees are in force for its strict regulation, Her Majesty's representative has to exercise the closest scrutiny to prevent their evasion, and to watch over the interests of thousands who are as yet incapable of looking after themselves. At that moment the Arabs, who had hitherto witnessed no practical demonstration of the resources of the protecting power, were learning with sullen discontent that these regulations meant the ultimate extinction of an institution which to them appeared a necessary condition of existence. Thirdly, there exist certain treaties between the sultanate and foreign powers dating, in one instance, as far back as 1846 (the date of the French Treaty with Muscat), by which European merchants and settlers were guaranteed against what was at the time of their conclusion a barbarous and fanatical Arab despotism. Under these treaties foreigners enjoy the privileges of the capitulations with which we are familiar in Oriental countries. They are only amenable to the jurisdiction of their own representative, their persons and houses are sacrosanct as far as the authority of the ruling sovereign is concerned. Moreover, with the exception of a uniform duty of five per cent on all goods imported, they have entire immunity from any contribution to the burdens of the state whose hospitality they enjoy, and even the taxation which the sovereign may levy on native produce is strictly defined by these agreements. Such instruments naturally hamper considerably the development of a new and equitable administration, but none of the powers concerned has as yet shown any disposition to abandon the privileges and immunities, which no doubt were absolutely indispensable at the time they were conferred, now that the situation is altered. Another arduous task imposed upon the representative of the protecting power was that of putting into force and giving practical application to the provisions of the Brussels Act for the suppression of the slave-trade, and for the protection of the native against the poisonous liquors and the cheap firearms with which the manufactories of Europe were threatening his extermination.

Gerald Portal at once set to work with a vigorous hand. The first and most difficult task before him was to obtain control over the finances, and after assigning to the Sultan's civil list a sum more than sufficient to cover reasonable expenditure, to secure that all revenue should pass through a Government office presided over by an English chief minister. For this office the services of General, now Sir Lloyd, Mathews, who had been appointed Consul-General at Mombasa, but who had not taken up his post, were lent to the sultanate.

The customs department was thoroughly reorganised, new storehouses were built, a new wharf completed in a very short space of time with steam cranes and every convenience—to be used, however, only by those who were prepared to pay for the privilege of landing their goods when they were guaranteed against the risks which they ran at the old incommodious landing-place. A post-office was organised under an English officer (Commander Hardinge, R.N.), and the provisions of the Brussels Act were promptly put into force. The army was also placed under a British officer, Brigadier-General Hatch, and as many of the numberless irregulars who fattened on the improvidence of the palace were disbanded as was possible consistently with the public safety. A department of public works was instituted, and a shipping-office, the Sultan having been induced to make over two of the smaller vessels which he had inherited to the Government service. The lighting of the town at nights was strictly enforced, and a number of minor reforms, such as the removal of petroleum stores to a place of security outside the limits of the populous town, were initiated. As may be imagined, innovations so sweeping and wholesale were not brought about without considerable opposition from all parties interested in the maintenance of the old system. The subjects of Her Majesty were naturally no less anxious than those of foreign powers not to lose a particle of the privileges secured them by the old treaties, and the Sultan grew more and more disposed to place difficulties in the path as he saw his power ebbing from him; but with firmness, patience, and goodwill these objects were all secured.

One change which needed considerable determination and courage was immediately decided on by Her Majesty's agent as vitally necessary to the existence of the Protectorate. The firm establishment of Germany on the mainland was beginning to attract directly thither a considerable portion of the import trade from foreign countries, which had hitherto been discharged at Zanzibar as the emporium of Eastern Africa, and Sir Gerald foresaw that while, owing to her valuable clove plantations which yield far more important results than any portion of the coast can for a long time compete with, Zanzibar was certain to attract ships to the port and provide them with freights, her import trade was in danger of falling off, and her commanding position as the universal market of the interior was menaced. He therefore boldly determined to abolish the five per cent duty on imports and to make Zanzibar a free port. This involved considerable loss of income, but it was anticipated that some compensation would be provided by the wharf rents and the storage of goods in Government go-downs, and the choice lay between accepting such compensation and witnessing an annual decline in foreign trade. Time has as yet been too short to judge of results, but hitherto, at any rate, Zanzibar has fairly well maintained the position which was undoubtedly menaced, while a better collection of taxes and certain new sources of revenue, such as a widely-extended system of registration of titles and contracts among the native populations, have further contributed to make up the deficiency. In spite of the great initial expenditure entailed by the reforms undertaken, the first financial year ended with a slight surplus, and the position appears to be steadily improving.

It was in the midst of the serious preoccupations caused by these reforms, and many other still inchoate schemes, that the summons to undertake the important Mission to Uganda reached Sir Gerald Portal towards the end of 1892, and he was compelled to direct all his energies to the new work before him, and to leave to other hands the task of completing the development of the new European administration—a task which has since been considerably facilitated by the death of the late Sultan Seyyid Ali, whose views grew more and more obstructionist as time proceeded, and by the establishment on the throne of the present enlightened ruler Seyyid Hamed bin Thwain, who has most loyally co-operated in every scheme for the improvement of the island and the condition of all classes of its inhabitants. For his services in Zanzibar and on the coast Gerald Portal was rewarded with the K.C.M.G.

How the Uganda Mission was organised and carried out he has told himself in the following pages, and no more need be said about it here; but, in conclusion, his services to his country in a career in which the younger members seldom are able to emerge from the body of their contemporaries, and find but rare opportunities of distinguishing themselves, may be summed up as having consisted in the work which he performed while only a subordinate in Cairo, in the adventurous expedition to Abyssinia, in his initial organisation of the Zanzibar Protectorate with which his name will always be associated, and, lastly, in the Mission to Uganda,—a considerable record for so young a man, and one which promised a career of great utility in the future had his life been spared.

Little more remains to be told. Sir Gerald had suffered from repeated attacks of fever both in Uganda and on the march, which, though never serious enough to give rise to anxiety, were undoubtedly very trying to a constitution already weakened by continuous residence in a tropical climate. He had, however, returned to Zanzibar in excellent health after his arduous experiences on the homeward journey, and he arrived in England in the last month of 1893 apparently strong and well in the full flush of success, eagerly anticipating the delight of home and the enjoyment of so much that he had been cut off from in his adventurous march of some 2000 miles through Equatorial Africa. Early in January he fell ill with what appeared to be a relapse of African fever, but after three weeks of varying phases the fatal signs of typhoid became manifest, and his strength, impaired as it was by a most trying climate, was unequal to contending against the ravages of disease. It was a hard fate for a man who had encountered so many adventures, and passed so often through the fire, to fall a victim to a sickness bred of city life; and he struggled bravely, as those who attended him bear witness, in that last unequal battle. But the end was near, and on the 26th of January the brief and brilliant career was closed, and Gerald Portal passed away from us, rich in the affection of many devoted friends, and in the sorrow of all his countrymen.

His character may fairly be judged by the ensuing record, and by the pages of the Report which he has submitted to Her Majesty's Government. The qualities which marked him most, perhaps, were the quickness with which he surveyed a given situation, a rapidity of decision, and a dogged determination in carrying out the line he had adopted. He was somewhat reserved by nature, and little inclined to discuss matters on which he had assumed the full responsibility, but he combined with this characteristic a generous appreciation of the work of others, and was staunchly loyal to his friends. Success had only done him good, and taught him a wider tolerance, and that passion to excel which had marked his youth helped him to make up the ground he may have somewhat neglected in early years, so that his general knowledge of a wide range of subjects made him the most agreeable of companions. At the same time there existed in him a softer side, by right of which he was a true lover of Nature, an ardent admirer of all things beautiful—a quality which from time to time finds voice in the following pages. He was a man eminently qualified by the strength of his personality, by his own natural inclination, and no less by the power of sympathy which he possessed, to carry out the Imperial policy with which his life was associated. The men of his own time and age, comrades at school, colleagues in his profession, and contemporaries in the sister services, will mourn him long and sincerely, while many of those who met him only once or twice will hardly fail to preserve the memory of a very winning smile.

Of his brother Raymond Portal something remains to be said in its proper place. Of both of them much has necessarily been left unsaid, but their own words will help to fill the vacant spaces. It is not easy for one who has grown up with them to write with the reserve which is due, for the two graves are still quite new, and there are many living for whom the pathos of their story is very near to tears.

R. R.

PART I

RIPON FALLS.
From a sketch by C. Whymper after a photograph by Colonel Rhodes.
[See page 139.

CHAPTER I

My appointment as H.M. Commissioner to Uganda—The staff of the Mission—Equipment of the caravan—The main body despatched to Kikuyu—A farewell state-visit to the Sultan of Zanzibar—We start upon our journey on the 1st of January 1893.

THE events which led to the despatch of a Mission to examine and report on the state of affairs in Uganda will still be fresh in every one's recollection. The Imperial British East Africa Company, whose first caravan, under the leadership of Messrs. Jackson and Gedge, had arrived in that country in April 1890, found, after some eighteen months' experience, that the task of exercising a control over a province at such a distance from the coast was beyond their strength, and announced their intention of withdrawing their officers and forces from the whole region. Fearing that such a course would gravely imperil the lives of the missionaries in Uganda, some friends of the Church Missionary Society subscribed £16,000 towards the expenses of administration, on the condition that the Company would maintain their forces and officers there for another year, till the end of 1892. The offer was accepted by the Directors of the Company, and the year was spent in Uganda: the first part in a sanguinary civil war, the remainder in efforts on the part of the Company's local officials to re-establish peace on a permanent basis. Nothing, however, occurred to induce the Directors to reconsider their determination to evacuate the country, and towards the end of 1892 the same problem, regarding the future disposal of Uganda, which had been shelved for a year by the munificent offering of the members of the Church Missionary Society, presented itself for final consideration and solution. Her Majesty's Government determined not to interfere with the Company's evacuation, but, in the hope of lessening the danger to the lives of missionaries and others which would be caused by a hurried retreat, and in order, at the same time, to enable them to receive fuller information as to the actual state of affairs in Equatorial Africa, they consented to defray the Company's costs of administration there for three months, from the 1st of January till the 31st of March 1893, and at the same time to despatch a Commissioner to Uganda to report upon the subject, and to suggest, if possible, the "best means of dealing with the country."

It was with great delight, not unmingled with some dismay at the magnitude of the task and the importance of the interests involved, that I received the offer of this appointment on the last day of November 1892. My next feeling was that the time at my disposal for organising and equipping the necessary caravan, and for reaching Uganda before the evacuation of the Company, was uncomfortably short. The usual allowance for a caravan to travel from the coast to Uganda was ninety days, and the date of the Company's retreat from Uganda was definitely fixed for the 31st of March, the 90th day of the new year. Even if, therefore, I were to count upon no more than to arrive in Uganda one day before its evacuation, this would only leave me the short space of one month for the recruitment of porters—who have of late years become most difficult to obtain—and for their medical examination; for the engagement of officers of the staff, and for their journey of three weeks from Europe to Zanzibar; for the selection and purchase of provisions, of equipment, of innumerable articles of barter, such as cloth and cotton stuffs of different qualities, beads of several sizes and kinds, iron, copper, and brass wire, small chains, looking-glasses and coloured handkerchiefs, of axes, bill-hooks, intrenching tools, ropes, canvas, tents and their equipment, medical stores, and, in short, of all the thousand and one articles which may sound like trifles and be easily overlooked at the coast, but the absence of any one of which 800 miles in the interior may be productive of serious inconvenience to the whole caravan.

Concurrently with all this work of preparation, innumerable outstanding questions had to be settled in connection with the somewhat complicated system of administration in Zanzibar, and the Sultan's assent had to be obtained to my taking 200 of his partly-drilled soldiers to serve both as escort on the journey, and, if necessary, as a sort of police force in Uganda itself. With regard to these soldiers, I may at once confess that almost from the moment of leaving the coast till the day of our return, I never ceased to regret, in an ever-increasing degree, the unlucky moment in which I consented to inflict their company on the Expedition. As events turned out they were almost useless from start to finish, and yet, in self-justification, it must be added that it was impossible to foretell this in December 1892. No one in Europe or on the African coast had any but the vaguest ideas as to the numbers and nature of the force which could be placed at our disposal in Uganda on the retreat of the Company. We knew that the Company had a certain number of excellent Soudanese troops who had been recruited in Egypt a couple of years before, but we were informed at the same time that the period of service of these men had expired, and that they would all have to leave Uganda with the Company's officers. It was also reported that some of the refugees from Emin Pacha's old province, ex-soldiers of the Egyptian Government, had been enlisted by the Company, but nobody could tell us either the approximate number of these recruits or the degree of efficiency which they had attained. It was evidently necessary, not only that the Commission should have complete liberty of movement both before reaching Uganda and in that country itself, but also that it should be throughout in a position of absolute independence: it therefore appeared expedient to cause it to be accompanied by at least 200 armed men with some knowledge of the use of a rifle. Moreover, the Zanzibar soldiers in their own town, with their clean white uniforms, presented a most creditable appearance. On parade they appeared fairly smart, they drilled in a way that would put some English militia regiments to shame, and they could go through the bayonet exercise faultlessly. I confess, indeed, to having often looked upon this Zanzibar force as a future factor of some value in the eventual settlement of the whole East African question. It was, therefore, with real disappointment that I felt compelled, after travelling some hundreds of miles in their company, reluctantly to acquiesce in the unanimous verdict of the other officers of the Mission, that these Zanzibar soldiers were the laziest, the most hopelessly and repulsively dirty, and the most untrustworthy collection of men with whom it had ever been our misfortune to come in contact.[1]

A few days after a telegram had been despatched to London expressing my grateful thanks for the honour which had been done me in selecting me for this task, a further message was received from H.M. Secretary of State, informing me of the appointment of the officers who were to accompany the Mission to Uganda. These officers were: Colonel Rhodes, D.S.O., Royal Dragoons, then Military Secretary to H.E. the Governor of Bombay, who is well known

---

[1] In consequence of these and other recent experiences, a new system of recruiting is being introduced with a view to securing men of a better stamp.—*Ed.*

for his distinguished services in two expeditions to
Suakim, and in the terrible fighting of the desert
column of the Gordon Relief Expedition, where he
served as A.D.C. to the late Sir Herbert Stewart, and
afterwards to Sir James Dormer, and who has,
moreover, gained renown both in the hunting and
in the cricket fields; Brigade-Major Owen, D.S.O.,
Lancashire Fusiliers, whose name is familiar in many
circles, both for conspicuous services rendered in a
recent expedition against the Jebus in West Africa,
and for innumerable laurels earned "between the
flags" as the most consummate horseman and the
best gentleman rider of modern days; Captain
Portal, my brother, of the Royal North Lancashire
Regiment, then Adjutant of the Mounted Infantry;
and Lieutenant Arthur, Rifle Brigade, at that time
serving in the army of the Sultan of Zanzibar: this
officer was appointed specially to command the
escort of Zanzibar troops. To these were added
Mr. Ernest Berkeley, a Consul in H.M. service, who
had for the last year acted as Administrator of the
possessions of the Imperial British East Africa
Company at Mombasa; Dr. R. Moffat, recently in
charge of a Scottish Industrial Mission at Kibwezi,
in British East Africa, whose services I was most
fortunate to secure as medical officer to the Mission;
and Mr. Foaker, lately of the I.B.E.A. Company,
who had already made one journey to Uganda, and
was now to act as caravan leader, whose arduous duty
it was to superintend all details of the organisation
of porters, the weight and distribution of loads, the

supply and distribution of rations,—in short, all the innumerable and troublesome details connected with the internal economy of a large caravan bound on a long journey. Another valuable addition to our strength was made later, in the person of Lieutenant C. Villiers, Royal Horse Guards, who happened to have arrived about this time in East Africa with the intention of starting on a private shooting expedition into the interior, and who, in reply to his own earnest solicitation, obtained, at the very last moment, permission from the requisite authorities to accompany us to Uganda. I should not forget to add to these the name of my servant Hutchisson, who at once volunteered to accompany me, and who, in a journey with me through Abyssinia at the end of 1887, had given ample proofs of his powers of endurance, his resource and pluck, in some very critical moments, and under circumstances of peculiar discomfort and danger.

After the appointment of this staff, I could but confess to myself that, so far as concerned the actual journey and the work to be done, no expedition had ever left the coast of East Africa with so good a prospect of success, and that if we were destined to meet with disaster, or to break down through any of the countless accidents to which caravans in Eastern and Central Africa are liable, not only the responsibility but also the fault would lie with myself. Let me add here a fact of which we may all be justly proud, and to which, I fear, claim can be laid by very few expeditions after a long journey in Equatorial

Africa, that not only did general good fellowship reign throughout the journey, but that never on any occasion was the harmony of the party disturbed by a single squabble, by any jealousies, by any hasty or ill-considered word, or even by a day's coolness between any of the officers of the Expedition from the moment of starting until, nearly ten months later, some of us again saw the waters of the Indian Ocean.

The first steps taken, in the early days of December, were to select the soldiers who were to accompany us, and to send forth emissaries in every direction to recruit a sufficient number of porters. The soldiers were a comparatively easy matter as soon as the Sultan had kindly given his consent to their employment in this manner. A call for volunteers from among the battalion of 800 "regulars" produced immediately more than the 200 who were required, and the necessary selection was easily made by the rejection of the weakest. The remainder were then medically examined, vaccinated, and equipped with two serviceable suits of "khakee" tunic and knee-breeches, putties, and two pairs of sandals each; and every man carried a Snider rifle, sword bayonet, and forty rounds of ammunition. The precaution of causing every member of the caravan to be vaccinated is one which should always, when possible, be observed by the leader of an expedition going into the interior of Africa from the East Coast. There is scarcely a single tribe between Mombasa and Uganda which is ever quite free from the scourge of small-pox; sometimes it does not make itself very conspicuous, while at other times, especially after a period of drought, scarcity, or, as at the present moment, of distress caused by the death of all the cattle, it breaks out as a veritable plague, and decimates the population of immense districts. Few greater disasters can befall a caravan than to get small-pox among the men, as frequently happens when this precaution has been omitted. If the first cases occur at a station or in the neighbourhood of some village whose inhabitants can be trusted not to cut the throat of any defenceless stranger, the patients may be left behind with no greater inconvenience than the necessity of distributing their loads among other already overburdened men; but if an unfortunate wretch is seized with the disease in some district far from any human habitation, or tenanted only by the murderous Masai, his chances are small indeed. The caravan cannot wait: it has only rations for a limited number of days, and must push on to the next food-supplying district; the man must be carried by two, or perhaps four others, which means that three or five loads must be either thrown away or added to the burdens of their companions. The ruin which therefore befalls a caravan if, as not unfrequently happens, ten, fifteen, or twenty men are attacked almost simultaneously may be better imagined than described. And yet, although instances of such disasters are numerous and well known, such are the conservative and *laisser-aller* properties of the whole atmosphere of East Africa, that not only does no rule exist regarding the vaccination of porters, but I have never even heard of this ordinary precaution having been taken with any other caravan than my own which has left Mombasa at any time during the last three years.

Meanwhile the work of collecting porters was proceeding but slowly, for several reasons. In the first place, I had insisted on none but volunteers being recruited. In the second place, the professional porters are seldom keen to engage themselves for a very long journey, such as that to Uganda. If we had been going to Mount Kilimanjaro, to Jabora, or to Kikuyu, we could have secured as many good men as we liked in a couple of days, but the idea of Uganda rather frightens them: the road is but little known, and they feel that it means a long and wearisome journey, sometimes on very short rations, and an absence of many months from their homes at Zanzibar. In the third place, while the supply of porters is diminishing every year, the demand is growing ever larger.

It is a great mistake to suppose, as do most Europeans when they arrive in Zanzibar to collect a caravan for a journey or shooting expedition, that any stalwart peasant or street loafer of Zanzibar will make a good porter. Such a man would break down in a week, whatever may be his physical strength. He would infallibly get sore feet or cracked heels; the skin of his head or shoulders would be rubbed by his load; these sores would develop into serious ulcers, and after walking a hundred miles the man would either have to be left at some friendly village, or would have to hobble along with the caravan, doing no work and eating precious food. The professional caravan porters form a distinct clique by themselves. They spend their whole lives in either travelling about the continent with loads on their heads, or in spending the money thus amassed with all possible speed and with reckless extravagance at Zanzibar. They are a cheery lot, with heads like iron, feet like leather, and with the stomachs of ostriches—miserable, like children, in cold and wet districts, or in times when food is scarce, but forgetting all their discomforts with the first ray of sunshine, or with the first successful shot at a rhinoceros, zebra, or other animal which will supply them with meat. The life is a hard one, and the professional caravan porter seldom lives to be an old man, while the increased facilities now offered to able-bodied men of earning a comfortable living at Zanzibar or on the coast prevents younger men from joining their ranks. The authorities of German East Africa have long foreseen this difficulty, and have not only employed many devices to attract all the Zanzibar porters to take up their residence in German territory, but have also enacted the most stringent, and, on the whole, effective measures to prevent these men from leaving the German colony. I shall have occasion to return later to this question of porters and the means of transport which must eventually replace them in East Africa.

The number of men which we calculated would be

required for the Mission amounted to nearly 400, and it may perhaps be of some use to future travellers if I describe briefly the nature of the loads which made this apparently large number necessary. To every European officer were assigned ten men, two of whom were to carry his tent, with its poles, pegs, etc. These are heavy and awkward loads, especially in wet weather, and should, when possible, be divided into three. One man carried the bed and bedding, and the remaining seven were available for boxes of clothes, boots, scientific instruments, canteen, cooking-pots, chair, table, guns, ammunition, and all the rest of the officer's paraphernalia. As our party consisted of nine European officers, this accounted for ninety porters, to whom may be added four or five more who carried the mess-tent and its appurtenances. To each European was allowed one box of European provisions per month : these boxes were not to exceed sixty-five pounds in weight, including some fifteen pounds for the box itself, which must necessarily be strong and solid enough to withstand much dropping and bumping and general ill-treatment. These were filled with those necessaries of life which are not procurable in the interior, such as tea, coffee, cocoa, salt, sugar, oatmeal, rice, lime-juice, jam (a most necessary anti-scorbutic), and a certain quantity of tinned meats. In absolutely foodless districts, such as the greater part of those through which the road to Uganda passes, it was found that one such box per month for each officer was very far from being a liberal or unnecessary allowance. As we were preparing for an absence of ten months, the European provisions for the party of nine officers amounted to ninety more loads, which were brought up to one hundred by medical stores, medical comforts, and one or two "extras." The soldiers were allowed ten porters for every company of fifty men, including officers; their four companies, therefore, absorbed forty porters, to whom may be added about ten more for axes, intrenching tools, small grindstone, ropes, etc.

Nearly eighty men were required to carry the "currency" of the different countries through which we had to pass, consisting of cotton cloth of several different qualities and sizes, coloured handkerchiefs, beads of several kinds, brass, iron, and copper wire, small looking-glasses, and so forth. These have to be most carefully selected and packed, as in the centre of Africa a piece of cloth damaged by water, or beads of the wrong sort, are of no more value than they would be as articles of barter in Piccadilly. It is also most necessary to have quite the latest intelligence as to the change of fashions in different countries, for it often happens that the large and bright blue bead which last year was eagerly sought after in a certain district, and for strings of which flour and corn were readily produced, may now be a drug in the market, while its place in the estimation of the native has been taken by a small white or red one; or, perhaps, what is even more embarrassing to the traveller, beads may be temporarily out of fashion altogether, and the cry be all for small coils of bright brass wire. I need scarcely add that the fashion in these matters is set by the ladies of the tribe, who assert their arbitrary rights and their monopoly of taste in matters of dress—even when that dress consists of no more than a few strings of beads or a necklace of wire—with the same successful determination as the other daughters of Eve in Paris or London. To these loads of so-called "trade goods" about ten more may be added for "odds and ends," such as presents for the king of Uganda or for the more important chiefs, stationery, etc. To the 340 porters thus accounted for we added ten per cent as a moderate allowance for sickness, desertions, or accidents, and the total number of 400 was completed by the addition of headmen, overseers, cooks, and tent-boys.

By the middle of December a sufficient number of men had been collected and vaccinated to enable me to send off the main body of the caravan and of the soldiers, under Mr. Foaker and Lieutenant Arthur, while I had to wait at Zanzibar for the other officers, who were due to arrive on the last day of the year. The advance party were instructed to push forward with all convenient speed to Kikuyu, about 350 miles from the coast, and there to use their utmost endeavours to purchase, and pack in loads of sixty-five pounds, a sufficient quantity of flour or other available food to suffice the whole caravan for the long march of nearly 280 miles through the absolutely foodless country which lies between Kikuyu and Kavirondo. Meanwhile the work of collecting the remainder of the porters and of packing the rest of the loads was being pushed forward with feverish haste, but, alas!

the supply was not equal to the demand. It is true that a fair number of applications were received for the two months' advance of wages which it is customary to give to porters before starting on a long journey, but it was perfectly evident, from the character and appearance of the applicants, that the money was the only object aimed at, and that they could be relied upon to desert before going fifty miles from the coast. Many others had to be rejected on account of their extreme youth or physical weakness; but at last a sufficient number were engaged, not inferior perhaps to many others who are in these days taken as porters by caravans, but of whom certainly a large proportion were quite unfit for this sort of work. The main body, which had already gone on with Lieutenant Arthur, consisted of a very fair lot of men, including some magnificent specimens of muscular development, but our second party, which had to make forced marches, and to overtake the others with all possible speed, could not, in spite of all our efforts, muster more than a small proportion of even moderately good men; the rest were boys or "shirkers."

Our difficulties would have been far greater—in fact, it may be doubted whether we should have been able to make a start within at least a month of the appointed time—had not Zanzibar been blessed, in the person of its chief minister, with an English gentleman of the true patriotic, honest, self-sacrificing, and sympathetic type, which has gone so far to make England respected above other European nations by many of the native races of Africa. The name of

General Mathews is as a household word throughout many hundreds of square miles in East Africa.[1] Not an English or American traveller has ever set foot in these regions during the last fifteen years without owing to him a heavy debt of gratitude. Scarcely a native family can be found in Zanzibar that has not had cause to bless his open-handed generosity or his unswerving sense of justice. He is known as the true friend of the upright Arab and of the struggling Swahili,[2] but a terror to the oppressor or the evil-doer; and the influence of the cheery and kind-hearted General, handicapped by his alien race and his Christian religion, is barely second to that of the sacred person of the Sultan himself. General Mathews would have given his eyes to have been allowed to accompany our expedition, and it need not be added that we should more than gladly have welcomed his presence and the invaluable addition of his experience; but it was out of the question that the man on whom, more than any other, depended the working of the whole new administrative machinery of Zanzibar

[1] General, now Sir Lloyd William Mathews, K.C.M.G., began life in the Royal Navy. While serving at Zanzibar on H.M.S. *London*, the station-ship for the repression of the slave-trade, his services were lent to the famous Sultan Barghash, who was anxious to have his troops drilled in the European fashion. In due course he left the navy and entered the service of the Sultan, whose friend and confidential adviser he became, conducting many expeditions on the mainland for that monarch at the time of his greatest prosperity. When Zanzibar became a British Protectorate, General Mathews was named British Consul-General for the mainland, but he has hitherto never taken up the post, his services having once more been lent to the Sultans of Zanzibar, where he acts as first minister in the European Administration which is now completely organised.—*Ed*.

[2] It is perhaps scarcely necessary to explain that Swahili is the name of the mongrel people on the East African coast, in the British and German spheres, whose language is the *lingua franca* of Eastern Africa.—*Ed*.

could be spared from that country in the then critical state of affairs.

Sadly realising this penalty of the value of his previous work, General Mathews, with an unselfish kindness and devotion which no words can properly describe, not only placed his invaluable influence, his time, and his experience at our disposal, but even insisted on going himself with this second party of porters to Mombasa, in order to ensure that all the preparations for our departure should be completed.

Early in the morning of the 30th of December, a signal flying from the flag-staff above the Sultan's great clock-tower announced that a French mail-steamer had been sighted, and a couple of hours later I was delighted to greet Colonel Rhodes, Major Owen, and my brother. The first of these officers had come from Bombay, and had joined this steamer of the "Messageries Maritimes" at Aden. The other two had left England on the 10th, having thus had barely a week to complete all their preparations for a long journey and an absence of eight or ten months in Central Africa. It was not surprising, therefore, that almost their first words were an entreaty for one day's delay at Zanzibar in order to enable them to complete the purchase of various necessaries which had been forgotten in the hurried departure from England. Fortunately it was possible to grant this request, as Captain Campbell, R.N., had most kindly offered to take over our party to Mombasa in H.M.S. *Philomel*, and this beautiful cruiser was the only vessel in these seas which could negotiate the run from Zanzibar to Mombasa between sunrise and sunset.[1] I was also anxious to have a clear day at Zanzibar in order to enable me to discuss with Mr. Rennell Rodd, who had come out in the same steamer to act as H.M. Agent and Consul-General during my absence, many complicated questions affecting the internal administrative economy of the Sultan's dominions.

As soon as this point was settled, the party separated to put on all the finery at their command, and with all the staff of the Agency we proceeded to pay a state visit of greeting and farewell to the Sultan Seyyid Ali.[2] The streets were lined for some distance with soldiers, a guard of honour was drawn up opposite the steps of the Palace, the really good Goanese band played "God Save the Queen" and "Rule Britannia," long rows of beautifully-dressed and dignified Arabs made a lane for us through the lower ante-room and up the stairs, at the head of which stood the Sultan himself. His Highness led us to the upper end of the long reception-room, which was already more than half full of gray-bearded princes and dignitaries; we sat down on gilt and velvet chairs in a row on the right of the Sultan, while on his left were placed his relations and the high-born Arabs in strict order of precedence. I may be allowed to add here that disputes about this same

---

[1] Mombasa, the most important harbour on the British East Africa coast, and the headquarters of the British East Africa Company, is the point of departure for all caravans proceeding to Uganda through the British sphere.—ED.

[2] The late Sultan Seyyid Ali, who died March 5, 1893.

order of precedence among the leading Arabs are not the least troublesome among the many complicated local questions which are constantly being brought for adjudication before H.M. Consul-General. After the customary cup of coffee and glass of iced sherbet, of which it was good manners to drink only a mouthful or so, we rose to take our leave, it being left to the guest, in, I think, all Oriental countries, to give the signal for departure even from the reception-room of a sovereign. Many good wishes and polite phrases were uttered by His Highness, whose manners on occasions of this sort were truly excellent,—a refined combination of the dignity of the potentate with the Oriental and graceful courtesy of the host.

On the evening of the 31st of December a great banquet was given to the members of the Mission by all the English residents at Zanzibar, in a large room of the new English Club, which was opened for the first time on this occasion. The whole affair was admirably done, and the room was tastefully draped and festooned with flags and bunting of all sorts by the deft fingers of blue-jackets from the three men-of-war then in harbour. Some fifty English gentlemen were present,—a fair muster for a place like Zanzibar, so lately almost unheard of in Europe. Speeches, some of which, by the way, were of a really high order of oratory, prolonged the entertainment until the midnight breeze from the Indian Ocean carried into the dining-hall the last moaning breath of the dying year, while the brilliant tropical moon smiling into the open windows brightly announced the birth of the year 1893. The party broke up amidst the cordial farewells and good wishes of true friends, to many of whom I owe debts of gratitude for help and support during some trying times at Zanzibar which I can never repay. There remained barely time to write a few last necessary letters, and to despatch the last outstanding matters of official business, and at 4 A.M. the staff of the Mission met me again on the hospitable deck of H.M.S. *Philomel*. Before the sun had risen on the first day of the new year the anchor was up, and we were actually launched upon our long journey into the very heart of the Dark Continent.

CHAPTER II

We arrive at Port Reitz—By the "Central African Railway" to our encampment at Mazeras—An awkward squad—The first day's march.

THAT we were able to equip and organise a caravan of men and 200 soldiers, thoroughly supplied with "trade-goods," provisions, stores, tents, and all the paraphernalia necessary for a journey then estimated to last for ten months, and that we could send off two-thirds of the party in the marvellously short time of fifteen days, and start with the remainder within a month, is due not only to the unwearied exertions and great experience of General Mathews, of whom I have already spoken, but also to the self-denying courtesy of the Imperial British East Africa Company. I am happy in having here an opportunity of placing on record my sense of gratitude for the invaluable help received from the Administration of that Company, without which, I have no hesitation in saying that we must either have been considerably delayed in leaving the coast, or else have started with insufficient equipment. From the Directors themselves down to the lowest clerk at Mombasa, there was not one who did not render assistance in this work to the full extent of his opportunity; the whole machinery of the Administration and the organisation of their transport office were placed at our disposal, and the officers of the Company vied with each other in giving us the benefit, not only of their invaluable experience in such matters, but also of their personal assistance, at all hours and with a self-sacrificing devotion of which every member of the Commission appreciated the result, and for which it is impossible for us to express our thanks in an adequate manner.

The first day of the year 1893, during which we accomplished the first 140 miles of our journey, was spent, so far as I was concerned, in the most prosaic way. I had been somewhat overworked for a month, and was thoroughly worn out by the last two or three days: there was a fairly strong breeze and a good deal of sea, with the general result that I spent the whole time of our voyage from Zanzibar to Mombasa in a most uncompromising and undeniable attack of sea-sickness. I only recovered in time to join the other officers in admiring one of the most beautiful scenes that can be offered by East Africa—the entrance into the magnificent harbour known as Port Reitz, on the southern side of Mombasa Island. For over a mile we steamed along between groves of cocoa-nut palms, relieved by the heavy masses and deeper green of mango-trees. Here and there appeared the gray ruins of an ancient Portuguese fort or tower, its crenellated walls tinged with purple and gold by the rays of the setting sun, as though in memory of their bygone glory. H.M.S. *Philomel* was at last brought to an anchor close to the little promontory known as "Railway Point," from which we would begin our march on the following morning. Here we were joined by Mr. Berkeley, with the welcome news that our men and loads had all been sent forward to a place named Mazeras, about nine miles inland, where a camp was already pitched in preparation for our arrival, and that a sufficient number of porters had been sent back to carry up the personal baggage which we had brought with us from Zanzibar. That evening, at the hospitable board of Captain Campbell, we enjoyed for the last time for many months to come the luxury of porcelain plates, fine linen, glasses, and wine (well iced) to put into them. Henceforth we were to be satisfied with iron enamelled plates, tin mugs, tea and coffee.

Early the next morning the baggage was sent ashore in native boats, followed by a gray pony, the joint property of four of us, on which we wished to try the experiment of a march to Uganda.

Just before starting my attention was drawn to some English newspapers which were put into my hand, and in which the opinion was advanced that our Mission was being despatched too late, and could not possibly arrive in Uganda before the evacuation of that country by the Company; that in consequence we should find on our arrival nothing but disorder, anarchy, and bloodshed, should probably have to fight for our lives, and that a strong military expedition would be needed to get us out again! My last official act before starting was, therefore, to send a telegram to H.M. Secretary of State, hazarding the prophecy that we should cross the Nile and enter Uganda on or about the 13th of March, and should arrive at Kampala about the 17th of the same month. The patient reader will see later how far these prophecies were justified by the results.

All the officers of the staff then rowed off to the landing-place in several boats, and, lastly, I was invited to take my place in the Captain's galley, in which a crew of officers, with Captain Campbell himself as stroke, wished to row me ashore. I am not ashamed to confess to having felt profoundly affected not only at the honour which was thus done me, but even more at the feeling of friendship and goodwill which dictated this signal compliment, nor was this feeling lessened when, after a salute had been fired from the *Philomel*, the whole ship's company sprang into the rigging and cheered us till the woods and cocoa-nut groves rang again.

We soon set foot on the mainland of the African Continent, but not even yet were we forced to trust entirely to our own feet for the means of progression. For about seven miles into the interior from the spot where we landed, the East Africa Company had laid, some two or three years before, a little 24-inch tramway, which was, I am told, opened at that time with great ceremony under the name of the "Central African Railway." Although it had never been used except for occasional picnic parties from Mombasa, this tram-line was still in a fairly serviceable condition, and we therefore placed ourselves as comfortably as we could on some flat open trollies, on which a box or inverted basket was made to do duty as a seat. Two of us were placed on each trolly, which was propelled by a couple of natives pushing from behind. Our nerves were highly tried a few hundred yards from the start by finding ourselves at the top of a steep incline, about half-way down which we could see there were "points" leading on to a siding. Colonel Rhodes was my companion on the leading trolly, and, to our dismay, on arriving at the top of the slope our miserable coolies gave the machine a final push, and then left it to its own devices. Away we went at ever-increasing speed, perfectly helpless, and with the boxes on which we were sitting gradually working themselves towards the end of the little rushing platform! The "points" which we had noticed with such suspicion had, fortunately, been left open, either by chance or by the last comer, and with a jolt and a crash we whirled safely over them. Safely, too, we charged through or took a flying leap over a heap of pebbles lying on the rail; and at last, having reached the bottom of the valley, began to rush, but with gradually-decreasing speed and with a comfortable feeling of security, up the opposite incline. Now it was our turn to look back and enjoy the danger and discomfort of our friends. By extraordinary good luck they all arrived safely at the bottom of this dangerous slope, but not so the baggage placed on the last few trucks. More than one ominous crash was heard, and more than one trolly was seen tearing up the ground with its wheels in the air; but, marvellous to relate, the damage done was comparatively slight, and did not extend much beyond the infliction of some deep dints in a few tin boxes, and the complete pulverisation of some extremely choice cigars which one of the officers was carefully bringing with him as a last relic of the luxuries of civilised life. Along the rest of the line the journey was fairly easy, and through scenery the beauty of which would have been a sufficient compensation for almost any discomforts. The only difficulty worthy of note was caused by the weeds, creepers, grass, and small bushes which had grown up all over the line, and thereby rendered progress a matter of very hard toiling and pushing for the unfortunate coolies. As my companion remarked, this hardly looked as if the traffic along the Central African line had been very great since the day when it was first laid!

I should here explain that the reason why this tramway is not used by caravans entails no reflection whatever on the administration of the Company. It is simply that the line does not run along the regular caravan route, and does not extend far enough to join that route at any part. If it could have been continued for another ten or a dozen miles, there can be no doubt that caravans would have been eager to make use of the line, but at present it is not worth their while to turn from their well-known road for the sake of only seven miles of rail. The work was laid aside at the time when an agitation was set on foot for the construction of a more permanent line under the guarantee of Her Majesty's Government. So far as we ourselves were concerned, we undoubtedly found that this tramway saved us the greater part of a hot and disagreeable day's march.

About seven miles from the coast the line came to a sudden end without any warning, except such as was given by a few heaps of rails and boxes of nuts and screws lying by the wayside. The work was evidently abandoned as hastily as it had been commenced; rails, bolts, sleepers, screws and nuts, sufficient for some seventy or eighty miles of line, lie in stacks and heaps near the beach of the harbour; not a living soul, until ourselves, had ever made use of the line for any practical purpose, and the whole work remains as a monument to good intentions overpowered by force of circumstances.

A brisk walk of about three miles brought us to Mazeras, where our eyes were pleasantly greeted by the sight of a neat camp already pitched in a shady spot, with the tents in two ordered rows, the porters already told off into companies and messes, and drawn up for inspection, and, most grateful sight of all, a sumptuous luncheon prepared for us by the indefatigable hospitality of General Mathews. The rest of the day was spent in telling off the men to their respective loads, in repacking some of the baggage which was found to be above the regulation limit of sixty-five pounds, and in distributing the surplus among lighter loads when such could be found.

Here, too, we were glad to make the acquaintance of the medical officer of the Mission, Dr. Moffat, a proof of whose energy and keenness had already been afforded by the fact that, although the offer of the appointment had only reached him at the Scottish Industrial Mission at Kibwezi on the 16th of December, he had at once started for Mombasa, had walked 200 miles under the broiling sun, in the hottest time of the year, and within six degrees of the equator, had replenished his medical stores from such supplies as were available at the coast, and was now not only ready to start on the journey to the centre of Africa, but also willingly consented to take upon his shoulders the additional and most onerous work of caravan leader and general superintendent, until we should join the larger body which had gone forward a fortnight earlier under the leadership of Mr. Foaker. Hardly had we arrived in camp before Dr. Moffat's professional services were requisitioned by two of our party, who had been completely overpowered by the cruel and unaccustomed heat of the tropical mid-day sun, to which we had been unavoidably exposed in consequence of the delay and slight confusion at starting inevitable on a first departure from the coast.

The next morning at daybreak we prepared for the start of our first real march with the caravan and with all our belongings. The tents were struck, and then, in spite of all the care, the forethought, and the explanations which had been expended on the porters the preceding day, there ensued a scene of squabbles, of confusion, and of abject helplessness on the part of two-thirds of the men, which caused our hearts to sink into the very soles of our boots as we thought of the long journey before us. The older and shrewder professional porters, who had been at this game before, at once seized and shouldered the lightest and most comfortable-looking loads, and marched boldly out of camp; others were endeavouring, with the hopeless awkwardness of inexperience, to fold up the tents into some portable shape; others, again, were feebly attempting, with the help of some very rotten-looking string, to fasten the bags containing their ten days' rations of coarse flour to the top of the loads which they had to carry; while some, probably the most weakly and the youngest of the lot, were not even pretending to do anything, but stared with idiotic dismay at the formidable-looking packages which had been left to them by their sharper companions, and to which they had to add the weight of their own rations. We at once sent messengers to stop the leading men, and the whole party was halted in a long line along the path about a quarter of a mile out of camp. Here every man was made to place his load on the path in front of him; packages and men were rapidly counted and checked, and a redistribution of loads more in proportion to the strength of the carriers was quickly effected; headmen and overseers were placed at intervals all along the line; Major Owen, Captain Portal, and Dr. Moffat were told off to bring up the rear for the day; and by eight o'clock the whole party of some 200 men, including thirty of the Zanzibar soldiers who had been left by Lieutenant Arthur as our escort, was at last ready for a final departure.

There now only remained the most painful part of the whole morning's duty—to say good-bye to General Mathews. There was not one of our party, even among those who had only seen him for the first time a few hours ago, who had not been fascinated by his kindly cheerfulness, his indomitable self-sacrifice, and his unfailing energy; there was not one of us who did not wish that the General could accompany us to Uganda and back; but for myself, to whom his sound common-sense, his honest advice, and his marvellous influence over all classes at Zanzibar, had been simply invaluable during the many months that we had spent working side by side during very critical times, I could only wish helplessly that I could find some words to express even a fraction of the gratitude and of the confused rush of feelings which made me speechless. However, the graceful facility with which any son of the Latin races would be able to clothe his sentiments in fitting and picturesque words is denied to all but a favoured few of our tongue-tied and awkward nation, and our parting was what such partings always are between two English friends in any part of the world and under any imaginable circumstances,—a hearty grasp of the hand, perhaps rather more sustained than usual, and with an almost involuntary extra pressure at the end, and a simple "Good-bye, old fellow!" After all, is this much less eloquent, or does it convey much less meaning than the graceful phrases which have been unable to force their way through the confusion of real feeling, and to which one regrets half an hour later not to have been able to give utterance?

For a few minutes after the signal had been given to march all appeared to go well at last, and the picture then displayed before us would have been ample compensation to any lover of the beautiful in Nature for all the trouble, the time, the storms, the sea-sickness, and the heat incidental to a journey into tropical Africa. The long line of white-clad and black-skinned porters, bearing on their heads loads of every colour, size, and shape, slowly winds in single file along the narrow path like a brilliant and gigantic serpent, now almost dazzling to look upon under the rays of the morning sun, now gliding in dark and mysterious silence through the cool shade of a wooded valley. All around the richly-clothed downs and park-like glades of pasture are dotted with clumps of mimosa thorns, interspersed with flowering shrubs of every hue, which shine like rubies and turquoises against the dark and massive background of some gigantic mango-tree; the fan-palm thrusts its bristling head high into the air; the frowning severity of the black rocks, which here and there break through the grassy covering of the hills, is softened by groves of graceful cocoa-nut palms, to whose swaying stems cling masses of the most lovely flowering orchids; while the palms in their turn are compelled to bend their heads in unceasing homage before the ponderous strength of the mighty baobab, which on every eminence displays a bloated and unwieldy trunk, and, shaking itself clear from the festoons of creepers that try, as in mockery, to hide the ungainly nakedness, wildly stretches to heaven its distorted, gnarled, and leafless arms in a perpetual agony of despairing malevolence.

There was, however, but little time for the enjoyment of Nature's picture-gallery, for after a few minutes' walking the line of porters began to lengthen ominously. While the leading men still stepped out briskly with their heavy loads, others began slowly to drop farther and farther to the rear. Badly-tied loads, consisting of perhaps three or four separate articles, came to pieces, and the inexperienced youths could not adjust their burdens in a comfortable position either on their heads or their shoulders; they had not yet learned the older porters' trick of winding a good piece of cotton cloth tightly round their heads like the towering turbans worn by some Sikh regiments, in order to form a pad which keeps the actual load several inches above their skulls. These pieces of cloth, some seven feet long by four wide, were served out to every porter and every soldier before leaving the coast; by day they serve as a pad for his head while carrying his load, or, if he prefers it, as an additional garment in cold weather; while for the night two of these cloths stretched on sticks and leaning towards each other form an excellent little tent, under which the two owners can sleep in comfort and with less danger of fever from rain or dew.

It would have been hopeless to have attempted

more than a very short march on this first day. We had made a late start and the sun was fierce, the men had not got accustomed to their loads, nor were these as yet quite fairly distributed; both Europeans and natives were thoroughly out of condition, and would be liable to break down if severely pressed at first; above all, it had to be remembered that since they had received their two months' advance of wages at Zanzibar the large majority of the porters had probably been endeavouring to get as much value out of the money as possible in the few days yet left to them. It was safe to assume that every rupee which they had saved from the clutches of the Zanzibar and Mombasa ladies had been spent in cramming inordinate quantities of food and drink into their stomachs, and that, consequently, for the last few days about three-fourths of my caravan had been in a comfortable state of perpetual intoxication.[1] It was necessary to let all this work itself off by degrees; no more drink would be obtainable this side of Uganda, so that the physical training of the men was only a question of a short time, and it was above all things necessary to bring them pretty fresh to the edge of a long waterless and desert tract which lay a few days' march ahead of us, and which had to be traversed in one long scrambling march of nearly forty miles.

[1] In spite of the efforts that have been made, with purely humanitarian objects, to prevent the import into East Africa and the supply of spirits to the native, he is still able to satisfy his craving for alcohol with the fermented juice of the cocoa-nut palm, a liquor not less intoxicating; while the European trader has ingeniously found means to evade the line of prohibition by flooding Africa with a cheap and most pernicious spirit under the disguise of Eau de Cologne.—*Ed.*

On the first day, therefore, after a brisk walk of about six miles, we halted and camped at a place named Muachi, by the edge of some rather repulsive-looking water which, though apparently stagnant, feeds a slight stream, which eventually finds its way to the head of the great harbour of Mombasa (Port Reitz). The only thing worthy of note in connection with this camp is that although it lies within sixteen miles of Mombasa, the only means of crossing the deep, muddy water is afforded by a slippery, half-rotten, and twisted tree thrown from bank to bank, with no rail or artificial assistance,—difficult enough to traverse in dry weather, but a veritable trap for the wary or the unwary during or after rain. We made an estimate that the amount of losses suffered by caravans at this place during any average month would have been more than equivalent to the cost of construction and maintenance of a sufficient bridge for several years.

CHAPTER III

The day's programme—Crossing the great Taro Plain—The first station of the East Africa Company—A splendid view of Mount Kilimanjaro—Bad news from Kikuyu—A flourishing Industrial Mission.

LET not the reader be afraid, from the contents of the last chapter, that I am about to inflict upon him a detailed account of our proceedings day by day, after the approved fashion of African travellers. The hours at which we rose, breakfasted, marched, and halted, were no doubt of great interest to ourselves at the time, and so also were our numerous petty difficulties about porters, loads, food, and water; but I can scarcely hope that a faithful recapitulation of all these episodes of daily life would rouse the interest of even the most enthusiastic inquirers into African matters at home. It is sufficient to say that after the first few days of comparative confusion, the whole machinery of the caravan began to work smoothly. Headmen and porters soon settled down in earnest to their respective duties; the effects of coast-life, and especially of the final debauch, worked themselves off, the men's feet began to harden and their condition to improve, while the younger and more inexperienced porters soon learnt innumerable little tricks for tying up, packing, and arranging their loads in the most efficient manner, and at the same time in the most comfortable way for themselves.

SUDI BIN SULEIMAN,
Native Headman of the Mission Caravan.

There were, however, an ominous number who still continued to give the rear-guard a good deal of trouble, and who were constantly throwing down their packs and sitting down by the wayside on every sort of real or imaginary pretext. Some of these were really too young or too weakly for the work they had to do, others were suffering, almost from the start, from sore feet and ulcerated legs, but there was also a fair proportion of genuine "malingerers"—men as strong as donkeys, who simply calculated that by constantly dropping back to the rear, lying down by the roadside, shamming sickness, and so forth, they would succeed not only in escaping the necessary "fatigue duty" on arrival in camp, but that they would be given lighter loads, or even allowed to loaf along for some days with no burden at all.

The general routine of the day's work was as follows, and varied but little :—At 4.30 A.M. a drum was beaten, and the bugler of the Zanzibar soldiers sounded the reveille. Everybody then had to get up and hastily perform, in the dark, such toilet as might be thought necessary. While this was in progress the cooks were preparing some hot cocoa and porridge for the Europeans, which was devoured in immense quantities, and with hearty appetite, but in a hurry, between 5 and a quarter past. In the meantime the tent-boys were packing up the beds and bedding, closing and locking any boxes which might have been opened by their masters, and generally looking about to see that no articles of personal property were left behind. At the same time the porters told off to each officer were striking his tent, rolling it up tightly with its poles, pegs, ropes, and mallet in two loads, while others were engaged in fastening their own little properties, spare clothes, bag of ration-flour, etc., on to the loads which they were to carry. By about 5.30 A.M. everything was usually ready for a start, the signal was given by sounding the drum, and away we went as soon as the first streak of dawn was strong enough to show us the path. During the first part of the journey it was found desirable to halt the whole party for a few minutes about half a mile out of camp in order to give stragglers and clumsy packers time to join the rest, and also in order to let the headmen and officers of the rear-guard make a thorough search through the deserted camp to see if any load had been hidden or inadvertently left behind. We discontinued this practice after the first three weeks.

One of the English officers was told off, in rotation, every day, for the wearisome and disagreeable duty of rear-guard. It was his business, with the assistance of a headman, to see every porter, load, and soldier always in front of him; and it needs a few hours' personal experience of that task in order thoroughly to appreciate the amount of patience, good temper, and physical endurance which it demands. In the first place, it is always annoying to be the last man of a long column; secondly, the trail of a large number of Zanzibar porters, in the clothes which they have worn unwashed for some weeks, who themselves last touched water, except for drinking purposes, perhaps many months ago, is by no means savoury in the early morning; thirdly, within half a mile of starting there are probably a few men who have thrown down their loads and sitting by the wayside, swearing they are ill or lame. A hasty examination has to be made to see if the excuses are genuine or not: in the former case some arrangements have to be at once made for a substitute to carry the load, but in the latter, and far more frequent case, the "malingerer" has to be forced to shoulder his load again and urged forward to join the others. As the march goes on these events multiply, and, especially if the day be hot and the way long, it is by no means uncommon to come across a whole pile of loads lying by the wayside, and no carriers visible until a more careful search discovers them peacefully sleeping under a tree. It was customary, after walking about two or two and a half hours, for the officer in front to call a halt in order to rest the men, and to let the rear—by this time straggling a long way behind—close up again. The leading men now enjoy a good rest for perhaps nearly an hour, but not so the unfortunate officer of the rear-guard; for his arrival is the signal for a fresh start, this time probably for a longer spell, to the place where it has been decided to camp. The average speed of marching was about two and three-quarter miles an hour, and as we covered 820 miles in sixty-six marching days, the amount of ground traversed averaged twelve and a half miles a day, which, I may observe, *en parenthèse*, is far above the usual speed of heavily-laden caravans going up-country.

As soon as we reached the halting-place, generally between 11 o'clock and mid-day, suitable sites were chosen for the tents, which were at once pitched with the help of the Zanzibar soldiers. The camping-place for the porters was then marked out, cooks were set to work to boil water, make tea or coffee, and prepare luncheon; men were despatched for water, and others for firewood; every officer looked after his own tent and counted his loads as they came in; the general stores, "trade-goods," etc., were checked off, and deposited in an orderly heap in the middle of the camp, and then covered with a large tarpaulin; a strong "boma," or hedge of thorns, was made in which to enclose at night the donkeys or cattle accompanying us, and sentries were posted at such places as were thought suitable. After luncheon came the medical parade, at which the doctor had to spend a considerable time in dressing ulcers, administering quinine, and generally examining and prescribing for all those who presented themselves for treatment. Meanwhile, if not too tired, some, at least, of us would go out shooting, returning at sunset for dinner with or with-

MY TENT.

out spoils of the chase, and by 9 o'clock most, if not all, of the Europeans were safely in bed and sleeping the sleep of healthy weariness.

It would be difficult to imagine a more healthy life than this. Nothing stronger than coffee ever passed our lips except, perhaps, when the water was very high-flavoured and of a green or brown colour, an extremely diminutive allowance of whisky at bedtime; our only enemies were sore feet and fever; the weather was, on the whole, fine and pleasant, the nights cool, and the sun, after the first fortnight, not too hot; the result was, therefore, that the "hardships of African travel," of which we had all read so much, resulted, for the most of us at least, in the development of an amount of strength and of an abnormal appetite to which we had long been strangers in more civilised life.

It must not, however, be imagined that we had no troubles and no sickness in our party. We had our share of both, which shall be noticed later, and we even had cause more than once for grave anxiety; but, on the whole, for those who really kept well, the routine above described was about as health-giving a course as any that could be prescribed by a physician.

Even before the end of the first day's march, which I have endeavoured to describe in the last chapter, all signs of cultivation and of cocoa-nut plantations had disappeared. The country for the next fifty or sixty miles consisted of low undulating hills, covered with rank dry grass and stunted mimosa thorns, with a few small pools of extremely bad, thick, and stagnant water at long intervals. Occasionally, in the neighbourhood of one of these pools, was hidden a small poverty-stricken native village, inhabited, near the coast, by the Wa-Deruma,[1] and a little farther inland by the Wa-Nyika. Of these settlements and their inhabitants little need be said. Both were

---

[1] In the Swahili language, the *lingua franca* of East Africa, inflexions take place at the beginning of the word. *Wa-* is the mark of the plural.—*Ed.*

characterised by the extreme dirt and misery of their appearance; the few scant patches of grain or cassava on which the people depended for their subsistence were ill-kept, and could yield barely sufficient for the support of the villagers, certainly none for sale to passing travellers. The men carried a badly-made spear, with a small bow and poisoned arrows, and the clothing of men, women, and children alike consisted only of a single piece of very filthy and greasy cotton cloth, or an equally repulsive piece of hide. Neither men nor women showed any curiosity at our appearance, nor the slightest wish to enter into communication with the caravan, but, at the same time, they were not particularly shy, and did not run away at our approach; they appeared to be harmless, amiable, lazy, and imbued with all the philosophy of stolid stupidity. These people, the nearest in point of distance to the coast and to European development, as represented by the East Africa Company's headquarters at Mombasa, were morally farther removed from civilisation and of a lower type of intelligence than any whom we met on the whole subsequent journey.

Five days after leaving the coast we found ourselves face to face with the bugbear which had been looming before us ever since the start. This was a parched, waterless district, known as the "Taro plain," thirty-seven miles wide, extending from our camp at Taro, near a rock-hole full of green and almost putrid water, to a mountain named Maungu, in the blue distance, on whose extreme summit water is to be found during the greater part of the year. It was necessary to traverse this distance in one march, it being impossible to add to the loads already carried the weight and bulk of all the water which would be required for two days' march under a tropical sun during the hottest season of the year. The existence of this waterless plain is indeed one of the principal reasons which has caused Arab and Swahili traders to avoid the caravan route from Mombasa, and, in preference, to run the risks of attack from various native tribes to which they are exposed, by using the road from Bagamoyo or Pangani through German territory. This is less to be wondered at when it is remembered that the water at Maungu, at the north-western end of this plain, is by no means a certainty, and that when that pool is dry the march has to be prolonged from thirty-seven to about forty-eight miles, —a very severe trial for a loaded caravan, and one which, it is to be feared, has already cost many lives. I am only stating a self-evident fact in saying that this road from Mombasa can never become the main outlet for the commerce of Central Africa, so long as, in this district at all events, the only means of transport are the heads and shoulders of human porters.

It may be of some interest to give a brief account of our experiences during this march, which, it must be remembered, came upon us long before either the men or ourselves were in good walking trim. Most of us were rather stiff and weary from the un-accustomed exercise of the last few days, two of the officers and several of the men were pulled down by attacks of fever, and a large number, both of officers and men, were suffering from the blistered and ulcerated feet which are an almost inevitable consequence of the first few days' march under a tropical sun on a sandy path which burns like hot iron.

Before leaving the coast we had heard a good deal about certain wells, said to have been dug by the Imperial British East Africa Company at a place named Butzuma, in the midst of the Taro plain, and, relying on these wells, we had hoped that perhaps the greater part of the difficulty of this march had vanished, and that we should be able to halt and rest for a night half-way across. All illusions were, however, dispelled on the evening of the 6th of January, by the arrival at our camp at Taro of a party of natives who had just crossed the plain, and who told us that there was not a drop of water at Butzuma, and even laughed at our ignorance for asking such a question. In order to escape some hours, at least, the thirst-producing sun, and as, fortunately, we could rely with confidence upon a fairly bright moon, it was decided to do as much as possible of the journey by night. The men were therefore given an idle morning to lie about in the shade till 11.30 A.M., when tents were struck and the column slowly began to wind along a dusty path through a thick scrub of prickly mimosa. Soon after starting we sighted our objective point, the Maungu Mountain, standing abrupt and high out of the plain in the blue distance, and I think that our hearts sank a little as we took note of its blueness and distant appearance.

At mid-day down came the rain in a torrent such as is possible only in the tropics. Although this rather increased the difficulties of progression, and added materially to the weight of the loads, especially of the tents, the rain was received with sounds of welcome; for, we argued, now that the water is running off the rocks in little cascades, and that the path itself is churned by the feet of the leading men into a liquid slush, surely the Butzuma wells will be full of water, and we shall be able to camp there to-night and continue the march comfortably to-morrow morning.

After marching for between five and six hours we arrived at an open space, in which were two small square thatched roofs on poles. This was Butzuma, and these little squares of thatch covered the celebrated wells. The appearance of the place was not promising, and it was with a sinking heart that I went to examine the "wells." What I saw there would have been ridiculous if the attendant circumstances and the disappointment had not made it almost tragic: the much-vaunted wells consisted of two holes about eight or nine feet square by as many deep, covered over by a roof of grass-thatch in a state of considerable dilapidation; but as for water, I think I may safely say that the bottoms of these wells were the only thoroughly dry spots in the whole country within a circumference of ten miles! The afternoon was extremely oppressive and sultry, and we were all in the undignified position of being short of water with wet boots and clothes, and were also beginning to feel already that we had had enough walking for one day!

The tail of the caravan did not arrive at Butzuma till after we had been there a full hour, and the men had already, in their usual improvident manner, drunk most if not all of the water contained in the tin water-bottles which had been served out to them at the coast. It was thought advisable to make as much progress as possible before dark, and so, after allowing a short rest for the rear party, we started off again and marched till a little after sunset, i.e. for about an hour, and then stopped again. Even after this short spurt the tired rear lost a lot of ground, and did not appear till nearly an hour and a half after the leaders. Here we decided to wait till the moon should rise, and each of the Europeans contributed a little out of his water-flask into a common tea-pot, and we had some very refreshing tea and a biscuit, after which most of us got about two hours' sleep. At 11 P.M. the moon made her appearance, the tired men were kicked up somehow, loads were collected in the dark, in spite of the efforts of the "shirkers" to lose them, and once more we toiled along a pretty straight and good piece of road, which had recently been cleared for nearly ten miles by the orders of the East Africa Company. This time we struggled wearily along till 2.30 A.M., and then once more laid the seeds of future fever by lying on the ground for nearly an hour. At 3.15 A.M.

we were off again, limping forward, but now very slowly and painfully; all attempts at conversation had long ceased, and we felt inclined to regard a harmless remark addressed to any of us in the light of an insult.

With our minds a blank, our eyes fixed on the steep sides of Maungu, which in the bright moonlight now really began to look a little closer, we could do nothing but feebly hope for the end, and wonder whether we should ever get in, while the only sounds were an occasional deep curse in English or Swahili, as either a booted or a bare foot tripped over a stone or a root in the dark shadows. From time to time the ghostly form of some antelope, or the uncanny outline of a hyæna was seen crossing the path before us, or, with a hushed rustle of downy wings, some large night-bird would almost brush our faces, but the general impression produced by this forest of dry thorny scrub was one of deep, solemn, weird silence. At 4.30 A.M. the straight and newly-cleared path came to an abrupt end, and now to our other troubles were added those of sharp thorn branches hanging right across the road, which tore our faces, knocked the loads off the porters' heads, and caused additional loss of temper. At last, at 5 A.M., we arrived at a small clearing in the bush, and at the same time the first streak of dawn showed us each other's haggard faces. By mutual consent, and without a word being said, every one here threw himself once more on the ground for a little rest. The tail of the caravan straggled in within an hour, and at 6 o'clock we were off again for a last effort which should take us right in to Maungu.

By this time I don't suppose there was a pint of water left in the whole caravan, so that nothing but harm could be done by further waiting. To increase our difficulties the path now became the most circuitous, the most overgrown with thorns, and generally the most unkempt that it has ever been my fate to experience even in Africa. Our objective point, Maungu Mountain, was clearly visible, bearing W.N.W., but now we found ourselves marching sometimes due north, sometimes south, and sometimes even in an easterly direction—never seeing more than ten yards along the path ahead of us, always dodging under branches, and wrestling with thorns two and even three inches long, and as sharp as needles. Nothing, I think, is so tiring, so thoroughly heart-breaking, as the feeling thus engendered that, in spite of all one's walking and toil, one is not really making much progress, and countless were the anathemas hurled at the heads of the East Africa Company's authorities, as we realised how the expenditure of a few pounds, a few weeks' work for a few men, at any time during the five years that they have held their charter of administration, might have saved us all this trouble, might have cleared and straightened the road, and thereby shortened the whole of this accursed march by at least five miles.[1]

[1] I must here state, as Sir G. Portal would himself have done had he lived to revise these pages, that since this passage was written, a new road has been constructed by the patriotic enterprise of the late Sir W. Mackinnon,

At last, however, we began to ascend the foot of Maungu, and hoped our labours were at an end. Sharply, but in vain, we looked about for any signs of a watercourse or of a swampy piece of ground. Steeper and steeper became the path, till we felt that it only needed this ascent to break our hearts completely. By this time there was nobody anywhere near me except a couple of soldiers and a cook bearing an empty kettle. Higher and higher we climbed, despair alternating with philosophical resignation, until at length, at five minutes past 9, we emerged on an open space where there were evident traces of former camps. This, I was informed, was our destination. So far so good, and with a sigh of relief I sank down on the root of a tree, but where was the water? The irony of the situation, and the completeness of the "sell" devised by Nature, struck me as so successful that the answer only elicited a somewhat husky laugh: the water was at the extreme summit of the mountain, 1000 feet above the camping-ground! After a short discussion the two soldiers volunteered to go up and bring some water, and off they went, hung all round like Christmas-trees with the water-bottles of the men who had as yet arrived, and taking also the cook's empty kettle. For two more wearisome hours we had to wait, while a few more men dropped in, and then a shout of joy announced the return of the messengers. A very

executed at his sole expense, and continued by the public spirit of his heirs, which remedies all the defects alluded to, shortens the distance considerably, and, passing to the east of Maungu, avoids the wearisome ascent now about to be described. Reference is made to this work in chap. viii. — *Ed.*

limited drink was all I could allow to either myself or the men who had arrived, and then we sent back more volunteers with water for the tired ones scattered along the road for many miles. At the same time a fatigue party of the strongest men was despatched to help their weaker companions and to carry their loads in for them. For the rest of the morning haggard and limping men came staggering into camp, and it was not till nearly 3 o'clock in the afternoon that the whole caravan had arrived. There were many cases of exhaustion, and some of rather alarming prostration that afternoon, but I am happy to be able to add that not one ended fatally, and that there was, moreover, not one man unable to continue the march next day.

On the 9th of January we arrived, very stiff and tired, at a lovely spot at the foot of the Ndara Hills. Our camp was pitched in a grassy plain, shaded by magnificent trees, by the side of a sparkling stream of pure water which falls in a long silver thread from the summit of a lofty precipice, dashes proudly through the plain for a few hundred yards, and then loses itself suddenly in the thirsty soil. High in the precipitous mountains were hidden a few small villages of the Wa-Teita, a peaceful, harmless people, who complained bitterly of the oppression which they had suffered at the hands of passing caravans. They were very short of food, their meagre fields of maize and millet were parched and bare, and they could sell nothing to us except a few sugar-canes. In order to give a much-needed rest to the men, we stayed the whole of the next day at this pleasant spot, which gave an opportunity, to such of the officers as were not too footsore to move, for the production of guns and rifles of every calibre and every degree of modern perfection, in the anticipation of finding big game. The whole country was, however, too parched and dry; the game, which is usually reported to be in this neighbourhood, had evidently moved off to richer plains nearer the Sabaki river, and but little was seen by any of our party except a few zebra, two of which were bagged and brought to camp. The doctor was also fortunate enough to shoot a somewhat rare and curious gazelle, with a long, swan-like neck and long tail, known as Clarke's gazelle (*Ammodorcus Clarkei*). When bounding along, this creature bends its long neck backward and raises its tail over its back till they give the impression of a complete arch. I should add that not only all round our camp, but for miles in every direction, the plain was simply alive with small "button" quail. At every other step they were rising in twos and threes, and it is no exaggeration to say that every acre of grass concealed hundreds of these excellent little birds. Powder and shot was, however, far too precious to be wasted on quails of any sort.

For the next few days we pushed ahead without any adventure worth recording, crossing the Voi river, which entails nearly half an hour's walk through high rushes, water, and deep black mud of the most repulsive and odoriferous nature, and making generally rather long and forced marches till we arrived at the Tsavo river, where the East Africa Company had established their first "station" on the road to Central Africa, 140 miles from the coast. Somewhat to our disappointment, we found that this post consisted of nothing more than a mud house surrounded by a rough stockade of logs, in a dismal spot on the banks of the clear, quick-running Tsavo river, about twenty yards wide at this point. The Company's representative in charge of this station and of the surrounding district was a Portuguese half-breed youth of about seventeen years of age, who was apparently much depressed by the enforced companionship of a dozen "irregular" Arab soldiers, natives of the Persian Gulf and Hadramaut coast, deservedly looked upon at Zanzibar and along the shores of East Africa as being the veritable scum of the earth.

At Tsavo we found a quantity of flour and rice which had been sent up from Mombasa for us a week previously. From this, ten days' rations, at the rate of a pound and a half *per diem*, were dealt out to each man.

Two days afterwards, at a place named Kinani, notable chiefly for the thick, green colour and slimy character of its water, which lies in a marshy pool at the foot of a great mass of red granite rock, we obtained our first view of the mighty giant of East Africa, Mount Kilimanjaro. Late in the afternoon we had climbed to the top of the rocks and searched the horizon for the two lofty peaks, 21,000 feet above the sea-level. Before us opened an apparently endless vista of bold, rugged mountains piled up one behind the other till their outlines were lost in the red mist of the distance. It was with some disappointment that we selected the highest of these as being Kilimanjaro, and strove to make ourselves feel awe-struck and impressed with the grandeur of this monarch of a continent. But, as though the insult of this mistaken identity were too great to be borne any longer, suddenly, just as the sun began to touch the broken line of the horizon, a hitherto imperceptible mist was rolled aside as a curtain might be drawn back, and high above the highest of those ridges towered a gleaming mass of red-tinted snow and black rock. Frowning down upon the now humbled mountains around him, as though to reprove them for daring thus to depreciate his majesty, the snow-clad tyrant determined to show himself in his best aspect. Against his gleaming shoulder the setting sun nestled closer and closer; above and on either side dense masses of cloud enclosed the picture, the bold, irregular outlines of their inward edges gleaming with scarlet, purple, and gold, until the snow of the twin peaks caught the reflection and transformed itself into the richest mantle of brilliant velvet and satin. Near us not a sound was heard, all Nature was silent, the tongue of even a Rifle Brigade subaltern was stilled; spell-bound we gazed as slowly, tenderly, an imperceptible veil of mist was drawn before the face of the glory, gently and unwillingly, shrouding it as an Eastern Aphrodite dims her beauty with the transparent yashmak; darker, heavier grew the veil, until we gazed, as before, into a confused sea of gray mist and black peaks in the middle distance. Silently, and with a sigh as of relief from extreme tension, we turned away and wondered, was it real, this which we had seen?

After this incident our journey for a few days was most uninteresting. The road was fairly level, so that we managed to cover from twelve to fifteen miles every day, but there was no game, the country alternated between dense thorny scrub and sparse thorny scrub; water was only found in pools at long intervals, and was either thick, green, strong-smelling, and full of little animals, or else thick, brown, and full of mud. After an animated discussion a committee of taste decided that the latter was, on the whole, the best for culinary and drinking purposes. During these days we met an officer of the Imperial British East Africa Company returning from Uganda to the coast. He drew for our edification a most dismal picture of the general state of affairs, and of the life led by Englishmen in Uganda; but, what was far more distressing, he also brought news of a mutiny of the Company's troops at Kikuyu, and of the death at that place of Captain Nelson, who had done such gallant service and had passed through such terrible sufferings during Mr. Stanley's expedition for the relief of Emin Pasha from 1887 to 1889. Apart from the sincere sorrow caused by the news, it also gave rise to some anxiety on our own account, as Kikuyu was the station on which we were relying for the collection of a sufficient quantity of food to support the whole caravan of porters and Zanzibar soldiers across a foodless tract of some 250 miles which lay beyond that place.

On the 18th of January we struck into an excellent and well-kept road, some ten feet wide, along which the men stepped out bravely. It led us for three or four miles through a lovely park-like country, over a clear, murmuring stream, to the station of the Scottish Industrial Mission at Kibwezi, about 200 miles from the coast. The road had indeed been cleared some months before for nearly thirty miles, but all the rest of it had unfortunately been allowed to become so overgrown with bushes and long grass that the track is almost imperceptible. As we approached this Industrial Mission evidences of its work and beneficent influence were apparent on every side. Fields were being cultivated, the natives were at work, and, standing with confidence to see our caravan defile, shouted out cheery greetings to the men. This was a refreshing contrast to the conduct of the inhabitants of a village only two marches back, who had fled with every sign of panic at the sight of a white man, and who, when with difficulty they were induced to come into the camp, poured out bitter complaints of the exactions, the ill-treatment, and the violation of domicile which they had suffered at the hands of travellers.

At the Kibwezi Mission we were received with every possible kindness and hospitality, and a pleasant afternoon was spent in admiring the neatness of the gardens, the grass-built houses, the well-kept turf intersected by walks and hedges, and in noting with pleasure the trust and good-will shown by the natives of neighbouring villages. Although this Industrial Mission had only recently been established in the country—scarcely a year before—the progress it had made in the affections of the people, and the general good it had already effected in the neighbourhood, were really remarkable. The founders are to be congratulated on the success of their enterprise, which bids fair, if well supported, to rival in well-doing its elder sister, the Lovedale Mission of Southern Africa.

This establishment affords another proof, if such were needed, of the wisdom of introducing the true benefits of civilisation among natives, not in the time-honoured English fashion with a Bible in one hand and a bottle of gin or a Tower musket in the other, but by teaching simple, useful arts, or by inculcating an improved system of agriculture, the benefits of which, and the additional comforts thus acquired, are quickly noticed and appreciated by the imitative African. The ordinary African, by the way, is not half such a fool as he looks; he appreciates as much as any one the advantages of a warm blanket on chilly nights, or of an iron hoe to replace his wooden spud in digging his little field; and the man who can teach him how to earn these luxuries will obtain a proportionate influence over him. But even in Africa the general laws of supply and demand are as strong as anywhere else : it is useless to offer the ordinary tribesman wages to serve as a caravan-porter or as a coolie in some engineering work. The first he connects in his mind with heavy loads, sore and ulcerous shoulders, long marches, swearing headmen, and possibly a vision of a gang of poor fellows fastened together with chains; the second means to him continuous work, more brutal headmen, and probably over all a terrible white man with a long stick, freely used, and strings of loud oaths in a strange tongue. After careful consideration, the African comes to the conclusion that whatever may be the inducements offered in beads, wire, or even blankets, this sort of thing is "not quite good enough." He hates regular hours or anything approaching to discipline, but he is quite ready to improve his own material comforts, and even to work with that object in view, if any one will show him what to do and how to do it; but as the very foundation of his nature is suspicion, he must first have confidence in his teacher.

I have no wish to be led here into an essay on the means of disseminating civilisation in Africa: the whole question is a most complicated one and full of difficulties, and it has already formed the subject of several thousands of pages from far abler pens than mine. Theories of the most admirable nature have been laid down and clearly expounded; books, pamphlets, speeches have proved to the world that the African native is a suffering martyr or that he is a demon incarnate, and treatment has been recommended accordingly. Africa certainly cannot complain of having received insufficient attention during the last few years, and yet it must be confessed that but little progress has been made except in a few isolated instances. It is to be feared that the shortcoming has been in the practice, the *mise en exécution* of all the carefully-devised plans for the improvement of the lot of the negro. It is true that the long hide whip and chains of the white overseer are things of the past, and that slave caravans are now scarce, but it is to be greatly feared that the breechloader and the repeating rifles of the European officer and his half-disciplined troops are still emptied far too often in the cause of civilisation, and that the fire in which the African now finds himself is not much more comfortable than his former passive position in the frying-pan. All the theories, rules for guidance, and plans which have been evolved on this subject, are useless if the first principles be forgotten; the ordinary African native is a curious compound of suspicion, superstition, child-like simplicity, and mulish obstinacy: if he knows and trusts his leader he may be guided gently towards civilisation, may be made a useful member of society, and even a Christian, but he will resist with the whole force of his nature any attempts to kick him from behind into comfort or into heaven.

CHAPTER IV

The scene of a Masai raid—Our first rhinoceros—Arrival at Machakos—Victualling the caravan—On the war-path—I bag a lion—The Wa-kamba tribe and warriors—The Wa-Kikuyu.

At Kibwezi Major Owen had a sharp attack of gastro-intestinal catarrh, but, fortunately, it was possible to get him out of his tent and into a comparatively warm and comfortable house, and as the next day's march was to be a short one of only about six miles, he had a long morning's rest, at the end of which he was sufficiently recovered to be able to accompany the caravan on one of the invaluable ponies. Regretfully we turned our backs on the hospitable mission-house, where we had enjoyed the luxuries of fresh milk, butter, bread, glasses, clean tablecloths, and wine, to which we had been strangers since leaving the coast, and unwillingly we felt compelled to turn a deaf ear to the petitions of the men, who clamoured for a day's rest on the plea that they were being worn out by travelling at this unprecedented pace. As though to confirm the justice of their dismal forebodings, almost immediately after crossing the Kibwezi river we entered upon two or three miles of the worst bit of road which we had the misfortune to encounter during the whole journey. Loose slabs and lumps of lava piled one above the other, with points like needles and edges like razors, cut our boots into ribbons, and reduced the already limping caravan to a sorry plight. Several extinct craters, visible in a range of hills on our west flank, showed clearly the origin of this lava, which was satisfactory from a geological point of view, but of little consolation to a porter with sixty-five pounds on his head and with bleeding feet, or to the officer who sadly watched the dissolution of what was of more value to him than its weight in gold—his precious pair of boots.

So far our experience of Africa as a country for sport, or indeed for anything except rank grass and stunted thorn bushes, had been most unfavourable. We had walked over 200 miles, and except for the very few beasts shot by those who were well enough to go out at Ndara a fortnight ago, we had not even seen any four-footed animal larger or more dangerous than a well-grown field-mouse. The general impression was gaining ground that African shooting was "a fraud," that big game was a myth, and that former travellers had been addicted to romance. I may as well say at once, that long before we reached the end of our journey we acknowledged that on two of these points our fears were not justified. On 20th January, two days after leaving Kibwezi, we entered what really looked like a more promising country. Over rolling hills and open grass-land dotted with fine trees, we travelled through an immense park. At a mid-day halt for luncheon we counted over a hundred hartebeest and a dozen ostriches within a mile of us; later in the afternoon we passed two herds of that most beautiful of all animals, the "Grant's gazelle" (*G. Grantii*), besides several little "Kirk's gazelles." On every side were tracks of giraffe and rhinoceros, but I do not think that any of our party saw either of these animals. Unfortunately, we had but little time for stalking or shooting this day : we had to do a march of over seventeen miles, and it was therefore impossible to stray very far from the path without having to make up a most disagreeable amount of "lee-way" afterwards. A couple of hartebeest (*Bubalis Cokei*) and a Kirk's gazelle were, however, collected on the march and formed a most welcome addition to the meagre fare of the men, hardly any of whom had tasted meat since we left the coast.

As we neared the camping-place we noticed that some of the old hands among the men began to point significantly to the remains of a disused "boma" or thorn fence near the path, and to tell some tale evidently of a thrilling nature, in connection with the place. On inquiry, we learnt that at this spot, only four months ago, a caravan of Swahili traders were peacefully encamped for the night, dreaming of no danger, but congratulating themselves on approaching the end of their journey after an absence of more than a year. They had built the "boma" as an enclosure for their donkeys and cattle, but the men were confidently sleeping in the open ground outside.

Suddenly, at midnight, they were rudely awakened by a din as of the infernal regions. By the fitful firelight, as they started up, they caught a vision of immense weird forms, apparently above the height of men, towering high above whose heads were strange shapes and devices—horns of antelopes and of cows, crowns or halos of long eagle-feathers, the skins and grinning heads of monkeys, of leopards, and of cats, and as they moved there was a clash of many bells attached to their thighs, knees, and ankles; like demons these huge forms flitted and bounded about between the fires, while the light glanced from off their strange head-gear, their garters and anklets of bells, from great shields painted with patterns of red, black, and white, and, above all, from mighty spears seven feet high, with keen broad blades of nearly half their length. Not for long were the unfortunate Swahilis and coast-traders allowed to gaze in terror on these sights; barely had they time to realise that these tall and active forms were not ghosts or intangible visitors of any kind, but veritable Masai warriors in all their war dress, and that the hideous noise meant that their peaceful camp was the scene of a midnight Masai raid, when amid the shouts and clash of bells was heard the dull thud of sharp iron cutting into flesh and breaking through bone, and the ghoulish, triumphant laughter which burst from the leaping warriors was mingled with more than one despairing shriek, startling the prowling hyænas more than a mile away, but ending too often in an inarticulate gurgle as the broad blade crashed from breast-bone to spine. One shot only was heard, one Masai rolled on the ground, and one man of the doomed caravan had time to seize his gun, plunge into the friendly darkness of the bush, and escape, eventually reaching the coast with a tale of having alone resisted and vanquished a war party of 100 Masai after all his companions had been killed. Long before daylight the camp was silent, the "boma" had been opened, and the cattle driven off. The warrior band were already many miles away when the sun rose on the scene, and revealed a confused heap of broken bales, scattered boxes, and distorted corpses, through whose gaping wounds the life-blood was still welling as gaunt, mangy hyænas fought and snarled and tore the warm limbs asunder with their jaws of iron.

Not having the least desire for any similar experience, we made a formidable "boma" round our camp that night on the banks of the Kiboko (Hippopotamus) river, posting at suitable places round the camp pickets of Zanzibari soldiers, who took measures for ensuring the safety of the whole party by lighting great fires, by shouting out "Halt! who goes there?" to the immense astonishment of any porter happening to stray near them for the next hour, and by then going comfortably to sleep for the rest of the night, with the complacent consciousness of having done as much duty as could reasonably be expected of them.

The next day was rendered famous for the death of our first rhinoceros, which happened in this wise. After the day's march was over and the camp arranged, Major Owen, accompanied by a native boy, was pensively strolling with a rifle up a narrow, sandy, dry watercourse fringed on either side by dense thickets of thorny bush on high banks. Rounding a corner he found himself face to face with a huge rhinoceros, sauntering with equal deliberation towards him, and only ten or fifteen paces distant. Both were at first equally startled by the encounter, and stopped for a few seconds to look at each other. The rhinoceros, after pondering over the matter, evidently had no desire for a further acquaintance, and began to turn his unwieldy carcass round in the narrow path. This offered a fair side shot, of which the gallant Major took prompt advantage, and in another moment the huge brute lay like a great boulder across the torrent-bed. During the same afternoon I, strolling similarly in search of adventure, happened to strike on fresh rhinoceros tracks at some distance from this spot. Following the spoor I soon came upon unmistakable proofs that the beast could not be more than a very short distance ahead, and every faculty and nerve was therefore kept at full tension. Soon I heard a great crashing and crackling of bushes close to the right-hand side, where a small game track debouched on to the stream-bed which I was following. Down behind a rock sank my boy and myself, nearer came the crashing and crackling, rifle was held ready, and our eyes vainly tried to pierce the blackness of the jungle. At last, to judge from the sound, the animal, whatever it was, could scarcely be ten yards from our ambush, and in another second would give a fair shot. A louder tearing of thorns than usual was followed by an angry snort, clearly proving that it was no animal of the antelope species before us, when suddenly I was considerably startled by this angry snort being followed by a very distinct and articulate sound, in which we recognised the three good Anglo-Saxon words, "D—— these thorns!" For the second time that afternoon, as we advanced from our hiding-place, the Major was startled by an unexpected encounter in the bush. He then conducted me to the place where his rhinoceros lay dead across the path; the tracks which I had been following for so long led up to the carcass, and then ceased.

By this time the news of the dead rhinoceros had reached camp, where, as nothing in the shape of meat is unwelcome to the stomach of a Swahili porter, except ostrich, lion, and hyaena, it was received with shouts of joy. In a marvellously short space of time the ominous number of patients who were waiting their turn for treatment outside the doctor's tent had dwindled down to two or three genuine sufferers, and soon a solid mass of half-naked men, all flourishing long knives and yelling at the top of their voices, was tearing across country in the direction of the carcass. The scene which ensued on their arrival defies description. In the twinkling of an eye the armour-like hide of the beast was ripped open in a dozen places; great lumps of dark, coarse, repulsive-looking flesh were being hacked and torn off; knives dripping with blood were gleaming, slashing, and digging in

the most dangerous way in every available spot;
men behind were pushing and trying to climb over
or force their way under their more fortunate comrades in front; others were thrusting their long
sharp weapons over the shoulders and between the
legs of their rivals; several, drenched with blood and
offal from head to foot, were standing and struggling
actually inside the carcass; porters, who during the
morning had either carried their loads cheerfully and
with quaint songs along the road, or who had whiningly tried to shirk their duty by complaining of
sore feet or stomach-ache, were now transformed by
the sight of meat and the smell of blood into an
assemblage of wild beasts. The whole scene was
instructive, but absolutely sickening. A pack of
fox-hounds breaking up a fox were tame lap-dogs in
comparison to these men. I could think of nothing
in the annals of the human race to which they could
be likened, unless it were Carlyle's description of the
Megaeras of the French Revolution.

Without further adventure we ended a long and
tiring march on the 22nd of January, at the Company's station at Nzoi. The station itself consisted
of a small hut, inhabited by an elderly Swahili, who
was assisted in his duties by a small boy. These
duties consisted in taking care of certain stores of
food which were occasionally sent there for the supply of the East Africa Company's caravans. All the
way from Kibwezi the country had been gradually
improving in appearance, but from Nzoi its character underwent a complete change. We now entered

the mountainous district of Ulu, well watered, densely populated, and extensively cultivated with Indian corn, sugar-cane, potatoes, and beans. Here, too, for the first time we began to complain of the cold at night, and found in the morning that the men were most unwilling to leave the neighbourhood of their fires. The pleasures of starting to march at sunrise in a heavy wet mist under these circumstances were not increased by the fact that for the greater part of two days' journey our road lay along the course of a mountain torrent, up which we had to wade against a swift stream, sometimes on soft, yielding sand, and sometimes over loose stones or great boulders of rock. Although the nights and early mornings were so cold, the heat of the sun later in the day was very oppressive in the deep gully up which we travelled: the rays were refracted from every rock, no breeze could penetrate into the gorge, and as we marched along we felt our heads almost splitting and the skin being scorched from our backs, while our nether limbs were ploughing through the icy water. The people of the far-reaching Wa-kamba race appeared to be industrious, friendly, and intelligent, but it was not pleasant for an Englishman to notice that at the first sight of a European, these people, living on the main caravan road of British East Africa, fled with shrieks and with every sign of terror. When some of the neighbouring chiefs had, with some difficulty, been induced to visit our camp, we were the recipients of a string of bitter complaints against caravans which had previously passed along this road, and long stories were told us of burnt villages, looted cattle, and of volleys poured into flying crowds. Into the merits of such stories it is outside the scope of this account to enter, and I would only remark that Africans are wonderfully good hands at making a big business out of a small one, and that native evidence can seldom be taken *au pied de la lettre*.

After a steady ascent of four days from Nzoi, for the most part over rounded grassy hills and through a pleasant country, we saw in the morning of the 26th of January the Company's flag flying over a strong, well-built fort and stockade, surrounded by a ditch and wire entanglement enclosing a well-arranged collection of good buildings and an orderly garden. This was the station of Machakos, 300 miles from the coast, and 4500 feet above the sea-level. Around the station crowds of Wa-kamba were walking about in the most friendly and confident manner, herds of cattle were grazing, and the whole scene was a picture of peace and prosperity in which the frowning stockade, ditch, and armed sentries stood forth in strong contrast. Our eyes and appetites were agreeably tickled by the sight of trim beds bright with well-known English flowers of every kind, side by side with a flourishing kitchen-garden well filled with lettuce, cabbages, beans, green peas, and all sorts of luxuries to which we from Zanzibar and the coast had long been strangers. Greedily we were anticipating the pleasures of a much-needed day of rest in this delightful spot, when our joy was effectually damped by the news that the main body of the caravan under Mr. Foaker had indeed arrived safely at the Company's station at Kikuyu, but only to find a state of war existing between the Company and the surrounding native tribes. Not an ounce of food could be collected there by love, money, or force. For their daily sustenance the Company's people were sending out foraging parties to dig potatoes in the fields of the natives, to cut down their sugar-canes, or to drive in their cattle. It was not surprising, under these circumstances, that Mr. Foaker's invitation to the tribes to come forward and sell food for our caravan had remained without effect, and that he had consequently been unable to make any preparation of any sort for the 280 miles of foodless country which lay before us. Fortunately, at Machakos there was both peace and plenty: had we arrived during one of the not unfrequent "tiffs" between the Company and the neighbouring Wa-kamba, the chances of the Expedition reaching Uganda before the evacuation of the 31st of March would have been small indeed. As it was, with the energetic help of Mr. Ainsworth, the Company's local representative, about 400 loads of flour were collected like magic; 100 natives agreed to carry loads to Kikuyu on condition that we undertook to escort them back again; we were able to engage the services of all the porters and donkeys of a Swahili caravan which happened to be stopping at Machakos on its way to the coast; and thus, by leaving behind all the other officers with their tents and baggage, and impressing their porters into the food-carrying service, Colonel Rhodes, the doctor, and I were able to start at daybreak next morning with a long string of people carrying nearly 500 loads of flour.

To the reader unaccustomed to African travel this amount will no doubt appear excessive for the requirements of a caravan, unless he will give himself the trouble to do a short sum in simple addition and multiplication. The problem before us was this: we had a caravan consisting of some 400 porters and 200 soldiers, in all 600 hungry stomachs, to lead across 280 miles of uninhabited country, throughout which not a spoonful of food of any sort could be procured except such game as might be shot by the Europeans. To every man was allowed a pound and a half of coarse flour *per diem*—a small enough quantity on which to walk twelve miles a day over a cold and mountainous country with a load weighing from 60 to 70 lbs. on his head; the caravan would thus consume 900 lbs. of flour a day, or 22,500 lbs. in 25 days; adding to this the very small allowance of 250 lbs. for loss from leaking sacks, from rain, from flooded rivers, or any of the thousand and one accidents which happen to such goods in such a country, we thus had to start from Kikuyu with at least 22,750 lbs. of flour, in addition to all the other loads, which already seemed as much as the men could manage to carry. The difficulty was no slight one; some of the strongest men might perhaps be able to bear an extra weight of some 20 lbs., but if we were to overload the whole caravan we should not only incur a charge of cruelty, but should also run a grave risk of defeating our own object by breaking down the men, or by "breaking their hearts" in a way that is fatally familiar to many an owner of gallant horses condemned to run under the "top weight" in handicaps. To increase the number of men was out of the question; no more were procurable in these countries, and in any case this would only have added to the difficulty by doubling the number of mouths to be fed. Our only hope was in donkeys, which by East African custom are supposed—though, as we afterwards discovered, most erroneously—to be able to carry a weight equal to two men's loads, *i.e.* 130 lbs., and to pick their own living by the wayside. We had relied on being able to procure a sufficient number of these animals at Kikuyu, and in ordinary times should no doubt have been able to do so, but what were our prospects now that we learnt that the Kikuyu tribes were practically holding the Company's station in a state of siege? It appeared as though our only chance of reaching Uganda in time lay in leaving nearly all the officers to kick their heels in idleness for two months at Machakos, while one or two of us pushed forward with all their porters laden with food. It will be readily understood that it was with no little anxiety that we said good-bye to those who were to remain behind, as we turned our faces towards the distant blue mountains which rose from the plain between us and Kikuyu.

As though to compensate us for our somewhat

gloomy situation, the road from Machakos to Kikuyu lay through some of the most delightful country that it is possible to conceive, and absolutely at variance with all accepted notions about Equatorial Africa. As we walked along that morning over rich pastures and rolling downs, breathing mountain air exhilarating as that of the Scottish Highlands in August, the flagging spirits of the men, somewhat sulky at having been defrauded of their promised rest, rose at every step, until great herds of antelope were seen galloping away as the echoes were roused by some ringing—and usually obscene—Swahili chorus. As we sat that night in greatcoats round a blazing fire, we agreed that it would be impossible to feel ill in this district, and that if only communications with the coast were a little simplified, as they easily could be, no life could be more delightful than that of the first European settlers on these plains, with magnificent scenery on every side, clear streams of water, a practically unlimited extent of the richest pasture, any amount of what is now probably the best and most varied shooting in the world, and a complete immunity —at least for the present—from telegrams or "interviews," circulars or companies, dinner-parties or duns.

Next morning, wishing to get some shooting before all the game within a ten-mile circle should have been scared by our noisy caravan, I started with a single gun-bearer about an hour before sunrise, and groped my way ahead through a heavy Scotch mist. After about three hours' walking, during which ghostly forms of horns and heads had occasionally shown themselves as a rattling of hoofs announced the invisible vicinity of great herds of hartebeest or of the "Grant's gazelle," a sudden rift in the mist revealed to us that we were nearing a steep grassy hill. It disclosed at the same time a sight which caused my boy and myself to drop in our tracks as though we were shot, and to lie prone on our stomachs in the grass. Less than a quarter of a mile ahead of us a long string of natives in single file was crossing our path at right angles to it. A single glance showed us that this was no peaceful trading-party; no women were visible, no sheep or goats, nobody carried a load, but we clearly saw that every man was fully armed; bright blades flashed through the mist, a long bow was in every right hand, and a full quiver of poisoned arrows hung at every back. Swiftly and silently these warriors, on mischief bent, defiled before us as we crouched on the plain; 550 men we counted, and then the long procession passed slowly out of sight round the shoulder of a hill. As the last glittering spear disappeared we rose to our feet with a sigh of relief and looked back for any signs of the approach of our caravan. Hardly, however, had we turned our heads when our nerves were destined to receive another shock. At less than thirty paces from us, flat on their stomachs as we had been, watching us as we had been watching the native war-party, were three lions, whose tails were wickedly thrashing down the grass behind them as they appeared to be weighing the question of attack or retreat. Fortunately my gun-bearer was a sturdy, plucky youth, and not a native of Zanzibar, who would probably have turned and fled and left me weaponless; he remained motionless as he gently, almost imperceptibly passed a loaded rifle into my hands. As I raised the gun to my shoulder the three lions sprang up together, and I am ashamed to confess that a somewhat hasty shot resulted in a clean miss! The second barrel, however, produced the dull thud of a bullet penetrating flesh and bone, but to my intense annoyance there was no apparent effect on the lions. These animals simultaneously took two bounds forward, and again halted and crouched, while I was hastily ramming in a couple more cartridges. Before I had time to load they were up again, and off at full speed, but this time in the opposite direction. As soon as possible I prepared for a parting shot at the last of the three, but to our astonishment, before I touched the trigger, the lion suddenly turned a complete somersault, and then lay on the plain motionless. On running up we found the beast quite dead, with the clear track of my second bullet in at one side and out at the other, clean through the very middle of his heart! Since receiving this wound, from an express ·577 solid bullet, the brute had charged forward about ten yards, had crouched, risen again, and bounded away for nearly a hundred paces!

When at last the caravan arrived on the scene, a few inquiries from the local natives who were carrying flour elicited the information that the war-party which had passed us consisted of the warriors of all the Wa-kamba villages round Machakos, who were bound on a great raiding expedition against their hereditary enemies the Masai. It struck us, not unnaturally, as being somewhat remarkable that nothing should have been known of this expedition by the British Company's representative, from whom we had parted the preceding day, and who was, theoretically at least, in charge of the administration of the whole of this district.

These Wa-kamba, who thus dare to attack the dreaded Masai in their own country, are a somewhat interesting race. Not many years ago they were almost unknown outside a small district on the Ulu Hills, but while all neighbouring tribes have been exterminated or scattered far and wide beyond the ever-increasing radius of the Masai raids, the Wa-kamba have been able to hold their own, and are now, as we have seen, beginning even to assume an aggressive attitude. They are a fine, active, well-grown race of a dark brown colour, and, probably, of purely African origin. Their men, though not so tall as the gigantic Masai warriors, are frequently quite six feet in height, and present a grand picture of muscular development. They appear to combine, to a degree unusual among East African tribes, the instincts and tastes of a pastoral and of an agricultural people; and while we had practical experience of the ease with which the villages round Machakos could, at a moment's notice, supply us with about eight tons of grain and flour, we saw their hill slopes covered with great flocks of goats and sheep, intermingled with not a few cows. The terrible epidemic which two years ago destroyed nearly every head of cattle, all the wild buffaloes, and most of the wildebeest in East Africa, did not spare the Wakamba, who told us that they had then lost every bull and cow belonging to their tribe; but whether by honest purchase, or, as is more likely, by successful raids, they appear to have succeeded in again collecting a small stock for breeding purposes.

Although the climate in their hills is often extremely cold, and made both ourselves and our porters very loath to leave our beds at sunrise, the men of this tribe wear but little clothing, being usually content with a short apron of hide slung in front of them, supplemented sometimes by a similar apron behind. I observed, however, that in the principal villages near the caravan road some of the chiefs had already taken to wearing far warmer draperies of cotton cloth, and I have no doubt that should traffic through their districts be at all developed, in a very short time both men and women will barter the corn far more eagerly for cloth than they now do for blue beads or for small round looking-glasses. Apropos of looking-glasses, an assemblage of Wa-kamba warriors under the morning sun is literally one of the most dazzling spectacles to be seen in this continent. No article of civilisation is more prized than a small circular mirror, about two inches in diameter, and framed in some gilt metal, the whole thing costing at the coast about twopence. Every warrior who respects himself possesses one of these articles of luxury, which he fastens with a string of blue beads to the centre of his forehead. Then, when he has decorated his arms, legs, neck, and waist with many coils of brilliantly-polished iron or brass wire, and has smeared his sleek body with a thorough coating of castor-oil, he can stalk proudly about in the bright sunlight like an animated heliograph.

The arms of the full-grown Mkamba consist of a good-sized bow with a full quiver of poisoned arrows, a straight, spatulate-shaped sword, and sometimes, but not often, an oblong shield of thick hide. This tribe is almost the only one I know in Africa which despises the spear as an offensive weapon, and prefers to rely exclusively on poisoned arrows, with the sword for use at close quarters or for despatching the wounded. It goes without saying that with the bow and arrow they are extremely expert and powerful marksmen. The expenditure of a couple of cartridges to kill a brace of the huge kites which always hover around a camp is well compensated by the gratitude of a whole tribe of Wa-kamba, who prize the strong and wiry feathers of these birds above all others for binding on to the shafts of their poisoned arrows. These people appear to be somewhat more prolific than most of their neighbours; the number of children to be seen in their villages is considerable, and both men and women carefully eschew various articles of diet, among others eggs of any kind or in any form, which are supposed to induce sterility. More probable and practical reasons for their increasing population are that they live in a bracing climate, and above all, that they appear to practise but few of the horrible customs of infanticide, of executions for supposed witchcraft, and of public murders for various superstitious reasons, which year by year, and month by month, stain the soil of the continent with the blood of so many thousands of victims among the neighbouring tribes throughout almost the whole extent of British and German East Africa.

The result of the expedition, of which I had witnessed the march on the morning of the 28th of January, we never heard. Having been secretly planned and organised it was probably unexpected by the Masai, and therefore successful; but the chances are that at least a dozen or twenty of the warriors who defiled before me in the early morning mist were before the next sunrise lying stiff, with an enormous gash in their breasts from a broad-bladed Masai spear, or were already torn in pieces and scattered over the plain by a scuffling mob of strong-jawed hyænas. The *modus procedendi* in these Wa-kamba raids is nearly always the same: on approaching the village or district to be attacked, the whole party is divided into two bodies, of which the stronger creeps silently round to the rear of the unconscious enemy's position, while, after an interval to enable their companions to reach their allotted station, the other party makes a sudden and noisy rush, with much whooping and yelling, at the principal gate. The attack is generally made either at night or with the first streak of dawn. While the Masai warriors seize their great spears and rush out to engage the attacking party in hand-to-hand combat, the women, children, cattle, and old men stream out of the back of the village, to seek shelter in the bush or in some neighbouring and perhaps stronger kraal. These, of course, all fall into the arms of the hidden Wa-kamba of the main body, who rapidly knock the old men on the head, despatch or neglect the children, seize all the women, girls, and cattle, and hurry off with their booty, giving a signal to their friends, who are maintaining the fierce combat with the warriors, that the object being successfully accomplished they may now retire with all speed from the fight. The whole party then return as quickly as possible to their own country, and the Masai women and girls, if they are not sold to some Swahili slave-trader, settle down to be mothers of Wa-kamba children, with the same material philosophy and animal contentment that they had previously displayed among their own people. A retaliatory raid would surely follow an episode of this sort, but the Wa-kamba villages are perched in safe positions on precipitous hills; they are not so easily attacked, and they keep good sentries. The Masai have more than once burnt their fingers severely in attempting to exact their revenge.

For two days we continued to march across the magnificent plain of pasture; the Athi river by which it is watered was fortunately low, and offered no serious difficulty, and such was the abundance of game, that we three Europeans—Colonel Rhodes, Dr. Moffat, and myself—had no difficulty in furnishing an ample supply of meat for the whole crowd of our 600 followers. Among other beasts four rhinoceroses were killed—two of them by Colonel Rhodes with the new army Lee-Metford rifle and its microscopic bullet. On comparing notes in the evening, we found that we three had, collectively, seen during the day specimens of the following animals, some of them singly, and some of them in many hundreds: rhinoceros, buffalo, hippopotamus, lion, zebra, wildebeest, waterbuck, hartebeest; *Gazella Grantii, Thomsoni, Kirkii*; pah, mpallah, hare; geese, guinea-fowl, florican, partridge, and snipe. There are, I imagine, but few other spots left in the world where nineteen different sorts of game animals may be seen in one day.

On the morning of the 30th January we left the open plain and plunged into the darkness of a dense belt of forest, which forms the natural boundary of the regions inhabited by the treacherous, cunning, and usually hostile people of Kikuyu. Warned by the state of affairs which we had heard was prevailing at the Company's fort in this district, we were careful to keep all our people close together, every man within a couple of paces of his neighbour. One European marched in front, one in the rear, and one in the middle of the long line. The Wa-Kikuyu, as we knew, seldom or never show themselves, or run the risk of a fight in the open, but lie like snakes in long grass, or in some dense bush within a few yards of the line of march, watching for a gap in the ranks, or for some incautious porter to stray away or loiter a few yards behind; even then not a sound is heard;

a scarcely perceptible "twang" of a small bow, the almost inaudible "whizz" of a little arrow for a dozen yards through the air, a slight puncture in the arm, throat, or chest, followed, almost inevitably, by the death of a man. Another favourite trick of the Wa-Kikuyu is to plant poisoned skewers in the path, set at an angle of about forty-five degrees, pointing towards the direction from which the stranger is expected. If the path is much overgrown or hidden by the luxuriant growth of long grass, these stakes are sometimes of much greater length, and so pointed that they would pierce the stomach of any one advancing towards them. Keeping a sharp look-out for these delicate attentions, our progress was inevitably slow, but at length we arrived without further adventure at the strong stockade, ditch, brick houses, and well-guarded stores known as Fort Smith in Kikuyu, above which was floating the Company's flag.

CHAPTER V

A state of siege at Kikuyu—An ivory caravan—We push on for Uganda—The game-abounding prairies of Lake Naivasha—First introduction to Masai warriors—The Masai tribe—The Salt Lake of Elmenteita—Hartebeest and antelope—An African forest.

AT Kikuyu Fort we found Lieutenant Arthur and Mr. Foaker in excellent health, and evidently thriving on the superabundance of good things produced by the admirable garden which was tended as the apple of his eye by Mr. Purkiss, the Company's representative in charge of the station, and which, for the variety, the abundance, and the general excellence of its produce, would put to shame many of the kitchen gardens that are the pride of English country houses. Here, too, we met Mr. Martin, a caravan-leader in the Company's service, who had just arrived from Uganda with a large caravan, laden principally with some £8000 worth of ivory. It was satisfactory to learn from this gentleman that when he left Uganda, some seven weeks before, all had been apparently quiet in that country, and that he had experienced no unusual difficulties in the countries through which he had passed. The great stack in the midst of Mr. Martin's camp, of about 15,000 lbs. of ivory, was a curious and interesting sight, and one which could now be nowhere seen out of East Africa. It gave a better idea than could be gained by any amount of reading, both of the immense numbers of elephants which are wandering about the head waters of the Nile, and of the terrible slaughter of these animals which is annually, daily, taking place in order that

GROUP FROM A CARAVAN PREPARING TO START WITH IVORY.

Europe and America may be supplied with billiard balls and piano-keys. Many of the tusks were over 70 lbs. in weight, and one magnificent piece of ivory pulled the scale at 140 lbs.

For our edification, Mr. Martin had a parade of his "strong men," viz. the men who were carrying the heaviest tusks on the journey. At his call, some twenty grand specimens of black humanity

came forward, each seized a tusk over 80 lbs. in
weight, with a Hercules at their head carrying the
gigantic one of 140 lbs. As though they had feathers
on their shoulders, these men fell into line, and then
actually proceeded to dance under a weight which
would deprive most average Englishmen of the power
of motion. Round and round in a large circle they
danced, singing a weird, monotonous chant, from time
to time, on a given signal from their leader, swinging
the great ivories from one shoulder to the other, the
muscles standing out on their necks and backs in
great solid lumps, glistening in the sun. It was a
sight worth recording, particularly when we remembered that these men were not only capable of performing these feats of strength for our amusement,
but that, as a matter of course, they were carrying
these crushing weights for five or six hours a day,
over mountains, through deep morasses and rushing
torrents, week after week throughout the 800 wearisome miles which intervene between Uganda and
the coast.

To ourselves, however, whose thoughts were ever
fixed on Uganda and the means of getting there, a
far more interesting sight than strong men and traders'
ivory was a fairly large herd of donkeys browsing
within the precincts of Mr. Martin's camp. These
animals had just carried food for his caravan from
Kavirondo to Kikuyu; between this place and the
coast he would have no further use for them, and in
a short time the whole lot, except an ominously large
proportion who were suffering from terrible and re-

volting sore backs and withers, became the property of H.M. Government "for a consideration." They were not a good collection of animals, far from it, and moreover they had just completed a very trying journey of 280 miles under heavy loads; but there was no choice open to us, and by taking over all that were capable of going we made it possible for the whole party to resume the journey to Uganda together. Most of the beasts could at all events carry something, and by an East African fallacy donkeys are supposed to thrive on what they are able to pick up for themselves on the road, whether the season be wet or dry, and whether the grass be young and green or burnt and yellow. We therefore lost no time in sending back messengers, under escort, to tell the officers who had been left at Machakos to push forward and rejoin us with all possible speed.

A few days' compulsory rest at Kikuyu did good to all the men, and probably to the Europeans also, though it was rather a curious fact that most of us were laid up there for a day or two after our arrival; perhaps in some cases from over-indulgence in the unaccustomed luxuries of fresh vegetables, green food, and fresh provisions of all sorts. Outside the fort itself the state of affairs was not so pleasant to contemplate: we were surrounded, day and night, by a complete ring of hostile Wa-Kikuyu, hidden in the long grass or bushes, and for any one to wander alone more than 200 yards from the stockade was almost certain death. On the morning of our arrival, a porter of Martin's caravan, who had strayed down to the long grass at the foot of the little hill on which the station is built, was speared through the back, and killed, within 250 paces of our tents. A short time before, eight soldiers in the Company's service who were foraging for food—probably in an illicit manner— were all massacred in a neighbouring village; and a day or two before our arrival the natives had even had the temerity to try to set fire to the fort itself at night.

Meanwhile, as no food for the garrison could be bought in the neighbourhood, although the whole country was literally covered with cultivation, strong armed parties had been sent out every day to dig potatoes, cut sugar-cane and corn-cobs, and otherwise collect food for themselves. This system, added to the fortuitous and almost simultaneous arrival of Mr. Martin with some 600 men and abundance of guns from the west, and of ourselves with a similar number of men from the east, appears to have made the Wa-Kikuyu reflect that their true interests lay rather in the direction of peace than in the continuation of their inefficient blockade; and on the 2nd of February about thirty chiefs of as many neighbouring villages presented themselves at the fort gates, and informed the Company's representative that they had had enough of war and now wished to try a little trade. Terms of peace were soon arranged, and the remaining days of our residence at Fort Smith were in consequence a good deal more comfortable, although every one knew that, peace or war, no native inhabitant of this district could be trusted to keep his spear out of the back of a defenceless stranger, if ever he were offered a fair opportunity without much danger of retaliation.

The Wa-Kikuyu, and especially that section of them who occupy the neighbourhood of the Company's fort, are undoubtedly a treacherous, untrust-

GROUP AT KIKUYU.
Mr. Ernest Berkeley. Lieutenant Arthur. Sir Gerald Portal. Major Owen.

worthy crowd, and have for many years been a source of constant trouble to passing caravans; but, on the other hand, they are not without their good qualities. They are, above all things, industrious and careful agriculturists; their crops are plentiful, clean, and

well cared for; their sweet potatoes are twice or
three times the size of any that I have seen either
on the coast or in other parts of the interior, and the
same remark applies to their corn, beans, and other
produce; they appear to have no objection, unless
they happen to be at war at the time, to travellers
helping themselves from the fields as they pass, so
long as this system is carried on in moderation; and
they appear to cultivate, from very love of the work
and of the soil, far more than they can either consume
themselves or hope to sell to caravans. It was not
unusual to see acres of potatoes or beans allowed to
rot and run to seed in the ground, simply because the
natives had no need of them, and did not care to take
the trouble to gather the whole of their harvest. This
mania of theirs for planting and sowing is carried to
an extreme which is actually harmful to their country,
as in pursuance of their hobby, by constantly taking
up fresh land, they are year by year destroying
thousands of fine timber trees, and rapidly dis-
afforesting great tracts in a region which is already
not overburdened with woodland. It will, however,
be a matter of time and difficulty, requiring great
tact, patience, and firmness, to induce these Wa-
Kikuyu to have confidence in Europeans, and to
discontinue their practice of spearing or otherwise
murdering any defenceless Swahili porter whom they
may find straying away by himself. Their experience
of European travellers up to the present time has not,
it must be confessed, been calculated to inspire them
with any great love for the white man. They have

been given a bad name, which sticks to them like a burr, and the stranger arriving within their gates treats them accordingly. Long before I went into their country myself I remember being told by an African traveller of great renown that the only way in which to deal with the Kikuyu people, whether singly or in masses, was "to shoot at sight."

The Company's station is situated at almost the extreme southern limit of their territory; the inhabitants of that district are, I believe, the least admirable of the whole race, and are even looked upon as black sheep and outcasts by the more respectable members of the same tribe who live farther north. The country of the Wa-Kikuyu extends in a long strip from the neighbourhood of the Company's fort northwards to Mount Kenia and the river Tana. The whole of this region lies 5000 to 7000 feet above the sea-level, enjoys a perfect climate eminently suited to Europeans, is of the most remarkable fertility, producing, apparently, the grains and vegetables of England and of Africa with impartial luxuriance, and is well watered throughout by innumerable clear mountain streams.

On the 5th of February the second half of our party, which had been left at Machakos, arrived in safety and without adventure, and for the first time all the members of the expedition sat down to luncheon together. Only, however, for one meal was this the case, for before the evening our doctor, who for some days had been suffering from slight fever, was seriously ill with all the symptoms of that most dreaded of common African diseases, "Black water" or hæmaturic fever. All through the next day poor Moffat's condition gave rise to the most serious anxiety, but on the 7th he was so much better that we decided to push on with the caravan, leaving Captain Portal to nurse the doctor and to bring him on after us if he was able to move before the 12th. I am thankful to say that he was well enough to start on the 10th, riding a pony which had been left for that purpose, and that he and my brother caught us up on the 17th about a hundred miles farther on our road.

Our first march from Kikuyu was rendered memorable by a ludicrous, though to the sufferers, an extremely disagreeable *contretemps*. Walking in front as usual, I had arrived at a suitable camping place, and selected the site for our camp, but was surprised to find not more than a dozen porters with me. We waited for half an hour, growing more and more surprised at the non-appearance of the rest, as the march had been an exceptionally short and easy one, and there had really been no apparent excuse for such straggling. At last a man turned up with a box on his head, and to my somewhat anxious inquiries about the whole caravan answered the single word "nyuki" (bees)! This explained the mystery; and soon the demoralised and disorganised party began to straggle in twos and threes into camp, showing every sign of having passed through a severe engagement with their persistent enemy.

Eyes were bunged up, noses twice their usual size, lips prominent to an appalling degree even for a negro, and general ill-temper all round. When at last the other officers arrived the whole story was told. It appeared that soon after I, with the head of the column, had passed certain trees, several distinct swarms of bees, annoyed by the noise and singing of the porters, had made an organised attack on the whole of the rest of the caravan. They went straight for the faces and especially the eyes of the men, who without a moment's hesitation threw their boxes down with a crash and bounded off into the long grass, in which they rolled and crouched and crawled in the hope of escaping the common foe. Having thus routed the 600 men of the caravan the bees do not appear to have pursued them far, but in order to show that they were complete masters of the field, proceeded to settle in swarms on the abandoned loads, and to defy any one to come and take them. This was decidedly awkward, no one would go near the loads, and the whole affair seemed to have reached an *impasse*, till some brain full of resource suggested an attack with fire. Under the direction of the English officers, who had arrived on the scene, the crestfallen porters were set to work to collect great handfuls of dried grass; when all was ready, these were simultaneously lighted, and a gallant charge on the bees, led by the Europeans, resulted after a short sharp struggle in the complete victory of humanity over insects. The caravan was re-formed, loads were shouldered, and the whole column left that spot at a pace which has never been equalled by our party before or since.

The next few days passed without any adventure worthy of record; we soon passed out of the rich and cultivated Kikuyu country, and our road lay through parched, arid, and stony plains, covered with dust, refracting the rays of the sun in a pitiless manner, and generally productive of much thirst and discontent. A somewhat difficult rocky descent brought us into the deep wide gorge familiar to geographers as the great meridional rift. In this curious volcanic depression we camped for two consecutive nights in what is known as the valley of the Keedong river, a small stream of clear warm water which gushes from the precipitous walls of the escarpment. These two nights were, without exception, the most uncomfortable of the whole journey. Every wind of the heavens appeared to have been let loose, and buffeted our unfortunate camp first from one side, then from the other, from the front and from the rear. At intervals during these nights a sound of the tearing of canvas or of the crashing of boughs, followed by maledictions in English or Swahili, announced the overthrow or destruction of a tent or of a temporary hut-shelter built by the porters. Few of us, tired as we were, could get any sleep in the midst of the din, we could only lie still and wonder how much longer one's own tent would hold out. In the morning everything, clothes, boxes, camp-beds, faces, and bodies, were covered with a thick layer of black dust, which had even penetrated into closed packages, into gun-cases and gun-locks, and had generally made itself as disagreeable as can well be imagined.

On the 10th we passed over the shoulder of Mount Longonot, a most interesting extinct volcano, graphically described by Mr. Joseph Thomson, who tells us how, after a most arduous climb, he succeeded in reaching the edge of the crater, where he actually sat with his legs dangling over an immense hole thousands of feet deep, at the bottom of which he could descry trees and abundant vegetation. We had, unfortunately, no time to go and inspect these geological wonders; and the same day, after a long march, we camped near the edge of the beautiful fresh-water Lake of Naivasha, a remarkable sheet of water of unknown but immense depth, evidently filling a huge ancient volcanic crater. The lake itself is about twelve miles long by half that width. The water is as sweet and fresh as that of a trout stream; but the most remarkable phenomenon in connection with this interesting lake is that, although it is liberally fed by several fine rushing streams and torrents on the northern and western sides, the water has no apparent exit, while the evaporation from its surface, even under a tropical sun, would not, apparently, be nearly sufficient to counterbalance the constant supplies of water thus poured in. An exit of some sort there must be, either deep down at the very base of the crater or by some unknown subterranean channel, or by rapid infiltration through some very porous substratum at present undiscovered. In this respect

Lake Naivasha resembles, but on a much larger scale, the Lake of Ashangi in Abyssinia, which similarly preserves the sweetness of its water without any apparent escape for its surplus into the deep sandy plains lying thousands of feet below it within a few miles of its eastern shores.

Around Lake Naivasha the prairies were literally covered with game, especially with thousands of that beautiful little antelope first discovered by Mr. Joseph Thomson, and named after him (*Gazella Thomsoni*). Zebras, too, were present in fair numbers, though very wild, and a few hartebeest and Grant's antelope added to the variety; while the waters and swampy shores of the lake itself were alive with duck, teal, wild geese, and many sorts of water-fowl; and the hoarse note of the lordly and beautiful crown crane sounded towards sunset in every direction. It need hardly be added that we lost no time in seizing rifles and setting out in different directions to work for the pot, with the result that in the evening the whole caravan, porters, soldiers, and Europeans, were able to enjoy hearty meals of venison, zebra, and other game, a most welcome and indeed valuable addition, for the hard-worked men, to their daily allowance of only a pound and a half of black flour.

It was in the neighbourhood of Lake Naivasha that we first made acquaintance with the most dreaded, but at the same time the most interesting, of all races living between the Victoria Nyanza and the East Coast, the far-famed and much-talked-of Masai. In the immediate neighbourhood of our camp we had observed on arrival several immense herds of cattle, grazing peacefully, tended by a few stalwart men with long spears; but in the afternoon we received a visit from a party of some thirty young warriors decked in all the bravery of their best war-

MASAI WARRIORS IN THEIR WAR-PAINT.[1]

dress. Splendid fellows they were too, not one of them under six feet in height, with long sinewy limbs, under whose shining chocolate skin the muscles could be seen working like bundles of india-rubber and whipcord. Clothes they had but few; a couple of short leather aprons slung over the shoulders, one in

[1] The photograph from which this engraving was made was very indistinct, and the illustration does not give a fair idea of the impressive aspect of the Masai warriors in their war-paint. The figure reproduced on the cover of this volume is from another photograph by Colonel Rhodes of a Masai warrior.

front and the other down the back, and neither of them quite reaching the hips, were all that could really be classified as garments; the rest was decoration and ornament.

Most of the warriors added to their great height by wearing some lofty and ferocious head-dress, either an edifice like a guardsman's bearskin made of hawks' feathers, or a complete circle of long feathers round the head made fast under the chin, or in some cases the horns of antelope, or a contrivance of iron wire covered with wool in the shape of immense buffalo horns. The upper parts of their arms were covered with coils of brightly-polished iron wire, of which also many of them wore coils round their waists; to the left thigh was tightly strapped a circle of small bells, which jingled loudly in unison as the warlike party kept step in their march; round the ankles were rings of iron wire, and usually also an anklet of hide with long stiff hair, possibly from the zebra's mane, standing straight out at right angles to the leg. In a girdle round the waist every man wore a straight sword rather less than three feet in length with a small handle of horn, no guard, and a topheavy blade of a spatulate shape about two or two and a half inches wide near the point, and only three-quarters of an inch at the hilt. On the other side of the girdle was stuck a heavy knob-kerry, either of wood or, more frequently, of rhinoceros horn. In the left hand was carried the splendid shield which is characteristic of the Masai alone; oblong, about four feet in height, slightly convex, and made either of buffalo or giraffe hide, it affords a perfect protection from spears or arrows to the warrior crouching behind it; but the most striking feature of these shields is the curious heraldic device and distinctive family badge with which each of them is painted. The only colours used are black, white, and red, but the different patterns are infinite and often very graceful. In the right hand was grasped the mighty and now world-famed Masai spear, six feet in length, with a broad shining blade of at least two and a half feet by three inches wide, and shod with a square sharp-pointed piece of iron nearly three feet long; thus in most of these spears no more wood is visible than is sufficient to leave room for the grasp of the hand in the middle of the haft. The warriors take the greatest pride in their spears, which, it must be allowed, are beautifully made and finished, and are always kept as bright as a Life Guardsman's cuirass at a birthday parade.

For our edification the Masai warriors, who in the presence of our large party were both fearless and friendly, performed a war-dance, accompanying it with a monotonous chant ending in a savage chorus, the effect of which was materially assisted by the clash of their thigh-bells as they stamped in unison. The dance over, the warriors prowled in an unconcerned manner about the camp, looking like monarchs of all they surveyed, and it was amusing to watch the endeavours of a little Zanzibar sentry to prevent a huge warrior from approaching too near the stores he was supposed to be protecting. Most of the Zanzibar soldiers average less than 5 feet 5 inches in height, and the calm contempt with which the naked warrior gazed down upon the little cloth-clad figure shouldering his rifle might have been taken as a picture of the triumph of primitive barbarism over a foreign semi-civilisation.

Confidence being thoroughly established, a good

MASAI WOMEN AT LAKE NAIVASHA.

many Masai girls, or "dittos" as the unmarried ones are called, came into camp. In contrast to their gigantic brothers, these girls were singularly small and slight, with graceful figures, and sometimes with really handsome features of almost a true Asiatic type. These girls were all sufficiently clothed for purposes of decency, and many of them wore as ornaments immense quantities of rings of bright wire, wound

MASAI CUSTOMS

tightly—too tightly, it seemed, for comfort—round their necks, from wrist to elbow, and from ankle to knee. The weight of metal thus carried by one extremely prepossessing little iron-clad girl must have been a really serious burden and impediment to progress.

Of the habits, manners, customs, morality—or rather immorality—of the Masai, I can say nothing which has not already been said with far greater authority and experience by Mr. Joseph Thomson in his interesting book, *Through Masailand*; but for the comfort of future travellers in these regions, I may safely assert that the Masai of to-day are no longer the dreaded, all-conquering, and triumphant "bogie" of ten years ago. "Ichabod"—the glory is departed from them, the terrible disease which a couple of years ago slew every buffalo in their country did not spare the cattle on which the Masai depend for their sole means of existence. Their cows and bulls died by tens of thousands, the whole race was reduced to the verge of starvation; women, old men, and children did indeed die by hundreds from want of food or from the plague of small-pox which attacked them at the same time. Even the young men, the warriors or "El-Moran," deprived of their sole articles of diet—blood, beef, and milk, seem temporarily to have lost their spirit; many sold their spears and shields for food, and in some parts of the country they so far changed the whole traditions of their race as to begin to sow grain and to till the ground. They have now recovered to some extent from their recent misery, a persevering system of raiding on their neighbours has enabled them to collect together a fair number of cattle, and their young men can once more enjoy their deep draughts of warm blood. In fact, although we saw a good many of the older men and women, and some of the children, looking as if they had not had a "square meal" for many a long month, the stalwart young warriors and their female companions the "dittos" presented a remarkably sleek, shiny, and well-fed appearance.

But another and better reason for the decadence of the Masai power is the introduction into East Africa of firearms, and especially of arms of precision. The Masai will not desert their old traditions and methods of fighting so far as to exchange their spears for guns, even if they could obtain them; but nevertheless they have a thorough dislike to seeing a rifle pointed at them, more especially if behind those shining barrels they descry the white face of a European. They are discovering that to people with guns, unless taken by surprise and overwhelmed by great disparity in numbers, the broad-bladed spears, the painted shields, savage head-gear, and jingling bells have lost more than half their terrors. The Masai will still, if they get an opportunity, and if their great superiority in numbers gives them courage, attack small parties of Swahilis carrying mails or messages, or, more rarely, small ill-supplied Swahili caravans; but they openly say that they do not wish for a feud with the white man, that they do not think it "good enough," and they have completely ceased either to expect or to demand any tribute whatever from caravans led by Europeans which may pass through their country. They are still, however, a great curse to the whole of British East Africa; their sanguinary raids, added to the terror of their name, not only check the development of all neighbouring tribes, but render desolate and absolutely uninhabited many hundreds and even thousands of square miles of fertile and healthy territory. Nevertheless, the Masai are of a distinctly higher order of race, intellect, and physical development than any of their more purely African-blooded neighbours, and there is no reason why, with patience, a firm administration, and even-handed justice, they should not, even in a short time, be converted into useful, docile, and pastoral members of the African community. Their stature, shape, clearly-chiselled and aquiline features, show the superiority of their Hamitic origin over that of the surrounding negro tribes, but, as in the case of their cousins the Gallas and Somalis, it is the very consciousness of this superiority which will probably offer the greatest resistance to the introduction of civilising reforms. Agriculturists they never will be; both the nature of their country and their racial traditions are adverse to this sort of labour, but when they have discovered that a better administration and an increase of self-confidence among surrounding tribes makes cattle-raiding and murder a losing game, and when they have learnt, as they are already learning, that they may trust to the word and honour of Englishmen, there is every ground for hoping not only that the once-dreaded Masailand will be a safe, pleasant, and healthy resort for European travellers and sportsmen, but that the Masai themselves will become valuable and expert breeders of cattle, donkeys, and horses (if these last are introduced), and that individuals of the tribe may be utilised as messengers, mail-runners, and even as disciplined soldiers or police.

Two days after leaving Lake Naivasha we arrived at the Salt Lake of Elmenteita, a long, comparatively narrow sheet of water, surrounded by a bleak, bare, and burnt country, intersected by cliffs of inhospitable-looking rock. On the road we had seen game of every sort and kind in vast numbers,—the bag during one day's march alone amounted to three zebras, seventeen *Thomsoni* antelope, one *Grantii*, and three crown cranes, which was sufficient to keep the whole caravan in meat. Unfortunately, however, at this time one of the keenest sportsmen among us, Major Owen, was suffering from such a badly ulcerated leg that he was not only quite unable to join any shooting party, but, as he became incapacitated from walking at all, was obliged to travel for the next 250 miles in a hammock slung on the shoulders of the most stalwart men that could be found. It may be mentioned by the way that this hammock, over which the Major had constructed a sort of shelter with a blanket thrown over the pole to protect him from the fierce rays of the sun, gave rise to all sorts of rumours and expectations previous to our arrival in Uganda. The natives of Kavirondo and

Usoga who saw the caravan pass with a number of white men on foot, and a covered litter carefully carried, not unnaturally jumped to the conclusion that in this closed conveyance must lie a lady. A rumour to this effect therefore flew ahead of us into Uganda, receiving additional confirmation and credence every day, so that on our arrival we not only found all the Europeans in Uganda making preparations to greet the wife of the Commissioner, but that King Mwanga himself was on tiptoe of excitement and expectation, as he had been told by his courtiers, and fully believed, that the mysterious lady was an English princess, sent as a suitable present to him by Her Majesty the Queen!

Close to Lake Elmenteita we passed the scene of the massacre of an entire Swahili caravan of some 300 men, which took place about twelve years ago. Three porters only are said to have made good their escape, and to have arrived after a marvellous series of adventures at the coast, where they narrated how their caravan had been attacked by the branch of the Masai known as the Wakwavi, and had successfully held their own for two days and a night, but that on the second night, all their ammunition being exhausted, in attempting to get away quietly under cover of the darkness, they had been discovered by the enemy, and, with the exception of the three lucky ones, massacred to a man. These Wakwavi, who used in former times to occupy all the country lying between this place and Kavirondo, are a somewhat degenerate branch of the Masai tribe, of whom they appear to have all the vices and none of the virtues. After a series of sanguinary battles and campaigns, the details of which are given by Mr. Thomson in his book, they were finally defeated by the true-blooded Masai, and driven to settle in Kavirondo, where they remain to this day, scattered all over the country in different native villages, stealing what they can, domineering over and terrorising the more timid inhabitants, doing little or no agricultural work, and generally making themselves a curse to an otherwise friendly and peaceful collection of village communities.

Thence we passed along an easy road to the salt, or rather brackish, Lake of Nakuru, a not very imposing piece of water some four miles long by the same in width. The country was still full of game, the only change being that the common hartebeest of the plains (*Bubalis Cokei*) was replaced by a larger and longer-horned species known as Jackson's hartebeest, it having first been shot by Mr. F. Jackson, recently an officer in the service of the I.B.E.A. Company. This animal, although more difficult to stalk successfully than any other game in the district, did not appear to be quite so wild as its cousin of the plains. But to whatever branch of the tribe they may belong, a herd of hartebeest never settle themselves to feed without first posting a sentinel on some spot, usually a tall ant-heap, whence he can command a good view of the surrounding country. Thoroughly conscientious, too, and vigilant these sentries are. They never attempt to browse or to "philander" with the ladies of the herd near them, but, standing erect, motionless, and somewhat ungainly, they incessantly sniff the breeze and scan the plains in search of a possible enemy. The instant that danger of any sort is suspected, the "look-out man" warns the rest of the herd by a stamp on the ground and a loud sneeze. At this signal up go all the heads, ten or twenty pairs of ears are pricked, and a similar number of sharp eyes are searching the grass and bushes on every side, while every nostril is distended and quivering for the slightest taint in the forest air. If, after the signal is given, the too eager sportsman makes the slightest mistake, if the sun strikes bright rays from his gun-barrel, if he incautiously shows even the crown of his helmet or treads on a dry stick, then good-bye to his chance of getting a shot at that herd. In a second the whole family, awkward and angular when at rest, are stretching out in a long-striding, graceful gallop, which would quickly distance any other species of antelope, or any other wild animal, in East Africa. When shot the hartebeest, if not too old, makes moderately good venison, though not particularly refined, the liver and tongue being perhaps the best parts of him. His flesh cannot be compared, in point of culinary excellence, with brisket of zebra, which is equal to the best veal, while the best of all fourfooted wild animals in East Africa, without the smallest doubt, is the beautiful *Grantii* antelope; of birds, the guinea-fowl, the florican, and, above all, the crown crane, are all worthy of a place of honour at Bignon's, or the Maison Dorée.

Ever since leaving the coast we had been gradually ascending into colder and better air, but two days after leaving Lake Nakuru, and having without difficulty crossed the Guasso (river) Masai, our ascent of the Mau Mountains began in earnest. On the 18th of February we camped at a spot fixed by the Railway Survey Expedition as being within a few hundred yards of the Equator, and bitterly cold it was. It was rather difficult to imagine ourselves almost exactly on the Equator, as we shivered that night in bed, covered with all the blankets we could muster, on the top of which were heaped coats, flannel shirts, and clothes of any sort which might help to keep in the heat, while most of us went to bed wearing two or more suits of night garments besides.

Unfortunately, the cold of the Equator Camp, added to the unpardonable stupidity or carelessness of some of the men, cost us far more than a little temporary inconvenience. In the afternoon when we made the camp, the donkeys, carrying the spare food and the sick men, were still a long way behind, and not expected to arrive for about a couple of hours. Our camp was surrounded by tall, dry grass, and the wind was blowing back along the road by which we had advanced. The men had several times been seriously warned of the danger of fire in this long grass, and already, a few days before, we had suffered some inconvenience, and I myself had been pre-

vented from entering the camp on my return from
shooting, in consequence of a grass fire kindled by
our men. But on this evening, some of the Zanzibar
soldiers, with the crass stupidity and wooden-headed
carelessness which distinguished them in most of
their proceedings, must needs set fire to the grass to
leeward of the camp. In five minutes there was an
immense wall of fire charging down the path by which
we had come, and along which, as we knew, the
donkeys, cattle, and invalids were painfully advancing! Nothing could be done, search parties were
sent to follow in the wake of the fire, but they
returned late and disconsolate without news. All
through that night there were no signs of the missing
party, and our anxiety may be imagined better than
described; not only were the lives of the men in
charge of the animals, and the invalids at stake, but
they had also all the food on which we could depend
to take the whole caravan either forward or back.
Porters and soldiers alike had left Kikuyu with
twelve days' rations already issued to them; this
was the twelfth day, a fresh issue was to have been
made that very afternoon; we were at least 120
miles from the nearest food-supplying district on
either side, and there was not one day's rations in
the camp! When the porters began to realise (with
empty stomachs) the full extent of the possible disaster which might be caused by the soldiers' stupidity,
they were almost ready to tear the latter in pieces.
At last, however, the next morning, one of the search
parties returned with the news that they had found

the missing men and animals safe from fire, in a damp nook near a stream. Soon afterwards the donkeys themselves came in sight, but it then appeared that two of the invalids had died during the night from exposure to the cold, as well as one donkey and two sheep.

One of these unfortunate invalids did not belong to our caravan, but was a poor old man whom I had found wandering alone some days before in a miserable state. His story was that he had been a porter in a caravan led by a Swahili, that he had fallen ill and had been unable to keep up with the others, on which the leader had quietly abandoned him to his fate. The unhappy wretch had been painfully hobbling along alone for five days when I found him. He was without food, almost without clothes, and without any means of making a fire at night. It appeared to us simply marvellous that he had not already died from exposure to the cold, or that he had not been killed by lions or even hyænas, who are quite bold enough to destroy a sick and helpless man by night. That these and similar acts of ghastly cruelty, amounting almost to cold-blooded murder, are done day by day, and have been done for the last fifty years in native caravans, there can be no doubt whatever; such caravans, when once they are fairly up-country, are free from all control; power, almost of life and death, over dozens of his fellow-creatures remains absolutely in the hands of the leader, who is perhaps a half-caste Arab, or perhaps a Swahili of a class from which domestic servants or private soldiers are drawn at Zanzibar; nobody asks or cares how many men, slaves or free, are taken or inveigled into coming as porters, and nobody knows or ascertains how many of these men ever return. The old man whom I picked up was some miles off the road, and, had I not happened to bend my steps that way in search of game, had no more chance of reaching any place where food could be obtained than he had of finding a balloon ready to transport him to his own hut in Mombasa. A thorough system of registration, inspection, and control of native-led caravans, both at the coast and at up-country stations, is one of the very first measures which should be carefully and thoughtfully devised and then efficiently carried out, if British authority or the British name is in any way, directly or indirectly, to be connected with this part of Africa.[1]

During the march on one of these days, our righteous English indignation was fired by what at first sight appeared to be a most abominable case of torture and cruelty in our own caravan. Our attention being attracted to a small group of men bending over a prostrate figure, we strolled up to see what was the matter. On arrival we found a porter, or soldier—I forget which—stretched face downwards on the ground, while two powerful men were pulling at his arms and legs in opposite directions with all their strength. Round each of the victim's ankles, separately, cords had been tied as tightly as they could be drawn, and the pressure still further increased by a

[1] Such steps have already been initiated in the Sultanate of Zanzibar.—*Ed.*

rude tourniquet made of a stick twisted in the knots, till they appeared to be cutting into the flesh. As though this was not sufficient torture, a third strapping big fellow was walking and even stamping up and down on the naked back of the unfortunate wretch, who was lying motionless, and, as we thought, without the power to struggle. Blazing with anger at the idea of this act of barbarism being perpetrated under our very eyes, we hotly demanded what it meant; but somewhat to our discomfiture the cold-blooded torturers only answered with a grin, and quite undisturbed by our anger, the single word "tumbo," while the panting victim raised his prostrate head and softly muttered the same not very poetical sound. "Tumbo" may be literally translated by the English colloquial expression "tummy"; in other words, the prostrate gentleman was suffering from apparently severe pains in the abdominal region, for which this stretching of the limbs, the tying up of the ankles, and the walking on the back constituted a favourite native remedy. The cure was rapid and complete, for on the termination of the operation the patient jumped up—a little stiffly at first—shouldered his load, and marched off in excellent spirits.

Before the end of our journey I saw this violent and original cure in operation on several occasions, and in each instance it was apparently successful; at all events I never heard of a second application being necessary, nor did the patients who had chosen to be treated by these methods apply to our doctor for any of his pills, chlorodyne, or other more civilised but milder modes of treatment.[1] A whole chapter might be filled by describing the wonderful native ways of treating different ailments, some of which have, at different times, come under my notice; for instance, in Abyssinia, some of my mule-drivers undertook the cure of one of their comrades who was suffering from a sharp attack of fever; the process consisted in first tying cords, with tourniquets of stick, tightly below each knee and above each ankle, while two men with small sharp knives made innumerable and apparently indiscriminate gashes all over the calves of the patient's legs. I am bound to confess that, whether in spite of or in consequence of the remedy, the fever was shaken off that night, but the next day the unfortunate man was far too stiff and sore to be able to walk!

On the 20th February we successfully crossed what is now known as "the Big Ravine," a precipitous descent into a cleft about 300 feet deep, with an equally steep ascent on the other side, the whole ravine not being more than 100 yards wide at the top. It took over four hours to get all the donkeys, loads, and men safely across this rather formidable obstacle. After this, for a day or two we had some experience of the true African "darkest forest" work, and as we cut, burrowed, and scrambled in the gloom over and through thick undergrowth, gigantic festoons of creepers, and rich, rank vegetation of every

---

[1] I have seen this rough-and-ready form of massage used by porters on the march for a strain of the muscles of the back, and I am informed that it is much resorted to for various ailments in Zanzibar and performed by the women of the house.—*Ed.*

sort, under the perpetual shade of towering forest monarchs, we could fully appreciate the true force of Mr. Stanley's graphic descriptions of the interminable Congo forest, and could enter in some small degree into the feelings of himself and his followers at their deprivation of air, light, and sunshine day after day, and even month after month. In our case, six or seven hours of work in this damp gloom was quite sufficient to make us long for the blessings of the open country, and we shuddered as we tried to realise what it would mean to be condemned to wander and toil painfully through a region so unfit for man and beast for hopeless consecutive months!

CHAPTER VI

West of the watershed—Extinction of the buffalo and eland—The Wanderobbo tribe—The fertile Kavirondo district—Mianda—We cross the Nile and camp in Uganda—The Ripon Falls—Amidst civilisation and rifles—We enter the Fort of Kampala on the 17th of March.

As we emerged on the 21st of February from the dense forest described in the last chapter, and camped, with a sigh of relief, on its edge, at a spot commanding a magnificent view over interminable downs, intersected by sparkling streams, and dotted with clumps of splendid timber, we found ourselves just 8600 feet above the level of the sea. During the first two hours of next day's march we climbed about 300 feet higher, and then, to our immense satisfaction, we began to observe that the little rivulets and mountain streams were no longer running towards us in an easterly or south-easterly direction, but were gurgling and tumbling away from us westward and north-westward. In other words, we had at last crossed the great watershed, at a height of just under 9000 feet, and the streams across which we now stepped so easily were all hastening to contribute their quota to the Victoria Nyanza, and were themselves some of the innumerable head-waters of the mighty Nile.

The descent into the great Central African plateau was gradual and comparatively easy, the nights by degrees became warmer and pleasanter; game, which on the top of the Mau Mountains had been rather scarce, again became plentiful, the men's chilled spirits revived, and every one felt more cheerful as we realised that most of our difficulties were now over, and that we had nothing before us but a few days' march downhill into Kavirondo, where we should again see living human beings, and be able to buy fresh food.

The general effect of the higher altitudes of the Mau Mountains and the Mau Forest was, I think, to produce a sense of gloom and depression of spirits among both Europeans and natives. The cold, at all events at night, was more than a mere inconvenience; we white men could make ourselves fairly comfortable in our tents with blankets and flannel clothes and a meat diet; we were, moreover, natives of a cold country, and might be expected to welcome a certain degree of chilliness as a homely feeling; but the half-clad porters, natives of the steaming coast, suffered severely in their little shelters of grass and twigs, as they huddled close together with their feet almost *in* a blazing fire, and their heads and bodies wrapped in the scanty bit of cotton cloth which constituted their only garment. The crossing of these mountains cost us altogether the lives of four men, all of whom died of acute pneumonia, contracted presumably during these cold nights. Another cause for a general sinking of spirits was perhaps the desolation and silence of the region. The absence of game, the paucity of birds, and the eternal wild sighing of the giant juniper-trees, all had a somewhat eerie and depressing influence, deepened by the sight of hundreds and hundreds of skulls, skeletons, and scattered bones of the unfortunate buffaloes, which only two or three years ago used to range in vast herds over these mountains.

A dreadful plague which, spreading southwards from Somaliland, overran, two years ago, the whole of East Africa, furnishes one of the most melancholy instances in the annals of natural history, of the sudden and almost complete extermination of a whole race of noble animals. Three years ago the magnificent African buffalo roamed in tens, and even hundreds of thousands over the Masai plains, over the Mau Mountains, over, in fact, the whole of what is called British and German East Africa; but now a traveller may wander for months in all the most likely or most inaccessible places, and see nothing of the buffalo except his horns and whitened bones scattered over the plain, or lying literally in heaps near tempting springs and cool watering places, to which the poor brutes had flocked to quench their consuming thirst, and to die. In South Africa the buffalo is still to be found, I believe, in some numbers, but there he is rapidly being exterminated from the south by the advancing rifles of civilisation, while on the other side there is reason to fear that this same dread plague, having done its fatal work in the east, is steadily and relentlessly pursuing its course southwards, so that, unless in the meantime the virulence of the epidemic mercifully dies out, the South African buffalo will inevitably share the fate of his northern cousin.

The stately eland, which was never so numerous as the buffalo, appears to have succumbed to the same plague, and the natives assert, though with what truth I know not, that there is not one left in East Africa. Certainly, although for days we passed through their former haunts, and diligently patrolled the country in every direction, not one of our party ever saw anything of an eland except a skull and some bones. It is to be feared, too, that the influx of travellers and sportsmen, which will inevitably take place as communications and means of transport are improved, will quite destroy any hope which might otherwise have been entertained that by degrees these two splendid races of wild animals would eventually recover, to some degree at least, from the recent effects of their deadly and almost unprecedented visitation.

As we briskly descended the western slopes of the mountains, it was pleasant to note by the wayside such old friends as the common daisy, forget-me-not, primrose, and buttercup, while blackberries climbed luxuriantly over the stunted bushes.

A little farther on some distant columns of smoke rising above a wood showed us that we were no longer the only human beings in this vast region. These fires, we found, were made by some wandering parties of the nomad tribe of Wanderobbo, a curious race of people who appear in some mysterious way to owe allegiance to the Masai, by whom they are tolerated and even to some extent protected. These Wanderobbo are clever blacksmiths, and it is they who, from iron wire supplied to them by the Masai, manufacture the beautifully-finished and finely-balanced spears which we had so greatly admired in the hands of the dominant tribe. But the Wanderobbo are above all things hunters; they live by the chase, and eat hardly anything but the flesh of game. It need scarcely be added that in this profession they are both bold and expert, and we all regretted that we had no chance of seeing them at work. They have no firearms, but, with nothing better than native-made spears, they manage to collect a considerable quantity of ivory every year, even though elephants have now become very scarce in their district.

The weapon with which they attack elephants is a short, heavy spear-head, deeply barbed, smeared with poison, and fitted loosely into a short socket of wood which is held in the hand. The sporting native, with this primitive weapon, crawls and glides silently and snake-like right up to the gigantic beast until he is within arm's-length of the ponderous body. Then, quick as thought, he plunges the poisoned spear-head into the belly of the enormous brute, withdrawing sharply the socket, which leaves the head buried in the mountain of flesh above him. Now, woe betide the native if he is not as agile as a monkey and as quick as a snake in getting himself out of the way and under cover! With a yell of pain the elephant turns round and furiously searches and sniffs for his unknown foe; failing to find him, the doomed brute crashes ahead through bushes, trees, creepers, regardless of impediments, leaving a trail behind him which his persistent enemy will follow, if necessary, for days, until the deadly poison has done its inevitable work, and, after swaying uncertainly backwards and forwards, and from side to side, the six tons of flesh, bone, and ivory fall to the ground with a sullen crash! I am informed that if the poison is well made and quite fresh, and the spear-head well driven home, the elephant will often succumb in about four hours from the time when he is first struck, during which he will perhaps cover some twenty-five miles of country. Sometimes, however, the Wanderobbo pursue a wounded animal for a hundred miles and more before securing their prize. In this way they will follow up a herd of perhaps eight or ten elephants until every member of the family is destroyed. Apart from their hunting propensities the Wanderobbo are a shy, harmless people, seldom seen, and usually living in small parties, in the heart of the thickest forest.

After leaving the mountains we descended to a vast, bare plain extending as far as the eye could reach, dotted with innumerable ant-hills eight or ten feet in height, but without a tree or shrub of any kind to break the brown and red expanse. There were on this plain a fair number of hartebeest, steinbuck, klipspringers, and other small gazelle, but in the total absence of cover, even the grass being at this season short and withered, it was almost impossible to get within range of anything, and but little damage was done by a good deal of shooting at impossible ranges. Luckily, through the very middle of this plain flows a small fresh stream with a few unhappy-looking bushes and trees on its banks, which gave us just sufficient firewood for the evening camp.

On the 26th of February, during the march, Colonel Rhodes and I were stalking some hartebeest a few hundred yards to the left of the head of the column, when we heard loud shouts behind us, which sent off our game at full gallop. Somewhat annoyed we looked round, and saw the leading section of the caravan in a state of wild excitement and confusion, while the other English officers were running at full speed to the front. The cause was not far to seek: at a little distance on the other side of the path we could see an enormous rhinoceros trotting steadily straight down on the porters, apparently with every intention of charging the whole crowd! Running and stumbling over the rough ground, we were on the scene in a minute, just as Villiers and my brother came into action with a couple of shots at over 100 yards' range. The rhinoceros apparently thought no more of these bullets than of flea-bites, and came steadily forward. Then followed a regular fusilade; Rhodes, Berkeley, my brother, Villiers, and myself blazed away, pouring bullets into the unfortunate beast at thirty, twenty, and at last even ten yards' distance. Close behind us the porters were yelling, jumping about, half-running away, and generally making a pandemonium of the quiet plain. The scene was so ridiculous that our laughter and haste seriously interfered with the accuracy of our aim, but at last the enormous brute gave a great lurch and a stumble, and, sinking down on its haunches, sat and looked at us at about five paces' distance, threatening us with its head and vicious horns, but no longer able to make a last charge. A final shot in the head put an end to the performance, and in another moment the carcass was surrounded, hacked, gashed, opened, and carved by a yelling crowd of black men, who had thrown down their loads anyhow, and were plunging with their long knives into what soon became a shapeless heap of blood, flesh, and unmentionable horrors. Fourteen bullets were found in the carcass, two or three of which had gone right through the heart, most of them being from ·577 express rifles. No better instance could be adduced to show the solid strength which had enabled this animal to stand, without turning or flinching, these terrific successive shocks, or the vitality which enabled it to continue its steady course, apparently unhurt, up to our very feet. The horns, which were not a very good pair, became the property of Lieutenant Villiers as having planted the first bullet.

The vitality of the rhinoceros appears, however, to vary considerably in different animals : a few days before I had come across one in an open plain, and put a bullet through his heart at a distance of about sixty yards, which had rolled him over stone dead like a rabbit, while on another occasion I had crept to within a few paces of a rhino-cow, and had given her a similar bullet in exactly the same place, which only had the effect of starting her off like a racehorse across the plain. She managed to cover nearly three-quarters of a mile in excellent time before pulling up, sinking slowly to her knees, and then dying. These were all the common two-horned black rhinoceros; of the white species we never saw a single specimen, nor do I believe that they now exist in this part of the continent.

On the 28th a steady climb brought us to the top of a pass over the Kabras Mountains, whence we had a magnificent view of the whole of Kabras and Kavirondo lying at our feet, bounded on the north by the huge mass of Mount Elgon (14,000 feet), towering high above the plain, his head wrapped in an almost perpetual veil of cloud, while in the blue distance ahead of us to the west might be faintly seen some of the hills of Usoga.

A 50 LB. TUSK BOUGHT IN KABRAS.

This really felt like the beginning of the end of our long tramp, and that evening, as we camped in the plains below, we had proof that we were no longer the only living human beings in the country, as black gentlemen and ladies, not wearing a single stitch of clothing, flocked into camp with a few heads of corn and half-starved-looking hens for sale in exchange for pink beads. The population on the outskirts of Kabras and Kavirondo is now very sparse and scattered, although, judging from the great number of deserted villages which we passed at frequent intervals during the march, this district must have been far more densely inhabited and thoroughly cultivated in quite recent times. It is the old story: Masai raids, extending year after year, have gradually driven these peaceful and timid people away to seek new homes out of the reach of their dangerous neighbours.

As we advanced farther into Kavirondo villages became more frequent, and on every side in their immediate vicinity were rich fields of Indian corn, millet, beans of several kinds, and sweet potatoes. The people were evidently industrious and skilful agriculturists, but, their wants being few and easily satisfied, quite four-fifths of this rich and ideal corn-growing land is still left to lie fallow. With peace, protection of the weak against the strong, and with rapid transit to the coast, there can be no doubt that Kavirondo could be converted into a granary capable of supplying vast quantities of every sort of grain at a merely nominal rate. If ever a railway is built to this part of the country, the freight charged on the transport of corn can be easily regulated in such a manner as to enable Kavirondo grain to undersell the produce of India at the coast, in Zanzibar, and even in Europe. The insignificance of the initial cost of the grain itself at the present time is sufficiently shown by the fact that, although only comparatively small patches are now cultivated by the most crude and primitive methods in the immediate neighbourhood of the villages, our 600 men were able to supply themselves with more corn than they could possibly consume, with eggs, occasional fowls, and fish, on the allowance issued to them of one string of small pink beads a day, in value something less than a farthing !

The people themselves are not particularly interesting, and are evidently related to the negro tribes of the Upper Nile. The men are tall, well-made, stalwart fellows, stark naked, or sometimes wearing a string of beads or one or two coils of wire round their necks, arms, or waists. They nearly always carry a long roughly-made spear. The married ladies wear a string—occasionally threaded with beads—round their waists, from which are hung, in front and behind, a couple of tufts like fly-wisps, or like a handful plucked from a horse's tail. The unmarried girls, with ingenuous simplicity, wear just nothing at all. As they never appear to oil, grease, or wash their bodies, their skins have a dull, rough, and unclean appearance, which contrasts most unfavourably with the sleek, well-oiled figures of the Masai youths and maidens. The villages of Kavirondo are all surrounded, for protection, by a deep ditch skirting a mud wall some six feet in height, through which the only entrance is across a very narrow causeway and through a low door, less than four feet in height, easily blocked by heavy beams of timber.

The village of the chief Mumia, at which the I.B.E.A. Company had established a small storehouse in charge of a native, is a favourite halting-place for caravans, and is in some ways already in advance of its neighbours. It is surrounded by more cultivation than most of the others, its inhabitants have learnt the instincts and the advantages of trade in corn and other food, and nearly all the principal men of the place have already begun to hide their nakedness in garments of cotton cloth, a demand for which commodity is, in consequence, rapidly being created.

At Mumia's we halted, out of pity for the hard-worked men, for a day's rest, and then, on the 4th of March, began the last stage of our journey of 187 miles to the capital of Uganda. A mile from the village we had to cross the Nzoia river, the most important stream which had yet opposed itself to our progress since leaving the coast. At the first glance it certainly looked rather formidable, being about forty yards wide, and running with a swift three-mile current between steep banks. It was, therefore, not surprising that among the leading men there was at first a good deal of hesitation about venturing into the water, which looked as if it might be of any depth, and haunted by innumerable crocodiles and other horrors. My exhortations and objurgations not having the smallest perceptible effect, I proceeded to lead the way in person, and walked, full of righteous indignation, into the brown current. The first step was only up to my knees, and I began to jeer at the timid porters, the second brought the water to my

CROSSING THE NZOIA RIVER.

waist, and though still triumphant, the jeers ceased of their own accord, but the fourth or fifth step saw me fairly swept off my legs, and Her Majesty's Commissioner was ignominiously striking out for the bank from which he had started. Foolishly, too, in my zeal and wrath I had not even taken the ordinary precaution of first divesting myself of my coat, so that the ducking was complete. After this we proceeded with more caution, and soon found a ford by which the whole party, with their loads, got safely across in little more than an hour.

For the next two days we made long, wearisome marches through a desolate country of abandoned villages, deserted and overgrown crops, and ruined huts. It appeared that a certain local chief, who had acquired rather more power than his neighbours, had been in the habit of raiding all over this country, till it was more than half ruined, and that then a "punitive" expedition of the Imperial British East Africa Company, directed against this chief, had overrun the district, and completed its desolation. The only incident of interest to us was that on the 5th we got our first distant view of the Victoria Nyanza, while our practical ingenuity was greatly exercised by the extreme difficulty of finding camping-places at which any firewood could be procured, the whole of Kavirondo consisting of rolling hills and plains, where the soil, impregnated with iron, is of extreme fertility, but almost without a tree. The marches through Kavirondo were quite the most uninteresting of the whole journey. The road was circuitous and aggravating to an unnecessary and heart-breaking degree, there were numerous swamps of evil-smelling water and deep black mud, and when on *terra firma* we were eternally toiling along over plains of burnt grass, without shade, with no scenery to admire, and nothing to look at except the dazzling iron-loaded soil, or a few very dirty black people without clothes.

On the 7th, however, the whole aspect of affairs underwent a complete and sudden change. We had camped that night almost on the shores of that part of Lake Victoria hitherto known as Sio Bay, which had been rechristened "Berkeley Bay" by the officers of the recent railway survey expedition. Our march the previous day had been, as usual, over monotonous, burnt, and barren plains, with occasional patches of cultivation round the villages; but now, without any gradation or preparation, we suddenly passed into a land of fine trees, of endless banana gardens, of cool shade, and intelligent-looking, chocolate-coloured people, completely clothed from head to foot in graceful togas of bark-cloth. We had crossed the frontier of Usoga. Now, indeed, were we in a land of plenty; great bunches of sweet, ripe bananas were brought to us at every plantation, and distributed to the porters by hospitable villagers without payment being demanded or expected. To us, who had seen no green or fresh food since leaving Kikuyu, the luxury was inestimable; the only serious danger which now threatened us was that the whole caravan should so over-eat itself in the midst of this abundance as to be unable to proceed.

However, although next morning, and on each of the subsequent days, many cases of "tumbo" or "tummy" came for treatment to our long-suffering doctor, no serious inconvenience was suffered by the community at large, and in high spirits the men stepped out bravely along well-kept paths, running between the cool and shady banana groves, over which towered here and there magnificent cedars, gum-trees, and forest giants of every description, while the divisions between the different plantations were marked by rows of the invaluable fig-tree, from the bark of which is made the warm and picturesque cloth worn by every native.

On the 8th of March we arrived at the large and prosperous village of the chief Mtanda, which is called on the maps "Wakoli's," after the name of the father of Mtanda, who was killed in 1892 by a porter in the caravan of an English missionary then on a visit to this place. Here the British East Africa Company had a stockade and a "station," in charge of a young German gentleman, to whom our hearty thanks are due for a pleasant and hospitable reception. Our men were supplied, free of cost, with goats, fowls, bananas, and every description of food, with the most lavish generosity, with the result that a good many murmurs were audible when their petition for a day of rest here was refused. I should explain that the bananas usually supplied, both to the men and ourselves, were immense bunches of green, unripe fruit, which are either boiled or, what is better, skinned and thoroughly steamed for an hour or so before they are eaten.

Having dealt out presents of wire, cloth, coloured handkerchiefs, and other treasures to all the hospitable chiefs, we pushed on for four more days through the same delightful, rich, and shady country, our appetites flattered by the good fare, our sense of smell by the sweet perfume of the various gums and of innumerable resinous trees and shrubs, and our eyes delighted by the fresh green and waving leaves of the bananas contrasting with the sombre hues of the stately cedar, while the red tulip-like flowers of the *Spathodia* vied with every shade of purple, yellow, blue, or white convolvuli, creepers, or flowering trees, in adding warmth, joy, and brilliancy to the smiling scene, to be themselves in turn almost put to shame by the thousands of brilliant butterflies of every hue and every size which rose in clouds from the path before us, and lightly defied competition in colour and beauty from any flower yet produced by Nature or Art. At intervals, as we rose over the brow of some green-clad granite hill, from which great gray masses of rock thrust their heads through the waving verdure as though to reprove the bright thoughtlessness of the vegetation, we could see below us, on our left, inlets and bays of the Victoria Nyanza. The water reflected every shadow and colour of the surrounding hills, lovely islands dotted the surface as it lay calm, blue, and peaceful under the morning sun, more beautiful than any Italian lake, but cruel as the very crocodiles which haunt its depths, treacherous and untrustworthy as the people who inhabit its shores and cut each others' throats in the name of the Christian religion.

At last, at 11 o'clock on the 12th of March, a muffled roar of water told us that we were approaching the frontier of Uganda, and in a few minutes a steep

THE NILE BELOW THE RIPON FALLS.

and rapid descent brought us to the head of Napoleon Gulf, at the very spot where the Somerset Nile leaves the Lake, and, severing all connection with its parent by throwing itself madly over the Ripon Falls, sets forth alone on its 3000-mile journey to the Mediterranean Sea.

A couple of long, light, but somewhat leaky canoes were ready to transport the whole caravan to the opposite bank, across a ferry some 500 yards wide. These canoes were fairly well constructed of strips of wood neatly sewn together with fibres of aloes and of bananas; they were built on a stout, solid keel, which projected some distance before the boat, and was then turned upwards till it towered proudly and gracefully above the water like the prow of an ancient Roman trireme. These lofty prows were always adorned in some manner as the taste of the owner might suggest, most commonly by a pair of antelope's horns, by a device worked in grass, by a pair of hippopotamus tusks, or some other trophy of the chase. It took nearly six hours to get all the men, loads, invalids, and animals across the ferry, the ponies, goats, and cattle being tied by the head to the canoe and made to swim, but before sunset that evening all the work was finished, the camp was pitched, and we could sit down with a clear conscience to our first dinner in Uganda, lulled by the hoarse murmur of the Ripon Falls.

The following morning, the 13th of March, after sending on the caravan at daybreak as usual, my brother and I turned back to the Ripon Falls, armed with fishing lines and a luncheon basket, with the intention of spending a thoroughly lazy morning, and of overtaking the others at their next camp in the evening. As we sat on rocks just below the Falls, occasionally throwing our lines in a desultory manner, the grand beauty of the place fascinated us as thirty years before it had fascinated Captain Speke, the first white man whose eyes had ever rested on this spot. To describe the

EMBARKING TO CROSS THE NILE.

scene I cannot do better than quote Captain Speke's own words, which are as true to-day as when they were written :[1]—

The "stones," as the Waganda call the Falls, was by far the most interesting sight I had seen in Africa. Though beautiful, the scene was not exactly what I expected; for the broad surface of the Lake was shut out from view by a spur of hill, and the Falls, about 12 feet deep, and 400 to 500 feet broad, were broken by rocks. Still it was a sight that attracted me to it for hours; the roar of the waters, thousands of passenger-fish, leaping at the Falls with all their might, the Wasoga and Waganda fishermen coming out in boats, and taking post on all the rocks with rod and hook, hippopotami and crocodiles lying sleepily on the water, the ferry at work above the Falls, and cattle driven down to drink at the margin of the Lake, made, in all, with the pretty nature of the country,—small hills, grassy-topped, with trees in the folds, and gardens on the lower slopes,—as interesting a picture as one could wish to see.

While my brother and I spent a happy and idle morning at this lovely place, fishing with great perseverance, but contentedly catching nothing, we complacently reflected that this was the 13th of March, the very day on which, before leaving the coast, I had ventured to prophesy in an official telegram that we should be at the Nile. It was pleasing to realise that in spite of the unforeseen difficulties and delays at Kikuyu, and of various other impediments with which we had met on divers occasions, we were at last actually in Uganda, and even one day ahead of our time.

Innumerable incidents and details now seemed to combine in order to demonstrate to us that, as

[1] Speke's *Discovery of the Source of the Nile*, p. 466.

compared with the countries through which we had
been wandering since the beginning of the year,
we had arrived at the home of African civilisation.
Great as had been the contrast between the people
of Usoga and the naked blacks of Kavirondo, the
superiority in bearing, in dress, and in manner of the
Waganda over their cousins and neighbours on the

THE NILE AFTER LEAVING LAKE VICTORIA.
Fish Cruise in the Foreground.

other side of the Nile was hardly less marked. Our
eyes were first opened by the refusal of a poor fisher-
man at the Falls to accept our proffered beads in
return for some bait, bananas, or other trifles which
we had bought from him, and by his asking, instead,
if we could not give him anything to read, whether a

book or a single page, printed in Luganda or Swahili? Unfortunately we were not supplied with any such literature, and the bargain was eventually struck for a few wax matches. That afternoon again, as we strolled on to rejoin the caravan ten miles ahead, we no longer stumbled in single file along a narrow path overgrown with grass and creepers, but walked freely and comfortably along a straight road, from ten to twenty feet wide, cleared of all vegetation, and that evening on arrival at our destination, we found the caravan encamped in a smooth, clear, well-kept, and well-swept open "square" in front of a clean-looking village, surrounded by crowds of sleek men and women, all decently dressed from head to foot in a softer and superior class of bark-cloth to that worn by the Wasoga. Finally, when at sunset I received the visit of the half-dozen chief men of the place, I was rather startled to find that they were all dressed in ample robes of the cleanest and most snowy cotton cloth of very fine quality, and that each man was followed by a slave bearing his master's chair or camp-stool!

Verily the wearied traveller entering Uganda for the first time across the eastern frontier, contemplates with unconscious relief the most ornamented, polished, and whitened side of the sepulchre, and, at first at all events, neither sees nor suspects anything of the festering bones, the foulness of iniquity, and the hideous decay which lie behind that pleasing surface!

Next morning at 5.30, after bidding a formal farewell and giving a suitable present of cloth to the hospitable chief of the village, Mondo by name, we had a most agreeable march of twelve miles through a fertile, hilly, and prosperous-looking country to our camping-place in another clean square in front of the village of the chief Mworogoma. The whole march had been along a broad, cleared road, evidently "done up" for the occasion; in fact, in several places the work was not yet finished, and some hundreds of women and children were busily engaged in scratching, tearing, or cutting away the grass and tangle which had been allowed to encroach upon the old path. During the day we crossed, dry-shod, several nasty-looking swamps which had been admirably bridged by a solid causeway of interlaced palm logs covered over with a thick layer of brushwood, grass, and earth.

About an hour before arriving at Mworogoma's we were met by a great personage named Zachariah, who holds the lucrative and important office of kangao or governor of the rich province of Bulemezi, besides being a most influential member of the Great Council of the king, and, I believe, a general of some reputation in times of war. In addition to his other dignities this Zachariah has now been ordained a deacon of the Church of England, and is thoroughly under the control of the Church Missionary Society. Having been sent by the king, with a guard of honour of twenty soldiers, to bid us welcome to his country, I am bound to say that Zachariah acquitted himself of his task to perfection; his appearance was pleasing, his clothes the very ideal of snowy white-

BRIDGING A SWAMP IN UGANDA.

ness, while his manners were a type of politeness itself, and would have fitted him for a post in any European court. During my residence in Uganda I had occasion to see a good deal of this man, and always found him intelligent, anxious to do his best in any matter that was required of him, and gifted with more common-sense and a less narrow mind than falls to the lot of most of his African brethren.

The guard of honour was a curious and motley crowd armed with at least half a dozen different kinds of rifles; one or two of them were clad in old tunics of English line regiments, others had coats of white cotton, evidently cut and sewn by themselves, but all, I noticed, had well-filled cartridge-belts round their waists. In my innocence, as I thought of all the thunders of the General Act of the Brussels Conference, and all the ordinances, enactments, and regulations which had been published thereafter by different Powers having possessions on the African coast, I wondered how, in the very centre of Africa, these people were enabled to keep their belts so well replenished with cartridges of different and of the most modern patterns. I had not been a month in the country before I had learnt that, for those who had the wherewithal to trade, guns, powder, lead, and all the instruments of destruction thereunto appertaining, could be as easily purchased in Uganda as in Pall Mall. This worthy guard of honour, having drawn itself up with mathematical precision in a line across the road as the caravan approached, proceeded to present arms in the most approved fashion, while

L.

Zachariah made his little speech of welcome, and suitable compliments were interchanged; but having said all we had to say, and being, on our side at least, very anxious to get on to camp and luncheon, the guard across the road offered a serious obstacle, and having got themselves into this unaccustomed attitude, much to their own pleasure and astonishment, the "soldiers" did not seem to know how to get out of it.

In vain I hinted, through the interpreter, to Zachariah, that we might now proceed on our journey —he only bowed and smiled, and replied that all must be as I wished. I pointed to the guard, but he thought I was only admiring them, and bowed and smiled all the more in modest deprecation. I then marched straight up to the guard, hoping that they might break their ranks and let us through, but they evidently imagined that I wished to inspect them more closely, and only continued to present arms with greater stolidity than ever. The situation was ludicrous, but was eventually saved by one of the porters behind me, who knew the Luganda language, shouting out a few words, which were afterwards translated to me as meaning, "Out of the way, you idiots." The guard then executed a wonderful manœuvre, which excited the admiration of the military officers of the Mission: they wheeled to the left and marched away ahead of us, still presenting arms, and with their noses apparently glued to the barrels of their rifles. For a mile or so they solemnly marched in this new fashion, and then one by one were observed surreptitiously to bring their rifles to the shoulder, or to some more comfortable position.

On the evening of the 16th, as we pitched our last camp at a small village only six miles from the capital, having received during the day's march at least half a dozen messages from King Mwanga, inquiring after our health and bidding us welcome, a brown pony with a somewhat seedy saddle made its appearance, with his black Majesty's request that I would ride the beast into the town next day in order that all the people might know which was the Commissioner. Until after sunset our camp was thronged by multitudes of brown-faced, brown-clad people, anxious to have the first look at the strange white men, who had been sent up by the far-famed Queen to set everything straight; and everything tended to show that the greatest excitement prevailed about our arrival. This became more evident the next morning, for although we got under weigh at the usual early hour, we had not gone a mile before we found the road crowded with people, while every ant-hill and post of vantage was occupied as thickly as are the rickety stands on the river-bank at the Oxford and Cambridge boat-race. As we approached the town the crowds, well-behaved and quiet, increased in density, while breathless messengers were continually dashing up with messages of welcome from the king and from various chiefs. At last a wooden palisade and a few mud huts on a low knoll ahead of us was pointed out as being the British East Africa Company's now famous fort of Kampala. After all we had read and heard of it, the fort itself and the mud huts in it appeared to us absurdly small and insignificant, and the available space was uncomfortably crowded with the highly-flavoured dwellings of the Company's Soudanese troops; but an inner enclosure, containing the storehouses and the mud huts occupied by the Europeans, was, though small, clean and well kept, and it was with a hearty sigh of relief that we entered the gates, leaving the picturesque, chocolate-faced, and bark-clothed mob outside, and surrendered ourselves to the cordial welcome and hospitality of Major Eric Smith of the 1st Life Guards, who was at that moment representing the Imperial British East Africa Company at the capital of Uganda. Captain Williams, Captain Macdonald, and other officers whom we had hoped to find here, were all away travelling in different parts of the country,—a welcome proof, at all events, of the pacific state of affairs in the provinces.

We were thus able at last to congratulate ourselves on having successfully accomplished our journey of 820 miles from the coast, and on having arrived at our destination the very day mentioned in my telegram sent from the coast, viz. the 17th of March. We thus entered the fort of Kampala on the seventy-fifth day after leaving the deck of H.M.S. *Philomel* at Mombasa. As eight days had been lost in a compulsory halt at Kikuyu, and two other days at different times were spent in complete rest, our marches had thus averaged about twelve and a half miles a day, a record which speaks volumes for the stamina and endurance, both of the European officers, and more particularly of the native porters, especially when it is remembered that for nearly 250 miles between the coast and Machakos, and again for 280 miles between Kikuyu and Kavirondo, we were travelling through an uncultivated and almost uninhabited country, and, consequently, that in addition to all the baggage, impedimenta, and stores of a large caravan going into the centre of Africa for eight or ten months, our heavily-laden men had sometimes to add the weight of twelve days' rations to their other burdens.

At certain periods of the journey—as, for instance, on leaving Kikuyu with full rations—many of the men had been carrying 75 lbs. or even 80 lbs. of dead weight on their heads, and with that crushing load had, without faltering and without murmuring, covered the day's march of ten or fifteen miles under a burning sun or through a chilling fog, over rocks and mountains, through swamps and rivers, with no certainty of anything to eat beyond a handful or two of the coarse black flour of mixed beans and corn which had been dealt out to him, and of which 18 lbs. were to last him for twelve days. It was indeed fortunate that by hard and constant work the Europeans had been able to keep the whole caravan so well supplied with game, that hardly a day passed without every man having a ration of meat to add to his supper. Without this addition I have no doubt that the work demanded of the porters would have proved to be beyond their strength. As it was, these half-savage Zanzibaris had performed a feat which could certainly not be equalled by even a picked battalion of beef-fed, cloth-clad Englishmen, and which would probably prove to be beyond the powers of any race of people existing in the world except the despised, crushed, and enslaved East African.

CHAPTER VII

A short survey of the conditions of the country—The districts suitable for European settlement—Facilities for traffic—Suggestions for improving the road—Proposed regulations for caravans and formation of stations.

BEFORE continuing the narrative of our experiences in Uganda itself, I would entreat the patient reader to accompany me through one chapter, which shall be as brief as possible, while we endeavour to analyse the experiences gained, and to recapitulate the lessons learnt by the nine Englishmen who had thus successfully completed their walk of 820 miles into the interior from the East African coast. So great is the responsibility in connection with the future of this vast continent which devolves on the present generation of Englishmen, so vital to the welfare, the prosperity, and even to the very lives of thousands—ay, millions—of human beings in this tropical land, is the decision which must without delay be taken by the inhabitants of that little island far away in the cold northern seas, that I have the less hesitation in following far abler and better qualified teachers than myself along some of the paths which they have trodden, and which they have, with immense labour, cleared of the undergrowth of romance and tradition, and of the impediments of surmise, for the benefit of their successors.

The present modest work, which is simply a list of our personal experiences threaded together as beads on a string, does not pretend to add anything to the scientific or geographical knowledge of Africa already in the possession of experts or even of ordinarily well-informed persons; it will have amply fulfilled its purpose if it succeeds in adding a few details or a little colour to the somewhat gray and blurred picture of the interior of this mysterious continent, of which the outlines have been sketched by the noble band of great explorers and travellers who for this end have sacrificed time, health, and too often life itself.

In the first place, let those who have not yet read Mr. A. Silva White's valuable book[1] realise that, roughly speaking, Central Africa consists of a vast plateau varying from 2000 to 6000 feet in height above the sea, the exterior margins of which, as Mr. White tells us, "will generally be found, as in those of other continents, to be higher than their central portions, thus presenting towards the sea a sort of natural rampart." This great fortification has for hundreds of years successfully withstood all attempts made from the outside world to penetrate beyond its frowning battlements. Rivers and lakes are, of course, the natural, and, before the wide dissemination of the use of railways, the sole means of communication

[1] *The Development of Africa.* By Arthur Silva White. London: George Philip and Son, 1890.

to any material extent, "but all the large rivers, not only in their upper, but also in their middle and lower courses, where they break through the margins of the plateau, have in consequence their beds filled with all sorts of rocky obstructions, and so great is their inclination that the accelerated waters become rapids, or break into cataracts, or fall down sheer heights, in their eager passage to the sea. And, unfortunately, from the fact of the inland or continental plateau approaching so near to the coasts, all the great rivers have their navigation obstructed at relatively short distances from their mouths."[1] It is this natural obstacle which has been one of the chief reasons why the whole of this vast continent, three times larger than Europe, has been allowed to lie dormant and undisturbed for so long. It is only in this generation that it has become possible, without swamping the undertaking by its initial cost, to organise means of transport which will overcome the opposition of Nature, and carry into the very heart of the interior the commerce, civilisation, and light of the outside world.

It has been already seen that the route which we followed is not connected with any of the great rivers or natural highways. An exaggerated fear of the Masai had kept it as a sealed book until Mr. Joseph Thomson made his celebrated journey from Mombasa through Masailand to Lake Victoria in 1883-84; but since that time it has been traversed by many caravans equipped at great expense, and painfully conveying

[1] *The Development of Africa*, chap. i. p. 9. By Arthur Silva White. London: George Philip and Son, 1890.

small packages of goods on the heads of long-suffering men. Such European parties as have come this way have always found it a very expensive business: native and Arab traders have sometimes been able to recoup their outlay, and even to make a profit, by a judicious combination of trade in ivory and in slaves, but I venture to think that even a cursory examination of the geographical, geological, and ethnological conditions of the country thus traversed will make it clear that all the commerce which can be carried, or all the intercourse which can be established between the coast and the interior under existing conditions of transport and communication, will be too insignificant in amount to have any important effect, or to confer any material benefit upon the central countries near the upper waters of the Nile, which are the objective point of most of these expeditions.

To render this plain, I will proceed, for the benefit of those who have not made any special study of the question, to make a crude and rapid dissection of the route which we have traversed.

In the first place, near the coast we find a narrow strip of land of recent geological formation, steadily rising from sea-level to a height of about 300 feet. This strip contains certain centres, usually in the neighbourhood of towns and villages, such as Mombasa, Malindi, or Wanga, where there is a fairly plentiful population of the curiously mongrel race known as Swahilis. The soil is fertile, and produces immense numbers of cocoa-nut palms, areca palms, great quantities of manioc, sweet potatoes, beans, some rice in suitable places, and, in short, most other crops which it may please the farmer to sow. Where the inhabitants are more scattered, and the ground has not been cleared for planting, there is a good deal of timber, sometimes of a valuable nature. Being exposed to the hot breezes and washed by the warm currents of the Indian Ocean, the mean annual temperature of this region is high, and averages not less than 80° Fahrenheit, while the mean range of temperature between the hottest and the coldest months does not average more than eight or ten degrees. The rainfall, which occurs principally in the months of April, May, and June, and again in November and December, is plentiful, and may be estimated at about sixty to seventy inches a year; on the islands, such as Zanzibar and Pemba, it amounts to perhaps ten inches more.

As will be gathered from the above figures, this region cannot be said to be well suited to European inhabitants. There are, it is true, a good many Europeans of different nationalities to be found living on the coast, nearly all of whom are either traders, officers of the Administration, or missionaries, but it would be difficult to find one who looks as if his residence there had done him good; all, except perhaps those who have just arrived from Europe, have that bloodless, washed-out look which is so characteristic of Europeans in Africa; white children do not thrive, and it would be better for the whole community if a universal rule could be made, that no foreigner should be allowed to remain more than two consecutive years on the coast without paying a visit of at least two months' duration to more congenial climates. The only exceptions to this rule might be the Indians and Portuguese, all of whom appear to be quite at home in this orchid-house atmosphere. It is to be feared, however, that such a regulation can only be made generally effective when men have ceased to struggle, fight, and strangle each other in the race for wealth, when international rivalries have merged into universal friendship, and when religious enthusiasm in Africa is tempered by broad-minded moderation. But although it is too much to hope that, until this millennium is declared, merchants, companies, or governments will afford to their sweltering employés the luxury of a biennial " run home," yet, if the East African question is seriously taken up, an opportunity may offer itself of giving fresh life to many an exhausted but patiently working subordinate, of restoring health and vigour to many an anæmic body or overtaxed brain at a merely nominal expense, by the establishment of hill stations and health resorts in the cool, healthy uplands only 300 miles from the coast. This suggestion, however, like almost every other East African problem which can be presented, resolves itself at once into the great all-shadowing question of transport.

Leaving the coastal strip after a couple of days' journey, we found at once a totally different aspect of country. The palms and all the rich vegetation and cultivation had disappeared, and were replaced by interminable scrub, thorny acacias, mimosas, and stunted, unhappy-looking trees of similar kinds. In the course of the next 250 miles we gradually—almost imperceptibly—ascended from 300 to over 3000 feet above the sea-level, the air becoming proportionately lighter and the temperature cooler. The rocks over which we walked, and the painfully dazzling red soil formed from them, were of the Mesozoic period, and lie in a sort of inner belt behind the coastal zone along the whole east of Africa, from Cape Town nearly to Cape Guardafui—sometimes, as in Somaliland, extending to the sea-shore itself. It was easy to see that this district derived but little benefit from the warm rains of the Indian Ocean; the general aspect of the country was parched, and the nature and appearance of the stunted trees and vegetation showed that they suffered from constant drought. The annual rainfall in the lower parts of this region probably does not amount to more than some twenty-five or thirty inches a year, increasing to about forty inches with the rise of altitude towards Nzoi and the Ulu Hills. The mean temperature decreases in inverse ratio to the rise of level, from 80 to about 72 Fahrenheit. The population, partly in consequence of the poverty of the country, and partly from inter-tribal wars and Masai raids, does not exceed about four persons per square mile.

This district, commencing some dozen miles from the sea-shore, and extending for 250 miles to the little station of Nzoi at the foot of the Ulu Mountains (where we camped on the 22nd of January), may thus be written down as almost valueless. There are, no doubt, here and there a few oases on the banks of some of the small streams found at rare intervals, where healthy young Englishmen might find life bearable, and where, as at the Scottish Industrial Mission at Kibwezi, their labour would be repaid by the soil; but, generally speaking, the heat of the climate, the want of rain, and the consequent absence of rivers, forbid us to hope that, at all events for many years to come, this part of the country will fulfil any *rôle* in history but that of a serious impediment in the way of reaching the more fertile and salubrious districts lying behind it, which it has shielded for so long against European invasion.

At 250 miles from the coast the nature of the country undergoes a complete and sudden change; we found ourselves climbing hills of the Palæozoic period, and as we ascended steadily to a height of 5000 feet at Machakos, and 5500 at Kikuyu, the air became proportionately cooler and more invigorating, while the smiling aspect of the country showed clearly that the rainfall was much greater than in the lower regions. The mean annual temperature may be safely said to sink with the rise of the land from 72° to about 64° Fahrenheit, and the rainfall would probably be found to be some 50 to 60 inches per annum, while the dews at night are heavy. As I have said before in the course of the narrative, the whole of this district appears to be exceptionally fertile, well watered by clear mountain streams, thoroughly healthy, and admirably adapted for European residents, while the first settlers, if their tastes inclined in that direction, would have the additional pleasure of living in the very heart of one of the finest and best-stocked game countries in the world. Labour could be fairly plentiful, as the population, especially among the Wakamba tribes in Ukumbi and the Ulu Hills, and again in the Kikuyu country, is dense; villages, huts, and native settlements are packed close together in every direction on the hills; and although the fear of the raiding Masai prevents the natives from settling on the more exposed and open plains, the population of the whole district cannot be less than thirty or forty per square mile, all the adults of both sexes being actively engaged in cultivation. It is this district, extending from the Ulu Hills to Kikuyu, which holds out hopes of prolonged life and health to the pale-faced residents at the coast, on whom a month or two among the hills of Kikuyu or on the plains of the Athi river would confer the same blessings as a visit to the moors of Scotland, without the crushing expense and loss of time entailed by the long sea journey.

Immediately after leaving the Kikuyu district there was another change. We entered suddenly into a barren, arid-looking district, of which the geological formation is purely volcanic or "eruptive." Extinct volcanoes reared their heads on every side as we crossed the great trough which furrows this part of Africa from north to south for some 600 miles, and in which lie a series of interesting lakes, from Lakes Rudolf and Stephanie in the north down to Lake

Naivasha. The height of Lake Naivasha above the sea is 6000 feet, and its climate cool and bright like that of Kikuyu, though in this part there would appear to be rather less rain; but after leaving the trough or "meridional rift" we rose rapidly to a height of nearly 9000 feet while crossing the Mau Mountains, before descending gradually to the level of 4000 feet in the plains of Kavirondo. In the higher altitudes the rainfall is naturally much greater than in the districts previously traversed; the moisture which is held in suspension in the warmer air as it passes over the plains, is at once condensed on arrival at the mountain range, and the higher parts of Mau receive probably not less than sixty to eighty inches of rain every year. The soil, formed by the decomposition of volcanic rocks, is generally rich, and the whole country well watered, but some days before reaching Kavirondo we were travelling through dry plains and over the undulating hills of the Palæozoic period. The whole of this country, across which our road led us for some 280 miles, would be well suited to Europeans so far as climate is concerned, but at present it is absolutely neglected, uncultivated, and almost uninhabited. Its only occupants are the Masai tribes, and these nomads cannot be reckoned at more than two or three persons per square mile of country.

In Kavirondo itself, which is also throughout of Palæozoic formation, the villages are in places fairly close together, but, on the other hand, there are many desolate tracts, extending for several days' journey, in which no human being can be seen; it would not, therefore, be safe to estimate the population at more than twenty to twenty-five per square mile. As the whole country lies from 4000 to 4500 feet above the sea, the climate is, on the whole, temperate; the nights are thoroughly cool, so much so, that although the variation between the hottest and the coldest months of the year cannot exceed five degrees, yet the average temperature throughout the year may be estimated at about 73° Fahrenheit. The annual rainfall, which occurs principally in the months of April, May, and June, and again in November and December, is probably forty inches.

In the last section of our journey, through Usoga and Uganda, we entered upon what is perhaps one of the oldest parts of the oldest continent of the world, the rocks being throughout of the archaic period. As, however, I shall have occasion later to speak more fully of these countries, I will here conclude this hasty and somewhat dry *résumé* of the different sections of our route, leaving the reader to draw his own conclusions as to the present or future value and prospects of the country described. Before leaving this subject I should add that for many of the statistics and figures which I have quoted above, I am indebted to Mr. A. Silva White's book, *The Development of Africa*, and to the valuable notes and maps compiled by Mr. E. G. Ravenstein, F.R.G.S., which form its interesting appendix.

I now come to one of the most important of all questions in connection with the future of Africa, viz. that of the road itself and the means employed for carrying traffic along it.

As regards what is by courtesy called the "road" but little need be said; it is well known that an African road consists simply of a footpath some ten inches wide worn in the grass by the constantly-passing naked feet of native villagers and caravan-porters. If, for any reason, such a path falls into disuse for a few months, especially during the rainy season, it is quickly obliterated by the rank grass, thorns, and creepers which always seem to ally themselves with the other forces of Nature in order to repel the invasion of the stranger. All marching is thus of necessity done in single file, and a large caravan, even without straggling, will often spread itself over a mile of country, while conversation is only possible by the leading man addressing his remarks to the empty air before him, and taking in the answers at the hollow of his back.

On fairly level and open plains, where the long grass has been burnt down, or before the young shoots have grown more than six or eight inches, these paths are good enough, and, if the weather is cool, the day's march is a real pleasure; but on the sides of hills, especially on hard soil, where the paths become runnels for rain-water, they are frequently hollowed into a deep and narrow gutter by no means well adapted for the comfortable progression of a man in boots. After the rainy season, when the grass of the plains has grown to four, six, or even eight feet in height on either side, it is frequently a matter of some difficulty for the leader to see the track through the overhanging masses of grass-heads and weeds, and, while his progress is seriously impeded by the tangle, the discomfort of the traveller is increased by his clothes being drenched through and through every morning by the heavy dew, or by the drops from the last shower which he brushes off the foliage as he forces his way forward. As the sun rises and gains strength the moisture is evaporated from the grass, and the pedestrian's clothes are gradually dried on him at the same time, but, nevertheless, it is an undoubted fact that this ducking, undergone with wearisome monotony from 6 till about 9 o'clock every morning, is the cause of many a bad attack of fever which is put down generally to the African climate.

These, however, are among the minor inconveniences inseparable from travelling on foot in uncivilised regions; what is a more serious annoyance, inasmuch as it causes unnecessary delay and fatigue, is the circuitous nature of the path, which twists, turns, and winds in a ridiculous and most irritating manner for no perceptible reason. In order to explain this peculiarity of African tracks, we must lay down three axioms: first, that the paths are made by natives; secondly, that to the native time has no value, and he is consequently never in a hurry; thirdly, that the native will always prefer to go round even the smallest obstacle rather than take the trouble of cutting or clearing it away for his own benefit or for that of his neighbours. Thus a fallen tree or an overhanging bough, a new ant-heap, or even a tuft of rank grass, will each be sufficient to cause the path to deflect perhaps for many yards; a similar occurrence will take place on the loop thus made, and so on, until in the course of years the road is made to trend for a considerable distance away from its objective point.

Frequently, towards the close of a long, weary, and thirsty day's march, our patience and our tempers have been sorely tried at finding ourselves following the path in a northerly, southerly, or even easterly direction, while we knew that our camping-place lay due west. If the road in such places were to be straightened, slightly widened throughout, and cleared even of such minor obstructions as would not demand any serious expenditure of labour, not only would the journey to Uganda be shortened by several days, but a still greater saving would be made in the muscle, stamina, and health of the overloaded men and donkeys. In forest countries and places where constant attention would be necessary in order to keep the road clear, it should be made compulsory on every caravan to be preceded by a small band of pioneers sent a mile or two ahead, armed with hatchets and bill-hooks, whose duty it would be to clear away such creepers, undergrowth, or overhanging branches as might have even partially blocked the path since the passage of the last party.

Again, an immense amount of delay and trouble to caravans could be easily avoided by the construction of a few bridges of the simplest nature; a couple or perhaps three slender tree-trunks laid side by side, and bound together by creepers or by rope, would in most cases be quite sufficient for the present, especially if these trunks were then covered over with grass, branches, and finally sods of earth, so as to make them passable for animals. There need be no fear of the natives destroying such bridges; on the contrary, they would appreciate the convenience thus offered as keenly as any European, and would most religiously preserve them. Only recently I heard of such an instance: a caravan was passing through a part of the country in which the natives had the reputation of not being too friendly to strangers; a small river offered an obstruction, and crowds of natives sat on the adjoining hills while the commander of the party superintended the building of a bridge by his own men. As soon as the work was completed, and the caravan had got safely across, the leader wished to take away some rope which he had used for lashing his bridge. Scarcely, however, had he touched the rope than down came the natives who had been quietly watching the proceedings: "No, no," said they, "you have made us a nice bridge, and we see the use of it as well as you do, but you need not think that we are such fools as to let you destroy it or take it away now that it is made; *pas si bêtes*, we thank you for your work, and now you may go in peace!"

It may be urged as an objection to all this, that labour is so scarce along the road to Uganda, that the expense and difficulty of any such undertaking as road-making would far outweigh its advantages; but, as a matter of fact, such is not the case. It has already been proved that near the coast the Wa-Deruma and the Wa-Nyika are perfectly willing to work for infinitesimal wages, if once they are sure of not being maltreated, of being punctually paid, and of securing protection for their homes from the attacks of more powerful neighbours during their absence. A little farther inland the Wa-kamba are ready to work on the same conditions; the Kikuyu people have been suffering under a bad reputation, and have never yet been given a fair chance, but there can be little doubt that with tact and patience their confidence could be gained, and a vast supply of labour thereby rendered available; the Kavirondo people are willing to do almost anything for a string of beads, and if they could see the chance of an occasional gift of meat, either from a bullock—price four or five dollars—or from the carcass of a hippopotamus, which could be easily shot at any time by the overseer, the supply of muscular men and wiry women would be found to exceed the demand twenty times over. In Usoga and Uganda this sort of labour is already organised to some extent by the native chiefs, to whom the execution of the work would have to be entrusted, and who already well understand the art of road and bridge making.

It is only just to those who have especially interested themselves in securing new fields for British commerce in Africa, to remind the reader that this question has not been entirely overlooked. It will be remembered that on the Taro plain near the coast we found that the Imperial British East Africa Company had cleared a road through thick bush for about ten miles, and a little farther on about double that length of road had been constructed by the energy of the Scottish Industrial Mission at Kibwezi. I am given to understand, moreover, that since our departure from the coast this work has been carried on at the personal expense of the late deeply-regretted President of the East Africa Company.

We now come to what is perhaps the most important of all questions in connection with the establishment of commercial intercourse with the rich countries of Central Africa, that of the means of transport of goods. It is well known that from the earliest times until to-day every parcel and package of barter-goods, personal baggage, or food has been carried on the heads or shoulders of men, occasionally assisted by a few half-starved and decrepit donkeys. So many abler pens than mine have written eloquent words about this system that I should be unwilling to say anything on the subject, did I not feel that it is the duty of every leader of an expedition who has been compelled by force of circumstances to use this only available form of transit, to lose no opportunity of entering his formal protest against it. From a moral and humanitarian point of view the arguments are obvious; they have, moreover, been set forth in innumerable books and pamphlets, and thundered from countless platforms, frequently with more zeal than accuracy of detail.

Therefore, passing over all question of humanity, or of the rights of man, and shunning all argument as to the equality or superiority of our black brothers, I will venture merely to touch briefly upon the utilitarian side of the question.

As an animal of burden man is out and out the worst. He eats more, carries less, is more liable to sickness, gets over less ground, is more expensive, more troublesome, and in every way less satisfactory than the meanest four-footed creature that can be trained, induced, or forced to carry a load. Why, then, is the question which naturally occurs to the stranger, has not some animal ever been substituted for man? The answer to this is, that until the last year or two, since Equatorial Africa has become a European field of enterprise, all commerce with the interior from the east coast has been a monopoly in the hands of Arabs and half-breeds, who have always tried to combine the slave-trade with a little legitimate dealing; for the former they require a certain force of men armed with guns, and this force is supplied by the porters, who thus serve a double purpose. In the second place, the porter is not quite such an expensive luxury to the Arab caravan leader as he is to the European. In the caravan of the former the men are all slaves, either his own, or those of friends who supply some of the capital, and "stand in" with him over the whole enterprise. Thirdly, the Arab has not much initiative, and, as beasts of burden are not easily procured at the coast, it does not enter his head—it would indeed be opposed to the Arab nature — to import them in any paying quantities. Unfortunately, in the damp, hot climate of Zanzibar and the coastal zone, no such animal appears to thrive, still less to breed. The few horses to be seen have all been imported, usually in open dhows, from Muscat or from India, and their price places them beyond the reach of the ordinary Arab trader. Camels are occasionally imported in small numbers from Somaliland, but they do not thrive near the coast, and neither the trading Arabs nor the Swahilis have the smallest idea as to how to treat these somewhat delicate animals. Donkeys are fairly cheap and plentiful at Zanzibar, but with them also the air or the food of the narrow coastal zone appears to disagree, and, even if they do not die, they lose flesh and muscle during the delay which always takes place on the coast before a caravan is ready to start. These reasons are sufficient to show why the Arab has always had his goods carried by men, with perhaps a few half-starved donkeys as a reserve; and the European companies, which during the last few years have begun to dabble in trade with the interior, have only followed the established custom.

Before discussing possible remedies and reforms, let us consider for a moment what is the common experience of a porter leaving the coast on a journey, let us say, from Mombasa to Lake Victoria under a native Arab leader. In the first place, he is utterly out of condition at the start, his muscles are flabby, and he has probably been more or less drunk for the last week. On the appointed day for the start he is given a load weighing some 60 or 70 lbs., to this he has to add his own rations for about ten days, say 15 lbs. more, bringing the load to a weight which few Englishmen would like to lift on to their shoulders, much less carry for ten miles a day. During the first days our porter, willing though he may be, feels that his burden is greater than he can bear; he lags behind, and at last drops his load by the side of the path while he lies down for a rest. From his pleasant reflections, however, he is shortly startled by the "thwack, thwack," of a hippopotamus-hide stick across the shoulders, which forcibly brings home to him the fact that the headman in charge of the rear of the caravan has arrived on the scene, and that it is time to move on if he values his own skin. In a day or two the labour and scanty food have very likely caused some small scratch on his bare foot to develop into a raging ulcer, but still he must get forward somehow, and carry a load. If the caravan be under a European, there may perhaps be a medicine chest, and he may have the chance of getting his wound dressed and sprinkled with "iodoform," but if it be an Arab trading expedition there is no such hope for him. Slowly and painfully he toils along, always getting whacked for lagging behind, his open sore becoming worse and worse until every step is an agony to him. At last comes the day when he can literally move no farther, and even the headman sees that the game is played out. If the poor fellow be near a native village he may creep there and take his chance, but if, as is more likely, he is in the midst of an uninhabited district, he need do nothing more than speculate as to the way in which the end will come, whether by lion, hyæna, or starvation. The caravan goes on, his load has been added to the already heavy burdens of his companions, and nobody will ever ask what has become of him, why he was left behind, whether he was murdered, or whether, indeed, he ever existed.

Meanwhile, there being no percentage or margin of spare men for such eventualities, the other porters toil ahead with 60 or 70 lbs. more on their shoulders than before. At last the caravan arrives at the top of the Mau Mountains, with the thermometer at night well below freezing-point. The improvident men have all left the coast wearing and possessing little more than a single loin cloth; the bitter cold penetrates to their very bones; in vain they huddle together, and almost burn their feet in the fire, the cold gets the better of them, and after forty-eight hours in this region the echoes of the night are roused by a long-continued chorus of painful coughing arising from every side. A few spare blankets, a little medicine, a couple of days' relief from carrying the hateful load, would now perhaps save half a dozen lives; but such an idea as that of carrying a load of blankets merely for the use of the men has never entered the head of the leader,—such an unremunerative bundle would appear to be the wildest extravagance. The result is that perhaps five or six more men are left to take their chance,—in other words, to die of cold, of starvation, or from wild beasts. I need follow this example no farther.

Let it not be thought that I have been guilty of exaggeration. There is not the smallest doubt that these things, and worse, are done every day in Arab caravans up-country, and it is whispered that they have not been unknown even under European leaders. The commander of the party runs no risk. Nobody asked or cared how many men left the coast with him, and nobody will ask or care how many come back. While up-country he exercises an absolute authority and power of life and death, and no inquisitive police or executive officer will ever make any awkward inquiries. Let it be clearly understood that all this does not apply to caravans of the British East Africa Company; in these the men are all duly enrolled, registered, and provided with a number stamped on a brass ticket; their leader is always provided with a certain quantity of simple medicines for the men, and there is often even a small percentage of spare men to relieve those who are sick.

Now we are met with the question, What is the remedy for the state of things sketched above, for surely all men will agree that it cannot be allowed to continue in a part of Africa which is supposed to be more or less under British influence? One answer to this question would of course be,—abolish altogether, once for all, the whole system of human transport. This, no doubt, will be the best solution if it is feasible; but time will be required before such a radical change can be thoroughly carried out, and an efficient substitute for men must first be found. Failing this, surely the first thing to do is to bring the whole traffic under as efficient control as the existing administrative machinery will allow. This is not the place in which to discuss all the steps which might or should be taken towards this object, but a few crude outlines of such regulations as could be most easily enacted may fairly be enumerated. In the first place, no caravan, whether under European or native leadership, should be allowed to leave the coast without being submitted to preliminary inspection by a competent officer. The names of all the men should be inscribed in a register, with their rates of pay, etc.; the number and weight of the loads should be examined, and a maximum weight fixed; while every caravan should be compelled to provide itself with at least 10 or 15 per cent of spare men to relieve those who may fall ill on the journey. No man should be allowed to go up-country who could not produce a certificate of having been vaccinated or of having had the small-pox. If the caravan contemplates crossing any of the colder regions, it should be compelled to take an adequate supply of cloth or blankets for the men, and should be also furnished with such simple medicines as might be safely used even by an ignorant man. The caravan should be made to report itself at every station of the Administration lying on or near its route, at which its papers would be examined and checked. Finally, if it be possible, no native-led expedition should be allowed to go into any region where slave-trade is suspected, nor indeed into any part of the country where its misconduct would have bad effects on the people, without being accompanied by a European official detailed off for the purpose.

Many other useful and necessary regulations could easily be enacted, if ever it be decided seriously to take up the whole question of the development of East Africa, and in the meantime important experiments might be made with animal transport. It is difficult to believe that camels would not thrive in the dry country between the coast and Machakos: the mimosa, their favourite food, is plentiful all along the route, the damp atmosphere, which is so fatal to them on the coast, is replaced by a dry climate less than twenty miles inland, and the route itself offers no natural difficulties or obstacles to their progress. An experiment with camels is said to have been made unsuccessfully some three or four years ago, but, from all accounts, it was so ridiculously mismanaged that the only wonder would have been to find that any of the animals survived the trial.

It has already been sufficiently proved that horses manage the whole journey to Uganda with ease. Several have been taken up there during the last two years: we ourselves started with a couple of ponies who did their full share of work in carrying tired, footsore, or invalid Europeans, and arrived in Uganda in far better condition than when they left the coast. Horses on the East Coast are too expensive for baggage animals, but henceforth no European who has the smallest regard for his own comfort, or who wishes to be fresh and able to shoot meat for his men in the afternoon after the day's march, should dream of leaving the coast to travel along our route without having provided himself with at least one pony.

Mules have never been tried, and I cannot recall ever having seen one in East Africa; in Abyssinia and its neighbouring countries the mule is the principal means of transport, and there is every reason to suppose that it would thrive equally well in East Africa.

The patient donkey is the only animal of which any use has yet been made, and he, poor beast, is overloaded, underfed, and maltreated to a pitiable extent. An idea appears to have fixed itself in the heads of all East African authorities, that the little native donkey, far smaller than a common English "moke," can carry a weight of no less than 150 lbs. for ten or fifteen miles a day, and can then pick up its own living by the wayside, requiring neither food nor attention. This crushing load is even tied on to the wretched beast with no saddle to keep the weight off his spine, but merely a rough pad of cotton stuffed with a few handfuls of grass or leaves! Loaded in this manner the unfortunate animal is beaten, pushed, and pulled by main force up and down mountains, and through swamps, from which he could scarcely extricate his legs even without the load on his back! Is it then surprising that on the long piece of road between Kikuyu and Kavirondo the hyænas are growing fat on the flesh of donkeys varied by that of an occasional porter?

Before leaving the subject of transport animals, let me repeat a suggestion which surely must occur to any traveller in this part of the world. The horse of East Africa is the zebra; active as an Arab pony, sturdy as a mule, hardy and swift, this animal is found all over the plains in hundreds and thousands. For some reason the zebra has acquired the reputation of being wild and untamable; as regards wildness, he is far more confident and more easy of approach than any other animal of his size in this country, and so far as I have been able to ascertain, no real and intelligent effort has ever been made during late years to domesticate a young zebra, except in South Africa, where we hear of a team of zebras being constantly driven about Johannesburg. Even if the experiment has been tried without success on the East African zebra in former times, would not the immense advantages which wait upon success justify a second trial on the spot, and with all the light of modern intelligence?

Finally, there is one other step which must be taken before there can be any hope of a really important English commerce with Uganda and its neighbouring countries. Readers who have accompanied me so far will have grasped the fact, that the greatest difficulties of the journey are those caused by the wide uninhabited tract of 280 miles between Kikuyu and Kavirondo. How to carry sufficient food for the whole party across this region is the great problem for every caravan. In our case it was solved by our good fortune in being able to secure nearly a hundred donkeys; other parties are not so fortunate, and have to contend with immense difficulties and privations. Apart from the purely economical aspect of the question, what must be the feelings of a man who falls ill or becomes very lame a day or two after embarking on this march. There is no hope for him unless he can struggle along somehow to the very end: the caravan cannot stop, if it did the food supply would run short; there is no possible resting place by the way, no hospitable village. In our caravan we had spare donkeys on which the sick were carried, but in other expeditions the unfortunate invalid must either push forward as best he can, must keep pace with the rest, or die in the bush.

The one thing which is a real necessity, if any effort at all is to be made to open up the country, is the establishment of a permanent station under European supervision half-way along this section of the road. The site, at twelve days' march from Kikuyu and a similar distance from Kavirondo, would be most healthy, about 7000 feet in height above the sea, and in a well-wooded, fertile, well-watered, and lovely country. The stores of grain and provisions which would be kept at this station would enable caravans to walk straight through from the coast to Uganda without any special preparations as regards food, never hampered by more than the twelve days' rations which can be carried by the porters themselves without extra assistance. As soon as the station is established, and is seen to be a permanency, providing adequate protection against the Masai, there would be no difficulty in planting a colony of cultivators around it who would be able to dispose of their grain to their great advantage as fast as it could be grown. It is unnecessary to go further into details on this subject; suffice it to say that with such a station, and with certain improvements to the road itself, such as have been indicated, the route to Uganda through the English sphere of influence would become one of the easiest of all East African journeys; without these reforms it is vain to hope that it will ever be a channel for commerce.

Throughout this chapter I have been careful to avoid any mention of a railway. It would hardly be proper for me to discuss here the pros and cons of this scheme. If a railway is ever built the whole way to the Lake, that would of course in itself settle all the questions which have been raised above. The suggestions which I have just ventured to make can only have any application in the event of no such railway being made, or of a line being constructed over only part of the whole distance.

CHAPTER VIII

The kingdom of Uganda : its climate and population—The King and Council—Provincial governors—Oppressive taxation—Intelligence and religion of the peasantry.

THE kingdom of Uganda, which during recent months has been the subject of so much "ink-slinging" and of such frequent oratorical efforts, hardly appears, at first sight, to deserve the amount of attention which has been bestowed upon it. The country is shaped like a somewhat irregular rectangle, or a "carpenter's square," of which the inner sides rest upon the Victoria Lake, occupying nearly 120 miles of its northern shore stretching westward from the exit of the Nile, and then turning southwards for 90 or 100 miles along the western coast of the Lake. The frontiers on the outer or land side are ill defined, but are seldom more than about 60 miles from the Victoria Nyanza. The whole country may be said to cover about 15,000 to 16,000 square miles, and is, therefore, roughly speaking, about the same size as Switzerland. Outside the limits of Uganda proper, its kings claim a sort of feudatory lordship over several small neighbouring states, such as Usoga on the east, and Toru and Ankori on the western side.

In some cases, as in Usoga, this claim is grudgingly recognised, and a small tribute is occasionally sent as a propitiatory offering to the king, but the more powerful or more distant chieftains, while careful in all messages and correspondence to address the king of Uganda as their "father" or "master," and signing themselves his "humble servants," would laugh to scorn any demand for a practical contribution towards the expenses of the central government, unless such a message were accompanied by a larger army than could be locally summoned into the field on the spur of the moment. All along the northern and part of the western frontier lies the powerful and jealous kingdom of Unyoro, whose kings and people, though less advanced in civilisation, are closely connected by blood with the inhabitants of Uganda and Usoga. The form of government of Uganda, which in the days of Speke (1862) and of Stanley (1875) was an absolute and bloodthirsty despotism, is now a monarchy, restrained, or hampered, as the case may be, by a supreme council of chiefs. At the present moment the country is nominally governed by a king named Mwanga, son of Mtesa, of which individual we shall have more to say hereafter.

Descriptions of Uganda and of its morals, customs, and form of government have been given to the world at different times since 1863 by Captain Speke,[1] by Mr. Stanley,[2] by Emin Pasha,[3] by several

---

[1] *Journal of the Discovery of the Nile.* By Capt. J. H. Speke. Blackwood, 1863.
[2] *Through the Dark Continent.* By H. M. Stanley. Sampson Low, 1875.
[3] *Emin Pasha in Central Africa.* Edited by Dr. Felkin. G. Philip & Son.

missionaries, and by divers other gentlemen who have taken an interest in African matters. But the evidence furnished by their respective works appears so contradictory, the country itself has undergone such violent political changes, and has suffered such terrible experiences, that it is a matter of great importance for a clear idea to be generally held concerning the actual state of affairs existing at the present moment. It may, therefore, be useful even at the risk of repeating what may be already known to give here a superficial description of the principal features, both physical and social, as they appeared to the officers of the English Mission on our arrival in March 1893.

As has been said before, Uganda is, geologically speaking, a district of extreme old age, that is to say, the rocks composing it are of the archaic period; and, by that very fact, where they thrust their gray and weather-beaten heads above the surface, they reproachfully convey to the traveller an oppressive sense of the countless ages during which they have grimly frowned on this expanse of land and water, silent witnesses of innumerable and untold deeds of nameless horror; the runlets on their battered sides filled too often with streams of human blood; hopelessly, until to-day, shut out from the light of the outer world in the very darkest centre of the vast continent of negroes.

Uganda is, however, essentially a country of contradictory impressions. The first feeling of gloom caused by the antiquity of the land, by its crime-laden history, and by the veil of mystery which is now being rudely torn aside, is dissipated as the eye ranges from the sparkling waters of the Lake over an endless vista of round or flat topped hills rising, close together in every direction, to a height of 300 to 600 feet above the level of the water. Nearly the whole country consists of little more than a close conglomeration of these hills, all of them clothed in the brightest green, a tropical character being given to the scene by the rich banana plantations which frequently cover their sides. Here again, however, the pleasant impression is shaken on closer inspection by the discovery that, except where its place is taken by the banana gardens, this wealth of verdure consists, not of growing crops and luxuriant cultivation, but of an impervious tangle of tall elephant grass, twelve to sixteen feet in height, whose close-growing cane-like stems offer an effective barrier to the comfortable progress of almost any living creature except an elephant or a field-mouse. It is, moreover, unpleasant to realise that between each hill and its neighbour lies an unwholesome-looking swamp, through the centre of which a sluggish stream of slimy water languidly struggles with the obstacles offered to its progress by dense masses of rushes, papyrus, and other rank and matted products of the marsh.

With a sigh of perplexity as he passes from the tangled waste through the carefully-tended and fruit-laden banana grove, from the bright air of the hillside to the death-dealing miasma of the fœtid swamp, the traveller as he raises his eyes towards the evening sun tells himself that at all events in the unearthly beauty of its sky-effects, and in the marvellous and utterly indescribable wealth of colour of its sunsets, Uganda surely has no equal throughout the world. In this he is probably right; for truly the magnificence and brilliancy of the visions I have gazed at, standing spell-bound on the shores of the Victoria Nyanza, have an overpowering glory, an almost defiant loveliness, unrivalled by the transcendental delicacy of colours where the sun sinks into the desert sands behind the Great Pyramid at Cairo, or by the weird beauty of the scene so often gazed at from the terraces of the Villa Medici at Rome. But again there is a revulsion of feeling as the cloud, just now so glorious with gold and purple, hurries across the sky, growing blacker and more threatening, till a few heavy splashes, followed by a blinding flash and a deafening roar of thunder, remind all men that hardly a day may be allowed to pass in this country without at least one thunderstorm.

During the three months that we spent in the country, although we did not have rain quite every day, I may safely say that at no time did twenty-four consecutive hours elapse without our having seen lightning and heard thunder. It is true that we were there during the wettest time of the year, but in Uganda there is rain more or less throughout the twelve months, though the greater part of the yearly supply falls during April, May, and June, and again in November and December. The average annual rainfall of the country is estimated at 51 inches, or about

30 inches per annum less than on the coast. Even during the wettest months the rains never appear to have the heavy persistency of the tropical downfall, but to come rather, as in Europe, in passing showers and local storms. In fact, the whole climate, the air, the general aspect of the country, make it difficult to realise that the capital of Uganda lies within one degree of the Equator. The general altitude of the country being about 4000 feet above the level of the sea, the air on the hillsides is fresh and light, and although the difference between the hottest and the coldest months is hardly more than 3° Fahr., the mean annual temperature does not exceed 70°. During the late morning, and in the middle of the day, the vertical rays of the sun are, as might be expected, too fierce for thorough comfort, and would make it unsafe for Europeans to walk about without some good protection for the head; but the evenings and nights are cool and fresh, and we all slept under at least one, and more often under two good blankets.

The inhabitants of Uganda consist, to speak correctly, of an agglomeration and partial fusion of many different races. Local tradition and internal ethnological evidence agree in supporting the theory that at some comparatively remote period, the date of which is hopelessly lost, the country was overrun by an invading horde from the north-east, possibly of Abyssinian blood, which drove most of the original inhabitants southwards into a district on the western shore of the Lake, where they were allowed to remain unmolested, being contemptuously known as Buddu (slaves). That part of the country has taken its name from this circumstance, and has figured conspicuously in recent history as the fertile province of Buddu. After the successful occupation of the country, the conquerors, as so often happens in Africa, mingled and intermarried freely with the subject race, losing by degrees nearly all trace of their distinctive language, and gradually acquiring more and more of the negro type, until we have to-day the curious mixture of negro coarseness of feature with slight traces of higher refinement, of African cunning with some real intelligence, of sensuality, cruelty, and immorality with polished manners and courteous dignity, which are among the most striking characteristics of the race of people known as the Waganda, who constitute by far the greater proportion of the present inhabitants of the country.

Leaving aside several unimportant Bantu tribes occupying certain parts of the country, who are all either connected with or in process of assimilation with the Waganda, we may say that the remainder of the population is supplied by the far more interesting, refined, and handsome race of Wahuma. Although the villages of the Wahuma are to be found scattered throughout the country, they keep themselves quite distinct from the Waganda, retaining their own language in all its purity; nor do they willingly intermarry with their neighbours. These Wahuma are a pastoral people, their villages are always to be found in a rich grass country, on which roam their herds of cattle. They live chiefly on beef and milk.

whereas the Waganda, with the exception of the wealthy chiefs, seldom eat anything more invigorating than bananas and pumpkins. The Wahuma are probably an offshoot of the Galla race, and although the sleek Waganda affect to look down upon the hardy but somewhat poverty-stricken race of herdsmen, this contempt is said to be cordially reciprocated; and one glance from the tall upright figures, the clear skins, the oval faces, thin lips, straight noses, and classically-chiselled features of the Wahuma to the lowering, coarse, and indeterminate faces, the thick skins and heavier bodies of the Waganda, shows at once on which side lies the pride of race and the purity of descent.

It is a curious fact that in spite of this real or assumed contempt on the part of the dominant Waganda, the royal family is reputed to be of Wahuma extraction, although by indiscriminate polygamy and concubinage it has now lost nearly all outward trace of its racial origin. Among the Waganda I never saw a handsome man, nor even a passably good-looking woman or girl; the latter after marriage, as in the case of most African races, soon "fall to pieces," and are wrinkled and old by the time they have reached their thirtieth year. In a Wahuma village stalwart, proud-looking aristocratic men are the rule rather than the exception, while the large, soft hazel eyes, the delicate lips gently parted over most brilliant teeth, the proud carriage of the little head, the clear velvety skin, the firm budding figure and elastic step of some of the

Wahuma maidens would be more than sufficient to turn the head of many a London sybarite.

Besides these two races, the inhabitants of the islands of the Lake present yet other distinct characteristics. They are divided into the Wa-Vuma, inhabiting the islands of that name scattered all along the coast from the eastern corner to about the centre of the northern shore, and the Wa-Sesse, occupying the Sesse archipelago on the western side of the Lake. These tribes, though quite separate one from the other, and speaking different languages, may be jointly described as being negroes of a blacker colour than the Waganda, more savage, more courageous, but altogether less civilised than the inhabitants of the mainland. The Sesse islanders have the reputation even of being cannibals, though it is said that if taxed with it they do not admit the soft impeachment.

As to the total population of Uganda proper it is difficult to arrive at any very accurate conclusion, though it may safely be said that it has been vastly overstated by several enthusiastic writers and speakers during the last few years. The almost incredible misgovernment, the barbarous enactments of its kings, the cold-blooded massacres, the wars of extermination, the raids, the murders, and the internecine conflicts under which the country has groaned for the last thirty years, have in many districts more than decimated the population, and have driven thousands into voluntary exile to the south of the Lake. In 1875 the population was estimated by Mr. Stanley at under

one million; in 1879 an English missionary put it at
five millions; more recently I am informed that one
of the authorities of the British East Africa Company
announced that the country contained three millions
of inhabitants, while a member of the Church Missionary Society has been heard to state that in
Uganda are nearly a million Protestants out of a
total population of a million and a half. On the
other hand, another officer of the East Africa Company, of local experience, held the opinion that there
were not more than 250,000 people in the whole
country. A careful, but at present incomplete, cal-
culation of the number of inhabitants, taking village
by village, and province by province, has been carried
on during the last few years by some of the French
missionaries in Uganda, and these gentlemen told me
that their labours had now progressed far enough to
enable them to predict that they would find the total
population to amount to about 450,000, but certainly
to fall short of half a million. We may, therefore,
in default of more accurate statistics, take 450,000 as
the figure, which gives us an average of about thirty
per square mile. To convey to the reader a sense of
the relative density of population, I would remind
him that Switzerland, in about the same area, contains three millions of inhabitants, and that in
England and Wales there is an average of 500
human beings to every square mile.

It is already well known from the accounts of
former travellers that in its political and social
economy Uganda stands forth in strong contrast to

all surrounding African nations; this indeed is one of the principal reasons for which this country has attracted so much attention, and has been the unwilling cause of so much heartburning among political, religious, and general circles at home. It has been the fate or the fortune of Uganda to differ in character and habits from its neighbours; its peculiarities and idiosyncrasies have secured public attention, and, like any private individual who is rash enough thus to single himself out from the common herd, it must now, whether for good or evil, prepare to incur the inevitable consequences of the sin of individuality.

I have already said that the government of Uganda is vested in the hands of a king (in the vernacular *Kabaka*), assisted by a council of chiefs. To define accurately the powers and functions of this council, or the limitations which it may exercise on the king's despotic authority, is, I regret to say, beyond my ability. Generally speaking, the authority of the council, as in England during the Middle Ages, would appear to rise and fall in inverse ratio to the strength of character of the monarch. In the days of Speke (1862) and Stanley (1875), when all men trembled under the tyranny and nonchalant cruelty of Mtesa, this council appears to have consisted of little more than a ring of fawning sycophants, who were beaten, fined, mutilated, or executed like the lowest of his subjects at the whim of the autocrat. To-day, under the weak and invertebrate Mwanga, although each chieftain is careful to preserve, in the royal presence, all the outward signs of abject submission and grovelling humility, nobody knows better than the king himself that if his wishes, advice, or commands do not happen to coincide with the opinions or interests of his council, they will be ignored or disobeyed without the smallest hesitation. The council itself consists of some ten or twelve chiefs, all of whom assist at its deliberations in virtue of divers offices held by them, and to which they have been previously appointed by the king. The majority of them are governors of certain of the ten provinces into which Uganda is divided; the remainder hold posts, which need not be detailed, in the king's household.

In theory this system of government by the king and his council would appear to be well enough, but, unfortunately, on our arrival we found that neither the one nor the other exercised any authority whatever over more than a portion of the whole country. For instance, the Catholic party had recently been driven away from the northern shores of Lake Victoria, and had been given the province of Buddu as their portion. The governor of Buddu was *ex officio* a member of the great council, but not only did he and every other official in the province decline to come near the capital—and indeed it would have been as much as their lives were worth to do so—but the whole province and the Catholic party looked upon the king and his chieftains as the representatives of a foreign and hostile power, and absolutely ignored their authority. Again, the British East

Africa Company had recently brought into the country a large number of Waganda Mohammedans, and had caused them to be allotted three provinces in which to settle, their own chiefs being made governors of the provinces; by all of these also the orders, writs, mandates, or exhortations of king and council were treated with calm contempt, and merely disregarded without any show of overt hostility. It will thus be readily understood that we found the central administration in a very limping, dishevelled, and unhappy condition of mind and body.

Below the governors of provinces, the country is cursed with an endless and complicated network of chiefs, sub-chiefs, petty chieftains, and jacks-in-office, from the wealthy court favourite who exercises his sway over a district of a hundred square miles, daily fawned upon by dozens of grovelling underlings, down to the poverty-stricken headman of a miserable village with its half-dozen tottering reed-built huts. In a few rare cases the chieftainships of districts are recognised as being the legitimate inheritance of certain families, but with these exceptions every one of these thousands of so-called "chiefs" who prey upon the country is, in theory at least, appointed by the king himself. The natural result is that the higher offices, governorships of provinces, seats at the council, and so forth, are held by favourites, who have generally served an apprenticeship at court, and have wormed themselves into the royal favour as "the king's pages." The minor posts are simply given to the shrillest and most pertinacious applicants, and to those who can "grease the palm" of the chamberlains and even of royalty itself in the most satisfactory manner. As soon as the coveted appointment is successfully secured, two qualities are simultaneously developed in the new chief, which are universal among his colleagues, and common equally to the highest and to the lowest of the fraternity. The first of these is that from the moment of his appointment he ceases to do a single stroke of work of any sort or kind himself, and the second is that he forthwith lays himself out to beat, rob, maltreat, and oppress the wretched peasantry or *bakopi* by every means in his power.

The working of the whole of this quasi-feudal system may perhaps be best illustrated by an example of the methods of procedure which are almost daily obtaining in all parts of the country. Let us imagine that the king, as is the habit of kings all the world over, feels a sudden desire for an increase of revenue to meet his real or imaginary needs. He informs his council of the fact, and after a short deliberation it is decided that a certain province shall be forthwith called upon to furnish the required contribution. It is perhaps scarcely necessary to explain that there being no money currency in Uganda, all taxes and contributions to the exchequer are made in kind—viz. in ivory, in cattle, sheep, goats, corn, bark-cloths, and all other produce of the country, besides a system of *corvée* or forced labour, for which men have to be supplied by the different provinces in certain proportions. As soon as the king and council have agreed upon the province which shall be the victim of the royal necessities, the governor is forthwith informed that he had better bestir himself, and produce what is wanted with as little delay as possible. He, nothing loath, for he has probably even intrigued that his province may be the one selected, departs from the capital with many promises and vows of loyalty. On arrival in his district he summons before him all the most important local chiefs, and to each one assigns the amount of the contribution for the production of which he will be held responsible. In this partition the governor is particularly careful to see that the aggregate amount, when brought in, will be more than double of what he has to pay over to the king; the rest will remain in his hands. Away go the sub-chiefs; the whole proceeding is repeated again and again in endless subdivision and gradation, and thus the hard-working peasantry, beaten and persecuted until the very last drop is wrung out of them, have to pay in the end five times, and even ten times, the amount at which their province was assessed. It is safe to say that scarcely one-tenth of what is paid in taxes by the people ever reaches the exchequer for which it is ostensibly levied; the remaining ninety per cent remains in the hands of those drones and curses of the country, the chiefs and petty chieftains of Uganda.

If, however, the sufferings of the *bakopi* were confined to extortions and robberies of this nature, their lot would not be much worse than that of the peasantry in several civilised but over-taxed countries which might be mentioned; but, unfortunately, the power of even the most petty sub-chief goes far beyond that of mere financial oppression. The whip, the stick, the cord, and the stocks are in constant use: the daughters of the people, if looked upon with an eye of favour by a great man, are taken without ceremony, and until quite recently even the lowest office carried with it the power of life and death over all subordinates. In the days of the late King Mtesa, and during the first years of the reign of Mwanga, executions on the most trivial pretext were of daily occurrence, not only at the capital and by command of the king, but all over the country, and at the mere will of these *batongoli* or district chiefs. An instance has been quoted to me of a man being put to death by an insignificant chieftain for the crime of dropping and breaking a gourd containing banana-beer; ears were cut off, eyes put out, hands amputated for yet more paltry reasons, and there was no redress for the sufferer; it was nobody's business to inquire into the case, nor could any greater chief be expected to put himself to any trouble about the ear, the eye, or the life of a mere peasant!

In this respect, however, it is satisfactory to note that during the last few years the influence and teaching of European missionaries, and the subsequent advent of European authority, as represented by the East Africa Company, have worked wonders. On this point, and it is to be feared on this one only, the missionaries of both the Catholic and the Protestant divisions of the Christian religion have been in full accord, and their joint influence has been brought to bear on every possible opportunity with a view to putting a stop to the whole system of off-hand executions, tortures, mutilations, and other cruelties. While Mtesa was still alive their representations and pleadings were met with a deaf ear or a scornful laugh, and day after day miserable wretches, courtiers, concubines, and even boys, were hurried off to execution at the whim of the king, whose example was imitated by the provincial chieftains until the whole country ran with blood. During the first years of Mwanga's reign things were no better, and the missionaries themselves had to leave the country; but when at last the Christian parties really obtained the upper hand, one of the first and best results of the newly-acquired influence of their teachers was the cessation of the deeds of blood which for many years had characterised the court and government of Uganda. As usual, the provinces followed the example of the court, and although there can be no doubt that oppression, violence, and extortion at the hands of his superiors is still the lot of the peasant, and although dark deeds are undoubtedly practised in country districts, of which the merest whisper scarcely reaches the ears of the white men many months afterwards, yet the actual life of the *bakopi* is now pretty safe, and he may even congratulate himself on a fair prospect of retaining and using his arms, hands, eyes, and ears during the remainder of his days.

In spite of the oppression of the lower by this self-styled upper class, there is no real aristocracy in Uganda.

The family of the kings is distinct, and as I have said above, there are a few offices and provincial chieftainships which have become hereditary in certain families, but with these exceptions the chiefs from highest to lowest were drawn originally from the *bakopi* class; a peasant girl may, without exciting any surprise, become the concubine of the king, and her son may succeed to the throne; nor is the promotion of the merest peasant to an important chieftainship a sufficiently rare occurrence to cause any gossip or even wonderment. Although, as soon as they have a grasp of authority, the chiefs treat the *bakopi* as a conquered race, the same blood runs in both, and the chief himself probably began his life as a peasant. He will possibly end it in the same condition unless he can exact enough from his district to satisfy not only his own requirements, but also the extortionate and constantly repeated demands of all his superiors. Similarly, the open degradation or the mysterious disappearance of the most powerful lord, or even of a dozen great personages at one swoop, would fail to excite more than passing gossip. The African, whether brown, yellow, or black, is thoroughly material in his tastes and sympathies, and so long as he sees a fair prospect of being able to fill his stomach with the daily ration of food to which he is accustomed, and to surround himself with what he considers his comforts, he is not in the least inclined to get up any show of indignation, or to "fash himself" in any way whatever on account of injustice, robbery, or death suffered by his neighbour.

It would, of course, be ridiculous on my part to pretend that, in the course of three months' residence in Uganda, I or any of the officers with me were able to acquire any thorough personal knowledge of the habits, thoughts, or distinctive modes of life of the Uganda peasantry; for information on these subjects we were forced to rely on the opinions of others, such as missionaries of various denominations, who had been longer in the country, and the very nature of whose work brings them into frequent contact with this class of the people. But here again, as in almost every instance in which we were compelled to appeal to Europeans of local experience, we were perplexed by the utterly divergent nature both of the evidence and of the conclusions brought forward by competent observers of different creeds.

On the one hand, we were asked to believe that the peasants of Uganda are an exceptionally intelligent and quick-witted race of people, eager to learn, diligent to work, quick to grasp the benefits of civilisation, and that they—or at least the Protestant section of them—had already in large proportion learned to read and write. On the other hand, we were told that these *bakopi* are little better than any ordinary African negro, that they were fairly good husbandmen, though not better than other African races, that they worked indeed, and kept the banana plantations clear of weeds, but only because they were cruelly beaten if they did not; that, as regards their deep religious fervour and the extensive purchase of religious reading-sheets sold by the Anglican Mission, which was so triumphantly quoted by the Protestant missionaries as a proof of the progress of their religion and of the education of the natives, these things merely proved once again that the *bakopi* would at once adopt any religion favoured at the moment by their masters,

A GROUP OF UGANDA NATIVES.

and would eagerly spend their cowrie-shells in purchasing these or any other "fetishes" which might appear to them to be connected with such religion; but that should Mwanga and the leading chiefs to-morrow become Catholics, Buddhists, or followers of Confucius, the peasantry would with equal readiness put away the reading-sheets for a fresh turn of the wheel, and crowd eagerly to the new church, temple, or joss-house.

As in the majority of such cases, the truth will probably be found to lie half-way between these two extremes. It is undoubtedly true that the peasantry do work, the women more than the men, and that they keep the banana plantations in beautiful order, free from weeds, cutting away the decaying leaves, plucking the fruit at the right moment, and so forth, but it is equally true that they would pass through some extremely unpleasant moments, the effects of which might last a lifetime, should the master discover that they had been remiss in any of these duties. As regards their general intelligence, it may, I think, be placed on a somewhat higher level than that of the ordinary negro tribes of the Nile valley, or of East Africa, but more than this cannot as yet be said; they are certainly far behind the natives of various parts of the coast of Africa, who have already for many years had their wits sharpened and their morals depraved by intercourse with Europeans. The religious feelings of the peasantry are no doubt such as might be expected among such a people. It would probably be easy to pick out men from each party, Catholic, Protestant, or Mohammedan, who, whether from sincere conviction or from obstinacy of character, would be ready to suffer any amount of inconvenience, and even death, rather than give up his beliefs at the bidding of another, but with the vast majority their creed is without doubt the creed of the strongest. The religion of the peasant is that of his immediate superior, that is, of the man who has most power to cause him constant inconvenience, and so on up the social scale, until we arrive at the chiefs of the great council and the king himself; and even in this august circle it would not be difficult to select men with whom faith and flesh-pots are synonymous terms.

The foregoing somewhat desultory description of the system of government and the division of classes has, I trust, been sufficient to show how greatly in Uganda the peace and prosperity of the country, and the welfare of the people, depend upon the individual character of the sovereign himself, and it is now necessary to devote a few pages to a description of Mwanga, son of Mtesa, King, or as the natives say, *Kabaka*, of this little corner of Central Africa which has unconsciously made such a stir in the great world.

PART II

FORT ALICE.

CHAPTER I

At Kampala—Visit to King Mwanga—Arrangements for a division of territories between the Protestant and Catholic Missions—The slave question—The queen-mother—From Kampala to the Ntebe Hills—Kaima's case—Illness of Captain Portal.

WITH the concluding words of the last chapter the written narrative is at an end. It was the intention of the author to have devoted the following chapters to a description of the court, the manners, and the resources of Uganda,—showing how it had passed from a condition scarcely rivalled by the horrible records of Dahomey to the promise of a rapid development under the guiding hand of the white man, only to relapse into an anarchy almost as disastrous through the political animosities which have found their opportunity and pretext in the antagonistic zeal of rival religious denominations. The concluding chapters were to have dealt with the homeward journey of the author and of Colonel Rhodes by the river Tana, passing in great measure through regions hitherto unvisited by European travellers.

The history of Uganda as he would have told it cannot be recorded here; such material as he had gathered has already been utilised in drawing up the

Report laid before Her Majesty's Government as the result of the mission entrusted to him. What has there been left untold must now be entrusted to other hands, and the sequel to the first eight chapters can only be found in the pages of the Blue-Book.[1] There remain, however, ample notes in a Diary kept from day to day with much neatness and care, from which may be gleaned the story of the homeward journey, and there are a few entries made during the months passed in the country itself, together with letters to friends and relations, which are valuable in supplementing information, but perhaps still more so in portraying the character of the writer himself. I propose, therefore, to include here such passages from the Diary as may fairly be made public, together with extracts from such letters as have come into my hands in their chronological order. Such a Diary possesses a special interest which a finished work might lack, in showing how days are filled up, and in revealing many of the details of life in savage countries. At the same time, it must be remembered that the events which are jotted down represent but a small portion of the activity of every day, and convey an inadequate impression of the immense quantity of work accomplished in a few weeks. It is easy in reading to pass over the infinite labour involved and the patience expended in such pioneer work as the establishment of the new headquarters, the transplanting of the colonies of Soudanese troops, and the slow conversion by drill and discipline of these half-

[1] *Parliamentary Papers*, Africa, No. 2. 1894.

savages into orderly and useful co-operators. Throughout the whole period covered in the present chapter the Commissioner was also engaged in collecting the information as to the country and its resources which he has placed on record in his Report, in studying a scheme for the pacification of the rival factions, in devising a temporary administration providing for future eventualities, and in working out the details of financial requirements,—no small labour with so multiform and singular a currency as that which Central Africa makes use of, the cost of which, moreover, depends upon the number of miles which it has been transported from the coast.

With regard to this Diary and the letters, I would claim that they should be read with the reserve and indulgence due to words written as purely personal memoranda or solely for the eyes of intimates. After mature consideration of their contents, I have come to the conclusion that little would be gained by giving publicity to any extracts either from the Diary or from private correspondence written previously to the Commissioner's arrival at Kampala, although the latter is far ampler during the early months of the Expedition. The foregoing chapters are so full, and deal so completely with every incident of the march, that such extracts would only read like repetitions of what has already been better told before. We will therefore take up the Diary at the point where the narrative breaks off:—

Friday, 17th March.—Started 6. Road cut very broad—unnecessary waste of much labour; but only heads and blades of grass cleared, roots left ; road will be choked immediately after rain. Crowds of people at various spots : messengers kept on arriving with messages of welcome from various chiefs.

Halted 8. Then rode Katikiro's pony, a screaming beast. Half a mile from town, met Raymond and Bishop Tucker, who had walked out. Great crowds near town. C.M.S. church at Namirembe conspicuous on the left front. Kampala ahead and Mengo behind.

Arrived Kampala about 9. Smith in charge.[1] Fort very much smaller than I expected, and crowded on E. and S.E. sides by Soudanese huts. Two rooms for self and one for Berkeley in mud house. One for Rhodes in another. Saw many chiefs, R.C. missionaries, and C.M.S.

18*th March.*—Got up 6.30. Prepared for king's baraza.[2] Officers all turned out in extraordinary kits, red coats, breeches, big boots, swords, etc., but heavy rain all morning, so sent to put off baraza till Monday, after waiting for two hours.

At 12, Macdonald and Wolf arrived from Buddu.[3] W. ill with lumbago. Report plague in Buddu: symptoms, swellings in glands under arms and in throat,—death in four days ; also great suffering there from jiggers. Jiggers very prevalent also here, attack toes and feet chiefly, cause great irritation, have to be cut out. Fleas innumerable ; few mosquitoes. Company's influence here seems very small. The Fort of Kampala in badly-chosen place, commanded by all surrounding hills. Smith against drilling or organising Waganda ; probably right. Visited Bishop Tucker : very fine, well-built church : holds 5000 people. All roof put on in one day. Mission houses very nice, of reeds, far superior to mud houses in Fort.

19*th March, Sunday.* — Long talk with Macdonald on situation. Mwanga sent to offer to come this afternoon ; told him No,—must go to church. Went to church at 4.30 with

---

[1] Major Eric Smith, 1st Life Guards, then acting in the I.B.E.A. Company's service.

[2] Baraza, general East African term for parliament, solemn reception, durbar, etc., originally the verandah or shed where such meetings are held.

[3] Captain Macdonald, R.E., in command of the Railway Survey Expedition. Herr Eugen Wolf, whose letters on Uganda have appeared in the *Berliner Tageblatt.*

MWANGA, KING OF UGANDA.

all members of Commission: none of Fort people. Writing Road Report.[1]

20th March.—Went to visit Mwanga 9 A.M. Staff in red, white, and all colours. Macdonald in full dress. Self in Zanzibar officer's sword and sash and Macdonald's plume. Escort of fifty Soudanese in front, then flag, then selves, then fifty Zanzibaris in rear. Through many courts enclosed by neat cane palisades to Mwanga's baraza. About fifty chiefs there. Mwanga on velvet chair given by Company, and carpet before

BISHOP TUCKER OUTSIDE HIS CHURCH AT NAMIREMBE.

him. Very grave offence for any one to tread on carpet. Bishop Tucker and English missionaries there, but not French: had not told missionaries. Mwanga's not a bad face, but weak; all chiefs talked as they liked—no discipline. He had a foolish habit of clasping the hands of any chief near him whenever a remark was made that pleased him. He is evidently nervous.

At 4 Mwanga came to call on me. Gave him tea and some presents. He asked for a khakee coat, also that I would kick out Mtanda, and put his brother on Busoga throne.

Dined with Bishop. Proposed scheme of paper currency.

[1] See Africa, No. 2. 1894.

21st March.—Further discussion with Smith about Toru Soudanese. He is against putting them near Guaso Masa. Smith declines Usoga command, only wants transport work, to bring loads and caravans from coast.

GROUP AT KAMPALA; 20TH MARCH.

Captain R. Portal.   Lieutenant Arthur.   Lieutenant Villiers.   Dr. Moffat.
Major Owen.   Captain Macdonald.   Sir Gerald Portal.   Mr. Berkeley.
Colonel Rhodes.

Went in the afternoon with Rhodes to visit the French missionaries at Rubaga. Splendid site, commanding king's hill and Fort. It was offered to Lugard. Pères Gaudibert and Guillemain there; very agreeable men; gave us an excellent glass of Algerian wine. In the evening Mr. Gedge [1] arrived from Buddu. He and Williams [2] had shot twenty-four Speke's antelopes.

[1] Acting as correspondent to the *Times.*
[2] Captain, now Major Williams, R.A., in the I.B.E.A. Company's service, and in charge of Uganda after the departure of Captain Lugard.

22nd *March.*—Writing Road Report all morning. Garden taken in hand and all available seeds sown, it had been terribly neglected and allowed to go to waste. Williams arrived in the evening.

THE KING'S DRUMS.

There is a letter of this date from Captain Portal to Lady Charlotte Portal, describing the Commissioner's arrival in Uganda, with a short note from the Commissioner himself, which may perhaps be most appropriately inserted here.

CAPTAIN PORTAL TO LADY CHARLOTTE PORTAL.

KAMPALA, 22nd *March* 1893.

MY DEAR MOTHER—You may observe that our walk is at an end, for the present. I think I wrote last about the 3rd or before, and since then we have been wandering through a country consisting entirely of banana groves, which took about five days to get through—miles and miles of bananas, which of course were brought in daily by the ton, for nothing.

On the 12th we crossed the Nile, and took all day over it.

Swarms of hippopotamus kicking about, of which I slew one. The next day Gerry and I let them walk on, and spent a lazy day at Ripon Falls, trying to catch some of the swarms of fish which were jumping up the Falls like salmon. We did not get any, however. The day after I went on alone with a dozen porters, to get to Kampala before them, and I got in on the 16th. It's a very civilised country compared to all the others we have seen. Gangs of women making a great broad road, and bridging the swamps, of which there are lots. The people are wonderfully good-mannered and civil, and are very intelligent. Nearly all speak a little Swahili, which is a blessing. It's damp and steamy rather just now, as it rains every day for a bit, but it seems to agree with everybody.

The rest of them got in the following day. Crowds of people went out to meet them, all the chiefs, and there was great excitement.

Next day we all went to see the king, an ordinary-looking person, who I believe doesn't count for very much. He returned the visit in the afternoon, which meant that he came to get his present. . . .

We are still living in tents at the Fort, as there is no room inside, but when the Company's people go, on or about the 1st, those of us who are here will get under cover. There are six Europeans at the Fort besides our nine. I shall be left here with two others, and some of the Company's people will stay on. I am not sure where I shall go, probably to the R.C. district about four days off. . . .—Your affectionate son,

M. R. P.

Sir Gerald Portal to Lady Charlotte Portal

Kampala, 23rd March 1893.

My dear Mother—We all arrived here well and strong on the 17th, the very day I had selected before leaving the coast.

Since then I have not had a moment's breathing time—interviews, writing, talking, and business of all sorts, from 6.30 A.M. till late at night, without a moment's respite.

I have only come to the conclusion so far that this is a far more complicated, difficult, and disagreeable business than any one anticipated. . . .—Your affectionate   G. H. P.

23rd March.—Decided to take over whole of Soudanese, both those here and those in forts ; estimated cost, Rupees 74,000 per annum. Also to send Owen and Raymond to Toru to recruit and organise men, and probably withdraw them from farther forts. Instructed R. and Owen to learn as much as possible of organisation of Soudanese here.

24th March.—Instructed Arthur and Berkeley to go to Usoga with ninety to a hundred Zanzibaris to take place of Soudanese there going down with Williams. Berkeley to examine question of succession to Wakoli, and decide whether to turn out Mtanda and put up his brother in his place. Muxworthy writes mail route interrupted,[1] probably by Wahehe or Wagogo.

Wolf better, says he is going (back to coast) by Usukuma.

25th March.—Gave Owen instructions about going to Toru and selecting site for new post half-way. Told Foaker to go to Toru to bring back the 1000 Soudanese—men, women, and children. Wrote to Zschatsch[2] and offered him Rs. 200 per month till 31st December. Rhodes and Williams making joint estimate of value of buildings.

26th March, Sunday.—Went with Smith, Macdonald, and Berkeley to the king's landing-stage on Lake, 7½ miles, pretty good road. A pretty place, but low and unhealthy, with large papyrus swamp alongside ; just opposite is the island of Balingugwe, the same of Williams' fight. C.M.S. steel boat lying there, and a small Berthon boat. Steel boat pretty good—two masts, lug sails, and jib, small cabin for storage forward, and six oars for calms. (?) Hire boat for Government for six months. Rhodes and Williams rode to another landing-place a mile farther up creek, and report it good spot for settlement of Soudanese.

27th March.—Bishop says he is willing to agree and help in partition of territory, and that arrangement would not have broken down if he had remained here.

Sent for Mwanga, who came with Katikiro, and told them object of my mission. They both said emphatically that if we go war will begin next day, and both they and all Protestants

---

[1] This refers to the mails regularly sent up by Messrs. Boustead, Ridley, and Co., of Zanzibar, through the German sphere to the south of Lake Victoria.

[2] A young German employé of the Company, referred to in Part I. Chap. VI., at Wakoli's.

will come out with us : said late war was not one of religion, but simply of ambition for power.

Promised to begin Toru road at once.

28th March.—Proposed to Owen independent command in Usoga, but he said he preferred Toru business. Immense stocks of ammunition in store. In our caravan no porters sick, but many Zanzibar soldiers, whose physique appears to break down after the journey even without loads.

APOLLO, KATIKIRO OF UGANDA.

29th March.—Messengers from Toru came in to Bishop, sent on here, say people won't obey Kusagama[1], and that K. wants Christian teachers. This probably a plan to prejudice division of spheres of influence.

Instructions to Owen about his mission issued also to Raymond.

Told Katikiro to send boat for French Bishop ——: long letter from latter.

Told king to send Usoga claimants back to Usoga.

30th March.—After immense fuss and many countings of

[1] The rightful native chief of Toru, driven out by Kabarega, and replaced in power by Captain Lugard.

LOWERING THE COMPANY'S FLAG AND PREPARING TO HOIST THE UNION JACK AT THE FORT AT KAMPALA.

loads and porters, Owen got off at 9.30 with 127 porters and 12 Soudanese: took Berthon boat. Armed all porters with carbines.

Rhodes and Williams busy about valuation and handing over of all arms. Saw chiefs of Mohammedans; told them at once to make road to Toru. They complained of having too little territory.

Long talk with Wolf as to future of Uganda. He thinks evacuation of Uganda would soon drive Germans back to coast. They could not afford to hold Uganda, and Arabs and Mohammedans would be so strengthened as to make tenure of Tanganyika and Usukuma impossible.

31*st March.*—Gave Smith instructions for return caravan of 320 loads if Government approve his appointment. Wrote to Rodd to support it, also that Smith is to organise whole transport system and be Road Commandant.

1*st April.*—Smith and caravan left at 8, well organised, every man knowing his load; no confusion or bustle. He took forty-four loads of ivory.

12 o'clock.—Hauled down Company's flag and hoisted Union Jack. Guards of honour and royal salute. King sent to me to ask for a flag like this; told him he could not have it.

A letter of this date from Captain Portal describes his departure with Major Owen on this mission to engage the Soudanese troops referred to above.

CAPTAIN PORTAL TO LADY CHARLOTTE PORTAL.

1st April 1893.

MY DEAR MOTHER—. . . I can't remember when I wrote last, but I think it was since we arrived at Kampala. I left there three days ago with Owen, and we are on our way to Unyoro, which is near the Albert Nyanza. We are going to some old forts they have there, to destroy two of them, and remove the garrisons, which consist of Soudanese troops, originally with Emin, who have been there for years without pay or food or anything, and live by raiding the surrounding country. They are believed to be about 4500, of which only 450 are fighting men, and the remainder women and slaves. We have got to move half to

Kampala and half are to be left in other forts, but first we are going to try and enlist the men, and put them on pay. I believe they are a wild lot, and no wonder, and it will probably be a hard job to move the mob to Kampala, also to feed the whole lot, as they are not to raid in the future, and there isn't much food in Unyoro, so what they are to eat I don't know.

This is a perfectly horrible bit of country, this part of Uganda. The road is very bad, and every day there are about four to six swamps to be crossed, some of them 400 yards long and up to your chest. Nearly all my boxes have been dropped by the porters in them by now, and as we have perpetual rain into the bargain, it is hard to be dry for a single moment, except perhaps for an hour or two in bed. It seems as if fever ought to be a certainty, but I never felt better, and it is the same with the others. These swamps are really all rivers, blocked, I suppose, by either papyrus or forest, as there is always one or the other. I can't make out how our cows and goats and sheep manage them, but they always turn up somehow or other.

I think it is likely that in a month's time, after we have settled the Soudanese, I shall go to look after Buddu, the province where the Roman Catholics are, and make a station there. I shall be glad if I do, for though it is much more pleasant to be with one of our people, it is better to have a job of one's own to do. If I do this I shall have to return to Kampala, probably with another body of Soudanese, who are to be settled near there, and there is just a chance I may see Gerald again before he departs for the coast.

There has been no shooting up here yet, though just now we are in an elephant country. I believe in three days we shall see some game, however. No mail has arrived for us yet. Just before I left Kampala the missionaries got one, with letters of November, but nothing newer; but as that looks as if the road to the south end of the Lake was open now, some letters may come up any day.

The Company's people were to leave Kampala yesterday. We are taking on three of them up here, to look after the stores, etc., and Macdonald, an engineer officer who has been surveying for the railway, has been left in charge of Uganda. I think under the present regime they will be peaceful here, but there will be nothing lasting about it. Now it's too dark to write, and we are short of candles [and of everything else it seems to me], so good-bye.—Yours affectionately, R. P.

2nd April, Easter Sunday.—Some of staff went to service. Church full, estimated 1500 people there. Busy with Williams taking over stores. Told Wolf he could have loan of a few porters to Usukuma. Williams keen not to destroy clan system here.

3rd April.—Williams started 9 A.M., ordered destruction of huts in Fort. Letter from Owen; has selected site for half-way post at Kibibi in Mohammedan country three and a half marches from here. Deserter from Owen with rifle and ten rounds of ammunition caught and put in guard-room.

4th April.—Parade of Zanzibaris and Soudanese troops at 9 A.M. Zanzibaris looked clean and did well, including the use-

SOUDANESE TROOPS AT KAMPALA—BAYONET DRILL.

less bayonet exercise. Soudanese have some fine men, but know very little drill as yet; in every sort of uniform. Hard rain in middle of parade. Deserter from Owen given twenty-five lashes with rope's end and one month in prison.

5th April.—French Bishop Monseigneur Hirth arrived, having walked all night from Mtebe, where he landed at 10 P.M. He seems a clever man, and a man of the world. (He is) bitter against the Fort and officers, also against the king and Protestants, but willing to be conciliatory. He eventually said he would be satisfied with Singo, Kaima, and Sesse, and the Katikiro, and Magisi. He also demanded that king's sister should be Catholic.

6th April.—Bishop Tucker came and said Protestants were signing a paper, undertaking not to give back runaway slaves from Mohammedans, and not to claim themselves. Bishop thought this an opening for stopping all slavery.

Went to Mwanga, 3 P.M. He asked anxiously about giving up runaway slaves. I advised getting Protestant and Catholic chiefs to agree about it, and to forbid all sale of slaves in country. He asked that Usoga cases might be tried here. I said Yes, for cases now actually here, but in future Usoga cases were to go to Resident there, except land and small cases, which are better judged by his baraza.

Went Rubaga and saw Mgr. Hirth. He agrees to meet Tucker at my house to discuss division of territory. Tucker also agrees; appointed meeting at 9.30 to-morrow.

The result of this meeting on the following day was an arrangement for the division of territory between the two religious denominations and the distribution of offices, which has been already recorded in the official papers. A letter from Sir Gerald, dated 7th April, refers to this interview.

Sir Gerald Portal to Lady Charlotte Portal

Received 28th June 1893.

KAMPALA, 7th *April* 1893.

MY DEAR MOTHER—I am, in fact we all are, growing rather tired of being without any mails or news from civilisation. The latest that any of us have seen was a paper of 24th December, which caught us up at Kikuyu at the beginning of February. It is made more trying by being a case of "hope deferred," as a mail through German territory to the south end of the Lake is long overdue, and we hear that the Arabs and others near Taboss have been in insurrection against the Germans, and have cut up one or two caravans from the coast which probably had mails. To make matters worse, a steel boat, belonging to the

East Africa Company, which I propose to buy for the Government, was sent to the south end two months ago, and should have been back here before my arrival. If she has come to grief and got wrecked it will be rather serious for us, as she is bringing cloth and stores, and the means of paying all our men for the next six months, and it takes a long time to get fresh

BABY ELEPHANT, BROUGHT INTO THE FORT AT KAMPALA, BEING FED ON MILK.[1]

stores—in fact, we cannot expect any before September. Everything is paid for here in cloth, including the pay and money for rations for all the men, so you may imagine that with a staff of 13 Europeans, about 600 soldiers, and 250 porters, the rolls of cloth disappear somewhat rapidly. It is this system which makes Uganda such an expensive place to hold, as to the original cost of the cotton cloth you must add the wages and cost of maintenance of the porters who carried it—the large

[1] It died in a few days.

proportion damaged by weather, by being dropped in rivers or muddy swamps—that lost by deserting and stealing porters on the road, the cost of the return journey of the porters who brought it up [for one cannot rely upon sufficient ivory to load up all the number], the risk of keeping it, the danger of rot, mildew, above all of white ants, and other burrowing insects, and the length of time during which all the money is locked up.

All these and many other similar problems make it by no means an easy task to arrive at an accurate estimate as to the cost of administration of a country like this.

A WAR CANOE.
Capt. Macdonald. Dr. Moffat. Sir G. Portal. Lieut. Villiers.

We are all very busy here now, and a good deal scattered, and although I have taken on in temporary Government service three of the Company's late employés, I still want two or three more good officers. Owen and Raymond and Mr. Grant are well away to the west, scattered between Albert Edward and Albert Lakes and near Mt. Ruwenzori : Arthur has gone to Usoga with 100 men, Berkeley is to go to Usoga in two days, another of the Company's late men has been sent to establish a station on the road to Buddu, half-way between the capital and the western forts, to keep open communication with Raymond and Co., and as soon as I can get clear of the most pressing questions, I am off to Buddu myself; I shall go there by canoe across the Lake, and then try and get by land to the nearest of the western forts, meet Raymond there, and bring him back with me, and also, probably, about 1000 more wild Soudanese—men, women, and children. After that, if I have time, I want to run down north for a week or ten days to have a look at the country, then back here, wind up outstanding questions, try to establish general administration in working order, and then off for home. Barring accidents, I calculate on getting away the last week in May, and, unless there is any reason for going personally through Usoga to settle more difficulties there, I shall probably try to get by canoes to the north-west corner of the Lake. I calculate on reaching the coast in seventy days, or at most seventy-five from the day of leaving Kampala, so that we ought to be at Zanzibar by the middle of August. I fear we can't return quicker than we came up, as, although there will be fewer and lighter loads, it is raining everywhere now, and will continue to do so till the middle or end of June, so that we shall find the small streams, which we walked through on the road up, swollen into rushing rivers, sometimes requiring two or three days' halt to make bridges; and dry ravines across which we stepped dry-shod will be quaking swamps, while all the red clay hill-sides will be slippery, and bring pain and grief to loaded porters.

I have had a very busy time here, every day from sunrise till night, and all the others who are still here are also kept pretty hard at work, but we are getting forward.

Yesterday I managed to get the Catholic and Protestant Bishops to meet in my room, to see if we could not come to an amicable settlement of these miserable religious quarrels. They and I were at it hammer and tongs from 9.30 till past 1. The atmosphere was rather electric once or twice. Bishop Tucker gave way to a certain extent, but would not go far enough for Monseigneur. At last they both agreed to leave me to decide the whole matter. I then warned them that if I did so, I should admit no further question, and should insist, by force if necessary, on my decision being at once carried out. To this they agreed, and I dictated the partition of territory and offices which appeared to me just, and then got them both to sign an undertaking that they not only accepted it, but would use their utmost influence and endeavours to get it carried peaceably into execution. After a lot more trouble I also got them to enter into an agreement as to future extension of mission work, so that the Catholic and Protestant missionaries may no longer continue to follow each other about, and plant new missions in the same districts, with the inevitable result of more war and scandal.

All's well that ends well, but I don't wish ever again to have a three and a half hours' skirmish with two angry bishops—one not understanding English, and the other knowing no French. The whole history of Uganda for the last ten years is more worthy the Middle Ages, or the days of the Edict of Nantes, than the end of the nineteenth century; but I don't think either side is more to blame than the other.

I had not intended to begin this third sheet of paper, as we are rather alarmingly short of that commodity, and it is disappearing rapidly in answering innumerable notes from bishops and missionaries, and from my own officers away in different parts of the country. I don't think there will be another mail from here till we go ourselves six or seven weeks hence, so don't expect to hear any more of me till you see the announcement in the papers that we have reached the coast.

As I said before, I hope to get Raymond back at headquarters before I start, if he can only get his job through pretty quickly. I propose that he should be chiefly here, and travelling periodically into the provinces.

I have not yet decided in the least what course to recommend with regard to the future of Uganda, nor probably, by the way, would I say what it was if I had.

All the Waganda are liars to the last man. They really lie—especially to a European—in preference to speaking the truth; and they regard successful lying as a fine art. A man who told the truth to a European unnecessarily, in preference to a plausible lie, founded on distorted facts, would be regarded as a mere fool, and would be distrusted by the others. As you may imagine, this does not make it easier to deal with the numerous complaints and quarrels which are always cropping up.

The climate here is distinctly good—the sun a little hot, but not too much so—and in the morning, evening, and at night it is quite cool, and one could wear European summer clothes with comfort,—in fact, we do so, except for the starchy shirts and collars, and at night I always have one blanket, and would have two if I had got them, over me, but a coat or mackintosh serves the purpose.

The country is nothing but a collection of steep hills with swamps between them, but looks green and pleasant, and the endless banana plantations give it a rich appearance. The only drawbacks are that the water is bad, and looks and smells very "swampy," and that the whole district is alive with creeping, crawling, and buzzing and flying insects of every sort and description, both by day and night—a paradise for a collector; and now, good-bye; love to all.

My prophecy is that this should reach Laverstoke about the 20th of July. I sent a letter to you on the 24th of March by the German route, but it is possible that some black chief may be reading it, as they are rather given to stopping mails on that road.—Yours affectionately, G. H. PORTAL.

8th April.—A paper given me signed by forty Protestant chiefs, saying they had determined to follow "coast custom" and free all slaves. This seems suspicious, also rather too radical, as throwing thousands of people free at once. It would make it impossible at first to get any work done by any one, and it is perhaps only a pretext to avoid work on roads, etc., by pleading as excuse no slaves. Mgr. Hirth is against the measure.

9th April, Sunday.—Very busy with mail.

11th April.—Berkeley left 9 A.M. for Usoga, with instructions to report, collect taxes, see chiefs, encourage trade, and get them to bring grievances to Englishman for settlement. Gedge accompanied him, going shooting elephants Chagwe.

10 A.M.—Saw all Protestant chiefs; explained arrangement with Catholics clearly; told them chiefs would be held responsible for peaceful execution. They raised many difficulties and objections, but these overruled.

3 P.M.—Went with Macdonald to Mwanga. Met all Usoga chiefs; told them Mtanda put on throne pending good behaviour; shambas to be given back to his brother Kaisema; explained

about taxes. They expressed themselves pleased. Mwanga made them good speech.

12th April.—Began writing book. Walked with Rhodes and Villiers to Mtesa's tomb; fine large house and well kept, but dark and not much to see. Broad stripe of red cloth all along roof. Curious wooden cannon lying there.

13th April.—Saw all Catholic chiefs; told them I should hold chiefs responsible that all goes quietly; all seem quiet and grateful.

TOMB OF MTESA, LATE KING OF UGANDA.

The entries during the next few days all deal with the difficulty experienced in bringing about a final settlement between the two religious denominations, whose representatives continue to wrangle over the distribution of offices, until at length, on the 19th, the draft agreement is signed by the Protestant chiefs, and by the Catholics on the 20th. In the meantime this note occurs on the 17th:—

Namasole (king's mother) came to visit me, riding on the shoulders of a strong man. She was dressed in a good leopard-skin tied on the right shoulder, and a good mbugu; nice intelligent old lady, with a cheerful, pleasant face; had at least one very good-looking girl with her; greatly admired my room; gave her a Cashmere shawl and some good silks.

22nd April.—Mwanga said he would come at 9 (to sign the agreement), but did not; said he would come at 3; waited till 3.30, then sent and told him to come at once. He came with Katikiro and several other Protestants; signed paper; other chiefs objected to Rubuga clause, but I suppressed them. Princes to be sent for immediately.[1]

Special messenger to Owen telling him to send Raymond back at once.

23rd April, Sunday.—Very wet. Rhodes sends note reporting favourably of Ntebe.

THE QUEEN-MOTHER (NAMASOLE).

24th April.—Offered Mgr. Hirth three canoes of Kakunguru to go to S. of lake and fetch princes. He refused, on ground that he would not accept any canoes of Protestants, nor allow them to have anything to do with princes; asked me to send Nubians[2] to fetch boys. I refused to send Nubians, saying they could not be trusted so far without officers, and that I would only take responsibility for boys on their arrival here.

25th April.—Tucker writes again about Rubuga and boys, saying Protestants object to clause signed by king. Answer that I cannot listen to chiefs against king, that I only recognise latter. Later T. writes chiefs accept conditions signed by king.

26th April.—Foaker and Reddie returned with crowd of Soudanese, but no list or papers.

---

[1] Rubuga, the king's sister, with a high official position. One of the chief points at issue had been whether or not this lady should be, as she finally was, conceded to the Catholic party. The princes had been detained with the Catholics since the war. See 5th April.

[2] The term Nubian is here used, as it frequently is, somewhat inaccurately for the Soudanese.

Macdonald went with Protestant, Catholic, and Mohammedan chiefs to apportion shambas[1] on Rubaga Hill. Great excitement among Protestants in consequence of decision. I said I would stick to Macdonald's judgment unless the natives could come to an agreement among themselves. Gave severe reprimand to Katikiro, who was impertinent to Macdonald.

27th April.—More excitement about shambas. Protestants object to giving up shambas on king's hill. Catholics refuse any others. Eventually Catholics say they will accept exchange and get bigger ones offered by king. Mohammedans ask for shambas on road to their provinces.

Gedge returned from Chagwe; got nine elephants; asked leave to accompany us to coast.

28th April.—Macdonald started for delimitation of road to Kaima. Called roll of Nubian soldiers from Toru, 85 in all. Told all soldiers and followers to go to Ntebe; cripples and old men to be settled in little shambas on opposite hill.

Namasole, the queen-mother, came to see me. Was *more* than friendly. Gave her a sheet of paper and red and blue pencil. She wanted to kiss me on going. Frank photographed her in gilt chair.

29th April.—Left Kampala 10.30 with Rhodes. Marched to Kisubi, fifteen miles: arrived there 4: good road all the way. Met Père Guillemain at Kisubi: very tired, but walked with him for two hours round shambas of Bugananowa and Kiballe, which French Mission want for a post and to try agricultural experiments. Kakuguni, to whom they belong, came there later: arranged with him for cession of Kiballe. Had very bad night: could not sleep: a terrible lot of mosquitoes.

30th April, Sunday.—Left Kisubi 6.30, and arrived Ntebe Hills 9.30; lovely place commanding peninsula: fine fresh air: walked to flat rocks running into sea: grand place for summer house. 3.30.—Walked all over high hills with Frank: grand site for fort, but far from water. Small-pox in village close by.

1st May.—Very bad night, millions of mosquitoes and heavy rain. Walked 9 A.M. with F. R. all over peninsula, and finally

---

[1] Shamba is the Swahili name for a garden or plantation, and hence for property in the country as distinguished from town-property.

settled on big hill. Moved camp up there and marked out road through future Soudanese village: hard work in long grass.

Foaker and Reddie with about 500 Soudanese arrived 3 P.M. Fine cool air up here and magnificent view.

2nd May.—Worked all morning allotting ground to Soudanese for their compounds: eleven yards by fifteen, and wide streets.

DR. MOFFAT AND DEAD HIPPOPOTAMUS, NEAR PORT ALICE.

Men seemed pleased. Also got Waganda to work on roads, and Swahili porters to clear road near hill: others to bring building wood. At 4 went to shoot hippos in Port Alice:[1] had four shots, all hits. Mgr. Hirth arrived and called, but I out.

3rd May.—Went 6 A.M. to see Mgr. Hirth: caught him just starting. On return found Bishop Tucker had arrived 8 P.M. Boys reported my two hippos dead: sent people: gave one to

[1] This name was given by Sir Gerald Portal to the new settlements, or, more strictly speaking, to the port at the foot of the Ntebe Hills.

Nubians, one to Swahilis. No quarrelling. Went on building house, also mess-house. Set Nubians to work on roads. Macdonald expected, but did not arrive.

4th May.—Bad night and rain. Macdonald arrived 8 A.M. with 120 Soudanese men and women. Cleared at 2 P.M. Went to sail steel Mission boat, but no wind. Letter from Berkeley respecting Usoga : satisfactory.

5th May.—Gedge arrived Ntebe, and Bishop Tucker left. Building tent-houses; both broke in ridge pole; soft wet wood : sent for wild-date poles.

6th May.—Wrote some of Report. Tent-house finally built, but, as very wet day, ground inside is soaked and unfit to inhabit. Letter from Raymond saying he leaves at once.

7th May, Sunday.—Letter from Berkeley reports Soudanese soldiers sent with letters of 4th to Unyoro were stopped by Kaima, maltreated, robbed of guns, and sent back. Sounds very serious, as they say Kaima was present in person. Instructed B. to make preliminary inquiry : I would come in to-morrow and hear case at 4 P.M. If Soudanese story true, must make an example of Kaima, and severely warn king and Katikiro.

8th May.—Left Ntebe 7.15 A.M. with three porters and the boys : walked right through to Kampala without a halt : arrived 1.10 P.M. : twenty-one miles in 5.50 hours. Spent afternoon examining Kaima's case, and taking depositions of Kaima and men.

9th May.—Gave judgment in Kaima's case : convicted him of stopping Queen's soldiers in execution of duty and of taking the Queen's guns. He condemned to go as prisoner to Kikuyu, and his man Mtobasa got twenty-five lashes in presence of Soudanese company. Kaima had to give back guns to soldiers. Drafted treaty with Mwanga, who sent to say he was coming, but did not.

10th May.—6.55. Got note from Mwanga, saying he would come at 8. Answered I was off to Ntebe. Started with Berkeley at 7 A.M. ; rained nearly all the way ; roads wet and bad : was dropped by old Sindano carrying me across river. Arrived Port Alice 2.30. Found Frank had had road cut to join caravan, also village streets finished. No mail heard of here.

11th May.—Worked all morning. Sailed Mission boat for two hours in afternoon in good breeze, but she is very slow,

FORT ALICE.

heavy, and undersailed. Macdonald returned with forty loads of cloth, and with steel boat in fair condition: reports Dzinga, an island, with three feet of water all round, Bunjako only two or three feet of swamp.

12th May.—Continued Report on existing situation.

13th May.—Writing Report all morning. Set Fundis[1] to work making new mast for steel boat. Berkeley left for Kampala. Heard case of complaint by five Waganda against five Swahili porters for entering shamba to assault woman—drawing knives: one Swahili was cut on shoulder by his friend. Sentenced two Swahilis to twelve lashes each, promising much more next time.

14th May, Sunday.—Left Ntebe 6.45, and arrived Kampala 1 P.M.: met pony on way and rode in; did not wait for Macdonald: very wet. Mwanga came to plead for Kaima to be let off with a fine: told him I consider; at last sent to say he might pay twenty frasilas[2] ivory. Went through proposed agreement with Mwanga, who said he would accept. Ordered 1st Company of Soudanese to prepare at once to go to Ntebe.

15th May.—Saw king; went through proposed agreement with him; he says he agrees to all.

Mail came in; Reuter's telegrams to 16th March; sent by Cecil Rhodes; Sultan of Zanzibar dead.

Explained situation and instructions to Macdonald (who was to be left in charge).

Letter from Raymond received by Berkeley; says he is ill and in great pain from head: probably sunstroke or malaria: due at Kibibi on 16th: Villiers offered to go to meet him.

16th May.—Villiers started 7 A.M. to meet Raymond; took pony and medical comforts.

Started 8 A.M.; arrived Port Alice 4 P.M.; dead beat and bad head; took quinine and bromide to give sleep.

17th May.—Sorting papers and writing Report all day: not very well.

18th May.—Finished Report and instructions to Macdonald 4 P.M. Feeling seedy and anxious about Raymond.

---

[1] Fundi is the general name throughout Eastern Africa for a skilled workman, from an elephant trapper to a locksmith.

[2] The frasila is thirty-five pounds weight.

CHAPTER II

Captain Portal's illness—He returns to Kampala; is joined by his brother—His death and funeral—Sir Gerald Portal's expedition starts from Kampala for Kikuyu.

WE now approach a very sad period in the narrative. I should not wish to dwell unduly on the painful details of a sorrow which cast its gloom on all the latter half of Sir Gerald's eventful journey, and yet there has seemed to me to be so fine a pathos in the simple record he has given of his brother's death that no word of it should be omitted in justice to them both. Nor is that all. When brave men die at the far outposts of Empire, doing the world's work at their country's call, perhaps amid the throb and hurry of life at home for a passing minute's space the shadow of a brief regret falls across the daily path when first the news comes in. But as quickly it is lifted; for all, except the very near and dear, the acuteness of perception is dulled by intervening distance, and it almost needs immediate contact to touch the imagination deeply. To those, however, who knew and loved the manly, generous nature that once was Raymond Portal, there will, I think, be a special interest in these last scenes of the life of one who never made an enemy, who inspired the warmest friendships, and whose compelling charm was recognised by all who chanced to come across him. There will be occasion to return to Raymond Portal later. In the meantime, such glimpses as have been already afforded of the hardships and difficulties of daily travel in the heart of the Dark Continent will serve to impress on those, who try to realise the conditions, some sense of that indomitable pluck which nerved him to carry out, with the heavy hand of sickness upon him, and the shadow of death before his eyes, alone, " without witness or honour," his last march back to die among his comrades in the mud house at Kampala.

It will be remembered that he had accompanied Major Owen into the Toru country, whence he was to march back with such Soudanese soldiers as it might be found possible to enlist, and the Commissioner had written to accelerate his return for reasons which are explained by the following extract from one of his letters home : —

> "I was anxious to get him to command the new station of Port Alice, where I have established the headquarters in a lovely, healthy spot, on a high hill overlooking the Lake. This would have given Raymond just the chance of independent and responsible work which he has been longing for, and which he would have done so well."

It was towards the last days of April that Captain Portal became aware of the symptoms of the fever, complicated perhaps with sunstroke, which had seized him in the Toru country. He was never very prudent or careful of himself, and a perusal of his Diary during the month of April will make it clear that the life he was leading in the Toru swamps could hardly fail to tell upon one whose constitution had already been severely tried with fevers on the West Coast and in the West Indies. At first he grew better and worse at intervals, but continuing to march in spite of pain and weakness, with scarcely any comforts or assistance, he wore out his little remaining strength, and was found at length by Lieutenant Villiers, who went out from Kampala to meet him, now far too weak to walk at all, and being carried by his porters, whose affection and fidelity he seems to have had a strange power of winning. Lieutenant Villiers had brought medical stores, and nourishing food and champagne, and at first it seemed as if these might not have come too late. Dr. Moffat was himself unable to put foot to the ground, but Dr. Baxter, of the English Mission, who had just returned tired out from a journey himself, no sooner heard of Captain Portal's illness than he set out immediately to meet him and bring him into Kampala. Captain Portal's Diary is published as a supplement to this book, and what more there is to be told will best be told there. These few words will perhaps suffice to explain the sequence of Sir Gerald's notes.

On the 20th of May the Commissioner, who was still at Port Alice, received the news that Captain Portal had been brought into camp, better, but very ill. He was at the time very far from well himself, but he started the following morning for Kampala at 9.30 A.M., being delayed till this late hour by terrific thunderstorms. The narrative of the Diary continues:—

21st May, Sunday.—Quite beat in five miles: had to drag along supported by whisky at intervals rest of way. Macdonald came to meet us on Rubaga Hill with some champagne! Found Raymond bad, very weak; but temperature down to 101°: had been 104½°; quite deaf; looking very poor, but knew me. Dr. Baxter more than kind, spends all his time here. Self very seedy; went to bed.

22nd May.—R. P. 102° and 103° all day. Baxter not very pleased. Self seedy, and fever. Mwanga came: went through treaty with him; he agrees to all.

23rd May.—R. P. temp. 101° in morning, then 100°, but up to 102° in evening. I sat with him all day, feeling very seedy. My own temp. 101° at bedtime. Took some Warburg. Sent for Moffat to come in.

24th May.—R. P. 101·6°-102°, 100°, and up again to 101·4°. Wandering a little in afternoon; took nourishment (Brand and milk and water). Pulse 86, and fairly good. Sat with him nearly all day. Self feeling better, but still seedy. Waganda Wa-Islam impertinent: claim province of Mugema, and say they won't work for king. Selim Bey wrote to me on subject.

25th May.—R. P. temp. 101° at 6 A.M. and 101·4° but steady; about 100·8° all day till 9 P.M., up to 101°; pulse weaker and wandering a good deal. Pulse rose to 100; Moffat arrived and consulted with Baxter: gave some champagne. Saw Selim Bey; pointed out the Wa-Islam not his business, he quite agreed.

26th May.—R. P. dreadfully weak and wandering all day, talking in Swahili a great deal; got no sleep all night, and very restless all day: temperature a shade better, varied only from 101·2° to 100·6°, till at 8.30 P.M. it went down to 99·8°; he had some sensible moments. Pulse rose to 120; he spoke to me sensibly at 4 P.M. Wrote officially to Owen, explaining situation as clearly as possible, got stores and Maxim gun ready to send out to him. Self bad head all day.

27th May.—Raymond's temperature not bad—about 100° to 100·6°; but pulse weaker, has risen to 130; breathing very laboured and rapid; had been given bromide, but without effect; has had no sleep for over two days now. Berkeley, Villiers, Rhodes, and Moffat had relieved each other through night; all report that he was restless, with quickened breathing and wandering. Rhodes and Moffat with him all morning. I had to work.

CAPTAIN RAYMOND PORTAL'S GRAVE.

At 1.30 P.M. I relieved Rhodes and thought R. looked worse. Temperature at 1 rose to 102°, and at 2 to 103°; gave him egg beaten in milk; he very quiet and motionless; at 4 temp. had risen to 104° and soon after to 105°; pulse and heart weaker. Moffat sponged him all over with cold water; temperature fell to 104·2°; weakness and difficulty of breathing increased. Gave hypodermic injection of carbonate of ammonia twice, but no effect perceptible. Dr. Baxter came. We prayed. All over about 5.30, quite quietly—motionless. Frank undertook to see to everything. He is more than kind and tactful.

28th May, Sunday.—Funeral was at 7.30 A.M. Frank had arranged everything: officers in full dress, four on each side; firing party of Soudanese battalion under Arthur. Went to English church at Namirembe; Bishop Tucker officiated; all done quietly and well. Kind letter from Bishop Tucker. Decided to start Tuesday morning.

EXTRACT FROM A LETTER FROM SIR GERALD PORTAL TO LADY ALICE PORTAL

KAMPALA, *28th May* 1893.

. . . . As you know, Raymond was sent out with Roddy Owen to the Toru country in the west. He was to have been sent back from there with a lot of Soudanese soldiers whom Owen was commissioned to enlist and send in to Kampala. (It is quite twelve to fourteen days' journey to where they were.)

On the 16th of May I happened to have come up here for a day from Port Alice—(the new headquarters 22 miles off)—and we received a note from Raymond saying he had started two days before, but was feeling very ill indeed, and feared that he might knock up on the way. As bad luck would have it, our doctor, Moffat, was quite a cripple from these infernal "jiggers," and could not put a foot to the ground, so he could not go; but I at once sent Villiers to meet R., with a pony and with every sort of comfort and medicine we could think of and scrape together. Villiers himself, poor man, was suffering from bad ulcers on the feet, also from "jiggers," but most pluckily limped off. Three days later there came a note from Villiers, saying that he had met Raymond with all his party, but that R.'s condition alarmed him, and he asked for farther help and advice. Luckily the Mission doctor had just returned from a journey that night, and though himself with ulcerated feet, at once most kindly consented to limp off and meet R. and Villiers. Rhodes and I had in the meantime had to return to Port Alice, whither we wanted R. brought, as it is a thousand times healthier than this hole, Kampala. However, by Dr. Baxter's (Mission doctor) advice they brought R. here, as it was a little nearer, and when he arrived Berkeley sent word to me (who was expecting him at Port Alice) to say that he was here, with a good deal of fever, but nothing alarming, though a great deal knocked up by the journey, and that I need not come in: this was on the 20th. However, Rhodes and I determined to come to Kampala, and started at daybreak on the 21st. I was a good deal out of sorts, and had had fever and headaches myself for nearly a week previously, so that 22-mile walk over hills and swamps that day nearly knocked me up altogether, but Frankie helped me along and kept on giving me whisky, and so we arrived somehow late that night. I found Raymond comfortably in bed looking much pulled down, but perfectly conscious, temperature falling from 103° to 102°, and in no pain. He knew me, and we spoke a little, but he was very drowsy, and I was half off my head myself, so Dr. Baxter turned me out and sent me to bed. The doctor was not anxious then at all.

Next day, 22nd, R. continued about the same, varying from 102° to 103°; he was quite sensible, and talked occasionally to me. I sat with him all day, except for a few hours when I had to see King Mwanga and some chiefs on business.

On the 23rd R.'s temperature went down to 101°, and then to 100°, and every one was beginning to think it was all right, but it rose again to 102° in the evening. I was with him all day, and he talked quite sensibly, and even cheerfully, though of course that was discouraged as much as possible. At night they would not let me stay, as I had been feeling very seedy, and had been over 100° and 101° myself all these days, and had bad heads every day.

On the 24th R. remained about the same, fever a little lower, but he was evidently a little weaker, though he took all the nourishment given him and his pulse was fairly good. He began to wander rather in the afternoon.

On the 25th still the same, though another very slight fall in his temperature; his weakness was great, and he talked a good deal in a delirious way, but he was often quite lucid and quiet, and knew me, and, in fact, if he was spoken to he always came to himself. Dr. Moffat arrived on this day; we had managed to borrow a pony to send for him. He was rather alarmed by R.'s general weakness, and they began to give champagne and stimulants.

The 26th, the weakness was very alarming, and both heart

and pulse were very feeble and rapid. R. was wandering all day, talking chiefly in Swahili, but in the evening about 4.30 he was conscious for a moment and knew me, and spoke to me quite quietly; after that he soon became very restless again. We all had great hopes still, as the fever was again less, and in the evening at 8 o'clock the temperature dropped for the first time to below 100°.

On the 27th the temperature was not at all bad, about 100 and 100½° till mid-day, but his heart and pulse were painfully feeble, and his breathing was very rapid and distressed; he was quite unconscious ever since he had spoken to me the day before. At 2 o'clock the thermometer showed his temperature had suddenly run up to 102°; we gave him some brandy and eggs beaten up in milk, which he swallowed. Then Moffat went to lie down and get some rest, and left me with R. alone again. R. was quite quiet, but his weakness was evidently growing rapidly. When I took the temperature again it had risen to 103°, so I called Moffat, who was evidently seriously alarmed. It soon after, at 4 o'clock, rose to 104°, and in less than half an hour to 105°; breathing very rapid and difficult. We then sponged him all over with cold water, which sometimes in desperate cases has a magical effect, but now it only brought it down a quarter of a degree. We gave champagne, which had no effect. Moffat tried strong injections subcutaneously, but it was evidently near the end. At 5.30 it was all over, quite quietly, and without a sign, except that the rapid, laboured breathing suddenly ceased. I am afraid I broke down altogether then; but the doctor went away and left me alone. Some time after Frankie came in and made me come away. He was so gentle and full of tact, and very much upset himself. He saw to all arrangements and everything. I cannot say how he helped. I felt I could not do anything. The funeral was this morning at the Protestant church. Bishop Tucker officiated. It was a military one, with a company of the Soudanese battalion. It has all been so miserable, I can hardly realise it all yet. It does seem so hard that it should be Raymond, the strongest and most active of all, who only wanted an opportunity to show what he really was, and who up here among a picked lot of officers had already proved himself far and away the best of them all. He was a different man here from in England, and was working hard and cheerfully all day. And it was my responsibility that brought him up here at all; that may be a selfish feeling, but it seems to make it all weigh much heavier.[1]

I am going to give this to Bishop Tucker, who starts to cross the Lake this week, and is going down by the German route. He may get down before our runners from Kikuyu.

Frank, Berkeley, Villiers, and I leave this place at daybreak the day after to-morrow, and it will be something to be on the road again instead of staying still.

There is another letter written, many weeks later during the journey home, to Lady Charlotte Portal, in which Sir Gerald, on the eve, as he believed, of returning to Uganda, tells over again the sad story which he had deferred writing home until the news had been broken. Here is a characteristic extract:—

The Mission doctor and I had prayed for him by his bedside at about 4 that afternoon. I fear I broke down completely then, and they put me to bed. I was very weak from the daily fever myself. He was buried at the Protestant church. The Bishop read the service, and volleys were fired by the escort of troops. I am sending a pencil sketch of the grave most kindly made for me by the Bishop.

The Bishop wrote a most kind letter, pointing out that a death like this, in doing his duty and trying to bring light to this unhappy country, was far nobler than one on the field of battle.

Two days afterwards I left Uganda. Going up there again the evening before, I met the Bishop, and we knelt by the grave while he prayed for help and comfort to you and all at home.

That is all I have to say. I can't tell you how dreadful it has been to me up here,—feeling that he came here at my

---

[1] A letter from Sir Gerald Portal to the editor of the same date, which contains matter entirely similar to the above extract, assigns malarial fever as the cause of Captain Portal's death.

instance and my responsibility. He was by far the best of all here, and would have really made his mark and got deserved distinction.

. . . . . .

The only thing I am glad of is that Raymond and I were never so much together in our lives, nor so close together in every way, as during these last four months.

29th May.—Busy day working and finishing up everything. Mwanga came in and signed treaty at 4 P.M. Had rather a stormy interview with Mohammedans in Mwanga's presence about their attitude; told them clearly they had no right to further territory, and must work for king; warned chiefs they would be held responsible. Went to say good-bye to Bishop Tucker, and arranged with him about his sending two telegrams for me if he gets to coast before us.

30th May.—Started from Kampala 8.15, with about 130 porters, 30 soldiers, and nearly 30 women, most of whom are to be left at Wakoli's.

March of 7½ miles; self very tired and utterly beat.

Berkeley left behind at Kampala to catch us at Bandu.

31st May.—Berkeley arrived 5.45 P.M., having marched from Kampala, 23 miles, in 7 hours.

CHAPTER III

The return journey—Difficulties of the march during the rainy season—Trouble in Uganda—Illness of Colonel Rhodes—Selim Bey is handed over to the Commissioner—Arrival at Kikuyu—Death of Selim Bey.

ON leaving Uganda it was Sir Gerald Portal's intention to follow the track by which he had come as far as Kikuyu, and thence to send off with all speed to the coast, by the established route, such of his despatches as were already completed. From Kikuyu he would then himself, accompanied by Colonel Rhodes, march in a northerly and somewhat westerly direction, passing through hitherto unexplored country, with the object of striking the upper waters of the river Tana, and of thus ascertaining whether its course, which was known to be navigable with difficulty up to a certain point, offered any prospect of providing an alternative road to Uganda. With a view to facilitating their movements I had, in accordance with Sir Gerald's wishes, taken steps to despatch up stream to a place called Hameye, in the neighbourhood of which they expected to strike the river, a number of native canoes sufficient to convey the whole party from there to the coast by water. Circumstances, however, delayed their journey, as will be seen farther on, and the departure of the canoes after many weeks of waiting added greatly to their difficulties. It is this journey at first through new country, and subsequently down the Tana, as it is described in the Diary and in letters, which it is most especially valuable to place permanently on record. The intervening notes, faithfully recorded day by day, of the journey between Kampala and Kikuyu, cover precisely the same ground as the latter chapters of the written narrative, and the road presents no new features beyond the increased difficulty of travelling, caused by the prevalence of the "great rains," which had now swollen streams into torrents, and converted muddy hollows into breast-high marshes. I therefore propose to extract from the Diary, during this stage, only such entries as appear to have any special interest, either as illustrating the character of the writer, or as bearing upon the nature of the country and its inhabitants:—

3rd June.—Two Zanzibari soldiers with letter from Zschatsch, saying Waganda still raiding all over Usoga: sent them on with note to Macdonald, advising him to fine Mwanga half his tribute; and said that I would tell all Usoga chiefs to catch and tie up all Waganda, and send them to officer at Wakoli's, who would flog them.

4th June, Sunday.—Lubwa's ferry: halted in shamba 7.45. Lubwa came to meet us in red coat. Went on 8.45 over hill with lovely view all over Usoga, and back over whole Napoleon Gulf: on by beautiful shady paths, full of thousands of the most beautiful butterflies of every size and colour, to Lubwa's chief village; did not halt, but went on to his son's a mile farther, where better camping ground. Lubwa came: gave two bullocks, six goats, six fowls, lot of eggs, and also a good shield. Told him station to be moved to his place with a European: he delighted. Also told him to settle all small cases among his people. He promised to build us ten canoes. Terrific storm.

8th June.—Mtanda's. Received letters from Macdonald saying Owen in difficulty. Five Swahilis from Salt Lake, sent as messengers to Manyema, taken prisoners by them. Kabarega has cut him off from forts one and two. Shukri killed; his position threatened. Wrote fully to Macdonald on subject, and said we would wait at Mumia's till 21st for news, and return if wanted.

9th June.—For three hours to-day marched through swarms of locusts, sometimes in thousands on path, sometimes thinner. They eat all grass and corn (wembe), but do not touch the bananas. Two hours into Kavirondo they suddenly ceased.

12th June.—Between Tunga's and Tindi's. Very wet long grass. At 6.45 reached strong running river, very deep, forty yards wide. In middle a rude weir of stakes. Waded up to middle to these, then great scramble across with ten men; found it impossible for men to carry loads across: so lined whole bridge (? weir) with men shoulder to shoulder hanging on to stakes, and passed loads from hand to hand, with relays of men at my end to wade waist deep rest of way to dry land. Much against expectation, nothing lost except one Snider rifle and some porters' goods. Pony swam across and got stuck, nearly drowned on landing side. Donkey refused, and got jammed against weir: pulled along by main force. Men swam across with cows, sheep, and goats. All over in three hours.

This passage is typical of an almost daily experience on the march through this region during the rainy season, and the crossing of these swollen rivers always involved a delay of some three hours. On the 14th the caravan arrived once more at Mumia's.

The following extract from a letter addressed by the Commissioner to Lady Alice Portal, dated the

14th of June, gives a consecutive narrative of recent events :—

My movements and plans are again unsettled by news which has followed us from Uganda. To begin at the beginning: I managed to finish up all work and business at Kampala, and left Captain Macdonald in charge, and gave him all necessary instructions, and started with Frankie and Villiers on the 30th; Berkeley staying back to finish some work for me, and caught us up two days later. I was still rather seedy with fever and heads, and the doctor hustled me off. Before going I went for the last time to see Raymond's grave at the Protestant church, and got Bishop Tucker, who sketches beautifully, to make a drawing of it for mother. Frank also took a photo. I was awfully knocked up by the first few days' marches, and, unluckily, a pony which Frank and I have bought between us for the exorbitant price of £130 was so weak and ill, and such a scarecrow, that he could not be ridden. I may at once say that both the pony and I are much better, and practically all right.

Well, after five days we crossed the Nile. We had divided into two parties, as I wanted to see a big chief, so Berkeley and I went one way with Arthur (who accompanied us for a week), and left Frank to conduct the main body of men with Villiers. We crossed at a place where it was three miles wide; it was a most beautiful spot, like the best of the Italian lakes, only prettier. Here all my men (fifty) and ourselves got into ten native canoes and raced across; the whole thing was like a perfect scene in a panorama.

In Usoga (at Wakoli's) I halted for a clear day for rest, and to arrange matters about those useless Zanzibar soldiers who were in garrison there, and of whom I am taking 120 with me, and leaving fifty behind. Frank and Villiers joined us there; the latter shot an elephant on the way.

Next day we marched ten miles, and then we were overtaken by runners from Macdonald at Kampala with rather bad news. He writes and asks advice. I have written fully my views, but added that if he found the situation getting really serious I would come back to Uganda, and that I would wait at Munia's (here) till the 21st for his letters and for the latest news, and would be guided by that. So after all I am not yet clear of that country. If I have to go back I shall go just with a few porters for my own things, and shall send on the caravan with the others to the coast. Frank says he would rather come back with me, and so does Villiers; but I don't know if that will be necessary. In any case I will send Berkeley and Foaker to the coast with all Zanzibar soldiers. I devoutly hope we *don't* have to go back. The journey here from Kampala, 170 miles, has been most disagreeable. The rains have scarcely ceased, and the whole country is a vast swamp. One day, for instance, I was for three hours up to my waist in water, with blazing sun overhead, getting the men and loads across a difficult and swollen river. Later in the same day we had to walk more than a mile in horrible-smelling black mud and water up to our middles, and then suddenly I in front found myself in up to my chin. I sounded with a long stick, and found that the next step the water would be about two feet above my head. And this has been the sort of thing every day, especially for the last week. When not actually in swamp and water and black mud, we are forcing our way through high grass usually two or three feet above our heads, which wets us to the skin in a minute. Again and again our pony has been all but drowned in the swamp, and as for the sheep and goats and bullocks which we are taking for food, it is a marvel how they have got across alive. We have been fortunate in not having rain during the morning while actually on the march, but we have usually had terrific storms with thunder and lightning towards evening, which makes the whole camp wet and miserable, and the tents awfully heavy to carry. I have been making very early starts, and usually have a big drum beaten to rouse the camp at 4.30, so that we get the tents packed, and can actually march with the first streak of dawn. I have told you very little about Uganda itself, and now I think of it, you know nothing of all that happened since I wrote to you about the 10th of April. Well, there is not much to say, and now I hate the whole place so since poor Raymond's death that I hate even writing about it. I had a very hard-worked time there. I moved the head-quarters from that close, unhealthy, and altogether hateful spot Kampala to a lovely place on the Lake; two great grassy hills,

NATIVES WITH HIPPOPOTAMUS (VICTORIA NYANZA).

like the Kingsclere Downs, rising almost straight out of the water; and a view over the Lake like over the sea dotted with a dozen islands. I put the European quarters on the highest hill, and the Soudanese troops on the lower one, and we marked out all the streets and divisions, giving each man a small compound, and established a market-place, and cut great wide roads in every direction. Before I left there was already quite a neat town of about 1000 inhabitants, ten times more healthy than at Kampala, and I left the officers there engaged in marking out allotments for each soldier to grow corn, potatoes, etc., which the Soudanese love doing. The name of the whole settlement is Port Alice. During the last fortnight I was busy with my final big Report, which you will see published sooner or later, I suppose. It is very curious on this journey, that after leaving Kampala all through Uganda and Usoga (ten days), one never sees a soul who is not dressed in cotton or bark-cloth from head to foot; then in one day across the frontier into Kavirondo, we find people nearly quite black, and not a shred of clothing of any kind or sort on man, woman, or child, except an occasional string of pink beads round the neck or waist, and perhaps a bracelet or anklet of brass or iron wire.

Whether I go forward or back, the rest here for a few days will do me good, and make me thoroughly fit. It is very hot to-day. I am writing in shirt-sleeves rolled up, and about 2,000,000 flies in my tent, but by night it is quite cool, and I sleep under two blankets. Frank Rhodes is our doctor on this journey, and is now in front of me applying ointments and dressings to all sorts of repulsive sores and wounds on a lot of porters. Villiers looks after the mess and the books, and the stores and firewood, candles, etc.

Instead of remaining at Mumia's, it was decided that they should press on to the Kabras Hills, there to await the expected mail from Captain Macdonald, as the higher country seemed likely to afford a more appropriate halting-place than the damp and running hollows at this season of the year. In the second

Kabras camp on the 19th the Commissioner suffered from a return of his old attack of fever, and his servant Hutchisson also began to sicken. On the 24th all the party were well enough to push on, and messengers from Captain Macdonald having brought in a report that the situation in Toru had improved, they were able to pitch their camp by the Guaso Masa, which was much swollen by the rains, and running with a very rapid stream.

Sunday, 25th June.—Guaso Masa Camp.—At midnight roused by messengers with another letter from Macdonald: he had received an improper message from Selim Bey; fears mutiny and trouble with Soudanese troops joining Waganda Mohammedans. Asks me to return.

Arranged self, Rhodes, and Villiers return with Hutchisson, and Berkeley to go on with Foaker and take despatches to England. Promised men returning double pay till next start homeward; no trouble with men; several asked to be allowed to come back.

Berkeley to catch French mail of August 3.

26th June.—Parted with Berkeley and Foaker, and then Rhodes, Villiers, and self turned back. Rhodes had bad head and rode.

This was the commencement of the very serious illness of Colonel Rhodes. With great difficulty, sometimes riding the pony, sometimes carried on a bed or in a hammock, he was brought back to Mumia's by the 30th. Thence Lieut. Villiers was despatched with all speed to Kampala, with orders to intercept and open all letters from Captain Macdonald and send them on, and further, to despatch stores to meet the Commissioner with as little delay as possible, since, owing to the necessity for the return journey, the difficulty in the food supply between Kikuyu and Uganda, and the division of the party, everything was beginning to run short. Meanwhile the Commissioner remained at Mumia's, awaiting news and nursing his sick comrade. In all this record of difficulties manfully faced and duties bravely undertaken, there are few things more touching as a simple testimony to the character of the chief of the Expedition than the entries which cover the next few pages. To reproduce them from the minute, but neat pencilling of the pocket-book would be difficult, and they would perhaps only be wearisome to the reader; the statement of the fact may therefore suffice. Throughout many weary days of doubt and anxiety, hour by hour of day and night, every variation in the temperature and pulse of his patient is noted with the scrupulous care of a hospital nurse, and opposite to each hour is set down the nourishment and the drugs administered. Interspersed with these tables are little notes of ominous import, telling how the scanty stores were ebbing fast, and all the port wine finished. Then the thermometer broke, and the tension of anxiety was only allayed when it was discovered that the interpreter Tembo had brought one with him. On the 4th of July news came in of the fighting with the Mohammedans in Uganda, which terminated in their defeat and the trial and exile of Selim Bey.

About the 7th of July Colonel Rhodes began to mend, but was far too weak from his long and exhausting attack to make a move in the direction of Uganda possible for at least another week. Messengers were therefore again despatched to headquarters to bring stores and carry letters to Captain Macdonald, pressing for his final decision as to whether the Commissioner's return was really necessary, in view of the news which appeared to indicate that the Mohammedan uprising had been suppressed. Meanwhile, when the period of real anxiety was over, the time of necessary waiting was chiefly spent in exploring the neighbouring region, in shooting and providing a hungry camp with meat, and in writing the earlier chapters of this book. On the 16th letters arrived from Captain Macdonald, stating that the situation no longer required Sir Gerald's presence, and that Selim Bey, together with certain Mohammedan Waganda chiefs, were being sent down as prisoners or exiles in charge of Mr. Gedge. But it was not until the 26th that he received from Mr. Gedge in person the Acting Commissioner's full report of the short-lived Mohammedan insurrection, now happily suppressed, and such satisfactory assurances as enabled him to continue without misgiving his journey to the coast.

One or two notes in the Diary during this period are interesting as illustrating the nature and resources of the surrounding country :—

12th July.—Munia's. Started 6 A.M. to go and shoot hippos down river to exchange for flour; 1½ hours from M. crossed Oelkom (? Welcome) river by curious swing-bridge of creepers about thirty yards wide. Crossing one by one took one hour for thirty men ; sent pony back, too risky for him swimming ; sixteen-mile walk crossing many swamps to village of Nyango ; 4 P.M. went after hippos ; shot six, but all carried right down stream, running too strong.

13th July.—Shot six more hippos, but only one caught going over falls. It is ridiculous to come and shoot here when the river is high : they are all carried down to the Lake, or at least many miles down stream. Many pitfalls for hippo along river bank ; I fell into one which was well covered over with twigs and grass : most of hippo meat taken by Kavirondo natives and porters.

14th July.—Two hippo recovered ; that makes three out of twelve ; at 11.30 a third dead hippo reported ; most of meat of three taken by natives and whole of one.

This district is very thickly populated ; innumerable villages and large ones ; fine crops ; eggs plentiful, and all provisions far more abundant than at Mumia's.

But the story of this anxious time is best told by Sir Gerald himself in a letter to Lady Alice Portal, dated from Mumia's on the 9th of July, and finished on the 5th of August :—

(*Extract.*)

As ink, like all other stores, is running very short, I must write in pencil, and tell you of all our misfortunes since I had to turn back from the Guaso Masa river.

As I told you by the letter sent on by Berkeley, I was roused at midnight on the 24th-25th June by a letter from Macdonald (who was left in charge in Uganda), saying that he anticipated Mohammedan troubles, and asking me to return. . . . Frank Rhodes, Villiers, and I turned back on the 26th, sending on Berkeley and Foaker with the mails. I was just recovering from a sharp attack of fever, and so was Hutchisson, so that forced marches were out of the question, and we came along steadily.

That very day Frank felt seedy, and had some fever—not much ; his temperature was 102 in the afternoon. Next day,

27th, we pushed on; he still had bad headache, and fever about the same. I gave him antipyrine (10 grs.), which did good; we could not stop, as there was no food in that district, and our men had hardly any flour left.

On the 28th we came on, Frank still with bad head, riding the pony. But after two hours' march he called to me, and said he felt faint and bad; he got off, and then fainted altogether; head burning hot, hands and arms and legs stone cold; was quite unconscious. Luckily I got hold of a little brandy, and revived him a little, but things looked very serious. Meanwhile, as we had been some way behind the caravan, going more slowly, I had sent on to Villiers, and told him to pitch camp at the nearest water, which unluckily was at least an hour and a half distant. After waiting three hours, and giving R. a little hot Liebig, we got a stretcher or litter and four men, and carried him on to camp. He was awfully bad, nearly unconscious, suffering from head, and feeling stone cold, though it was a blazing hot day. When at last we got him to camp and in bed I gave him carbonate of ammonia to restore him, and found his temperature run up to nearly 105°! He was bad all that afternoon; I did not know what might happen.

Next day we halted all day there, and Frank was decidedly better.

On the 30th we had to push on to get to a food country; so we arranged a covered hammock with a bed inside it, and carried him on for fifteen miles to this place. Though he was most carefully carried, there were a lot of swamps and bad places to cross, and it was impossible to avoid a little shaking. I gave him Liebig and Brand's essence on the way. On arrival here we put him to bed, but all that afternoon he had very high fever; temperature over 104°, at last going down. I treated him as well as I could, and then gave some champagne when his pulse got over 120, and he was evidently very weak and sinking.

Next day, the 1st July, I sent on Villiers to push to Kampala with all speed, while I dared not leave Rhodes. To cut the story short, ever since then till now it has been a terribly anxious time. Frank has again and again had these recurrent attacks of very high fever, each making him weaker, and my small stock of medical stores rapidly became exhausted. ... At last on the 7th his temperature became normal, and remained so for over fifty-six hours, and now I think he is quite clear of the fever, and I am ramming in the quinine as hard as I dare, but he is terribly weak and pulled down.

Meanwhile we are in a bad way for stores, which had been calculated just to take us to Kikuyu, where we have a fresh stock. Berkeley and Foaker took on half, Villiers had to take some more, and we are quite on our last legs.

The only thing which refreshed Frank when he was so bad was an occasional cup of tea. Providentially the tea, by great economy, just lasted till the fever left. Coffee was finished long ago. Salt will last us about two days more with great care. Sugar, none for a fortnight past. Port wine, which I want badly for Frank, none. We had only two bottles, and my fever and Hutchisson's used one. Whisky or spirits I have not tasted for a long time, nor any sauce of any kind to help down the daily dry goat. Rice none, white flour none, biscuits none, and oatmeal none! Candles and matches quite on their last legs, so that I shall have to go to bed at sunset. Tobacco running short!

Luckily I can get a little milk here and plenty of black flour, composed chiefly of sand mixed with crushed beans and millet, and there are plenty of goats. ... A little jam would be worth its weight in gold. Yesterday Hutchisson had a great triumph, and got a chicken (an oldish one), from which we made some soup for Frank.

Even the people here are uninteresting. They do not wear a single stitch of clothing, either men or women, and are very black and very dirty. Altogether our position is most distressful, and I don't think I have ever hated a place more.

Meanwhile in Uganda, Macdonald writes that the chief of our Soudanese soldiers tried to make a mutiny, and to get the men to join the Mohammedans against the Christians—but failed. The Mohammedans attacked the Christians and got thrashed. The Soudanese colonel is arrested and sent to an island, and all seems quiet. It was a local squabble. Now I expect him to write and ask me *not* to come to Uganda. The only cause for anxiety is Roddy Owen, who is on the other side of the Mohammedans, but as soon as we hear he is safe, I really see no reason for my going on to Uganda. I have written to Kampala for more stores, and hope to get them in about ten more days;—but, oh! this is a weary place, and I have had a terribly anxious time by myself nursing poor Frank.

10*th July*.—All yesterday afternoon and again this morning the whole air has been black with immense clouds of locusts. All the people are out round their fields of corn, lighting bonfires, beating drums, shouting, and waving rags and grass to prevent them settling. Millions and millions came through and over our camp, just out of reach of the hand. Thousands settled, and the men are catching them to eat. I tried some fried; tasteless, but not nasty. They are a great nuisance if they really settle here in their millions, as one can't move without squashing them, and they get into tents and everywhere.

11*th*, 12*th*, 13*th*, 14*th July*.—Nothing exciting. Frank getting stronger by slow, very slow degrees. On the 12th I decided I could leave him safely for a couple of days in Hutchisson's care, while I went about sixteen miles down the Nzoia river to shoot a few hippopotami, in order to exchange their meat for flour, as we are running short of beads and cloth for buying food. It was a long, swampy, tiring march, but at one place we came to a good-sized river about thirty yards wide, with a very deep and strong stream. There was a most picturesque bridge swung between two trees, over which we had to cross one by one. The bridge was simply made of creepers interlaced, with great holes and gaps through which one might easily tumble into the water. The whole thing was open work, like a very coarse net, and was swung at about this angle—

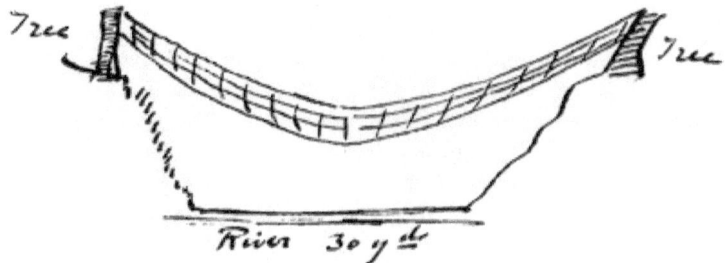

so that the climb up on the opposite side was rather a scramble. Inside the bridge was like this (*a*), and swung about with one's weight till often one found one's self like this (*b*). Oddly enough we dropped nothing  into the river, although on these occasions one usually loses one's most valuable box, or bed, or something of the sort. When I got to my destination, I found that there were

A CREEPER BRIDGE NEAR MUMIA'S.

lots of hippos, but the river was in flood, and running so strong that it was extremely difficult to prevent those shot from being carried over the falls, and right down out of this part of the country. I shot twelve, but we only could recover four. The others will all be found and eaten by the people lower down. Hundreds of natives came rushing along and tried to carry off all the meat; we nearly had a serious squabble and row. I had only thirty men altogether (porters), and ten had to remain in camp to look after it. However, after a lot of yelling and squalling, we managed to collect as much meat as the men could carry, and I returned on the 15th to find Rhodes getting on well, and also to find that we had received a present of a small tin of tea, and another small tin of salt, from a young German [1] in Usoga to whom I had written in our distress. This was real luxury.

On the 16th I got a letter from Macdonald, saying, as I expected, that all the trouble is over, and that my return is now unnecessary. We must, however, wait for our stores from Uganda, and for a final report from Macdonald, and then I trust we shall get fairly away from this hateful place and on the road home. If we get off on the 24th July from here, we should arrive at Mombasa about the 17th of September, and in that case would probably come home by the French mail of October 3, getting to London October 21, where at last I shall meet you again!

When Mr. Gedge at length reached Mumia's with Captain Macdonald's final report, he at the same time handed over to the Commissioner the mutinous Selim Bey in person, together with a miscellaneous crowd of Soudanese women and children who were to be taken down to the coast, as well as a brother of Mwanga's, Mbogo by name, whom it had become desirable to remove from Uganda, and who was also accompanied by a crowd of hangers-on. Great difficulties were experienced in providing all these additional mouths with food in a country where supplies ran so short, the more so as they had wantonly wasted the provisions distributed amongst them at the start to save themselves the trouble of carrying them. However, a start was made in the direction of the coast once more on the 27th, through an interminable

[1] Zschatsch.

cloud of locusts, which darkened the surrounding air for a space of two consecutive hours. The country to be traversed was in a terrible state from the continuous rains, and the record of the next three weeks' marching is only the same old story of flooded rivers and waist-high swamps, traversed with infinite difficulty and repeated loss of time, patience, and property.

A few extracts from the Diary will therefore suffice :—

31st July.—Guaso Masa. Found river in flood; ford impassable; all traces of bridge gone. Found spot with two fair-sized trees on opposite banks. Set all hands to work to cut them and make grass rope. First tree cut at 11 A.M., fell inwards into bank. Second tree fell into river, and jammed well, but not across. Cut many more small trees, and tied them with grass rope. Bridge made and ready by 3.30, but water rushing over in parts. Got all our men (loads passed from hand to hand) over by 5. Cows, pony, and donkey dragged, and swam with rope below. All over by 5.

2nd August.—Saw herd of eight giraffes quarter of a mile off, but they saw us and went.

5th August.—Gedge announced intention of going ahead to Kikuyu; gave him mails and twelve Zanzibar soldiers to take them on to coast. Told Mbogo to go on with Gedge; gave him two sheep. He begged for tea, sugar, and flour; told him I had nothing for him but the two sheep. He had been warned to carry twenty-five days' food.

9th August.—Equator. Self riding for sprained knee. 10.30 A.M.—Saw three elephants cross path in front. F. R. and I went after one, who separated himself; long tracking; I got a shot at 100 yards, and hit him too high, but through lungs. He came slowly towards us; both boys ran away. F. R. came up, and we followed him long way. Saw him standing at 250 yards, then lost him again. After some time I came across him, and shot him in neck. F. R. gave him two in neck. Mortally hit. Arrived camp 3 P.M. At 4.30 went after a distant rhino; after long, careful stalk came unexpectedly on him at twenty yards in long grass, head to us. He at once charged; boys ran away; Ramadan up a tree. Rhino came to within ten yards of me, then suddenly wheeled round snorting, gave me no chance of side shot; saw lots of game.

11*th August.*—Total bag, 5 zebra, 1 Grant.

12*th August.*—Lake Nakuro. I went after a Swayne's hartebeest, and got him after some trouble; two shots at him going full speed rolled him over. . . . Whole plain (S.E.) literally moving with zebra in parts: estimated we saw over 2000 in the day: counted one herd over 300. At one time about 400 trotted round our front within eighty yards, looking at pony which I was riding. Shot one Grantii doe. Decided not to shoot zebra to-day, as plenty of meat in camp already. View of Lake Elmenteita at 11. Country very dry; grass ready for burning; could see big fires ahead near L. Elmenteita, evidently Masai.

13*th August, Sunday.*—Marched to south-east side of Gariandusa river on Elmenteita Lake. Lots of zebra quite close; magnificent view over lake and volcanic country; small steep cones in every direction. Lake Elmenteita about seven miles long by two wide. Shot one partridge, large, with bright red legs; one Grant's; many long shots at Thomson's. Salt from lake no good; Mahomed Bau, one of the headmen, says he tried it with Martin, and it made all the men ill, probably natron.[1]

16*th July.*—Lake Naivasha, north-east end. At about midnight Selim Bey died of heart disease; had been as well as usual all day and evening; was found dead. Nubian women wailing all night. F. R. and I went to see him at 6 A.M. He

---

[1] The following is the analysis made by Messrs. Savory and Moore of a sample of water from Lake Elmenteita brought home by Colonel Rhodes:—

Chlorine, parts per million	590
Ammonia ,, ,, . . .	3·2
Nitrogenous nitrates, parts per million . . .	0
Total solids ,, ,, . . .	1210
Sulphuretted hydrogen, by volume . . .	0·065

The residue on evaporation was of a yellow colour and very deliquescent. The quantity of the water sent was insufficient for a quantitative analysis of the solids. It contained chlorides and carbonates of sodium and magnesium chiefly, together with smaller quantities of iron, aluminium, and calcium.

was buried close to camp. Shot a hyæna. F. R. got two mpallah [1] and one Grant's.

Three days more varied with plentiful sport in this magnificent game country brought the caravan to Kikuyu, where Major Eric Smith, who had come up from the coast, on his first journey as transport officer, had arrived with some 500 men. Long-expected mails from Zanzibar and England were awaiting them here, and a week was spent in resting and making preparations for the eventful journey to the coast by the Tana river, which will be dealt with in the following chapter.

After the dreary experiences of the last few weeks, it is pleasant to close with a letter written in a cheerful strain from the "camp of plenty" in Kikuyu :—

Sir Gerald Portal to Mr. Rennell Rodd

KIKUYU, *20th August* 1893.

MY DEAR RODD—I arrived here yesterday, and find Mr. Gedge, of the *Times*, had only arrived two days before me, and had not yet sent on the mails which had been entrusted to him. . . . I have received five letters from you all waiting for me here, the last of them being of June 10 from Zanzibar. Many thanks for all the trouble you have taken about our canoes on the Tana; of course our plans and times of arrival here have been all upset by Macdonald's alarmist views about the Soudanese in Uganda, and the boats may have already gone down again, but we have decided to try it, and to strike across to the Tana, hitting the river just below M'Kenzie, and marching to Hameye. Even if the special canoes have gone down, it appears that we may be able to get others by chance, and if not, that the road is not very difficult. Of course this makes the date of our arrival at the coast uncertain, but I should say about

---

[1] Mpallah (*Epyceros melampus*), a variety of the antelope family.

the 30th September or first week of October should see us at Lamu, or Mombasa, or we may strike across to Mombasa from Golbanti, only five days' march. Smith and Martin with their huge caravan arrived at this place just half an hour before we came in from the other side, and last night we were a happy party of seven—Smith, Martin, Purkiss, Hall, Gedge, Rhodes, and myself. Smith brought me up cigarettes, and champagne sent by that most excellent Berkeley, and we "roughed it" in the heart of Africa last night on champagne, gazelle, venison, excellent mutton, duck, fresh English potatoes, cabbages, beans, lettuces, beetroot, honey, eggs, milk, and every conceivable dainty. It was delightful, too, to wake up in the morning in a room, and to lie lazily in bed till 6.30, instead of getting up in the dark at 4.30 in a wet tent.

I shall rest here about four days; the men want it. I think I told you in my last letter from the top of Mau that Macdonald had sent me a crowd of naked Nubians—men, women, and children—whom he wanted to get rid of out of Uganda, and therefore packed off to the coast. I propose to leave the bulk of this lot here; they can be employed for work on the station in return for their food, and don't want any pay, and I shall get Gedge to take to the coast only the few people who claim to be entitled to a passage to Egypt from the Company or the Egyptian Government. Selim Bey himself died of heart disease at Lake Naivasha.

I am truly sorry to hear that you have had a sharp attack of fever, but it does not appear to have impeded the smooth current of affairs, and I must again most sincerely congratulate you on the great success of the whole show. I am very glad you have mopped up Witu, and hope you will secure Rogers. I fear that a radical change will have to be made in the whole force of Zanzibar troops. The class of men sent up with us—and they were picked men—will never be of the smallest use up country, but I will talk over all this on our arrival.

I am annexing Mr. Purkiss, and sending him up to Uganda; he has already resigned the Company's service. Love to Mathews, Hatch, and Company. We are both well and flourishing.—Yours sincerely, G. PORTAL.

CHAPTER IV

The Tana route to Uganda—Crossing the Malanga river—Difficulties on the route—The Grand Falls—Along the Tana river to Ndura—From Ndura to Witu—Zanzibar.

THE object of Sir Gerald Portal's Mission to Uganda, and the examination which he was instructed to make into its condition, resources, and capabilities, would hardly have been complete without the last most trying experiences entailed by the investigation as to whether an alternative route to the coast was practicable by the waterways of the Tana. The river had indeed been visited and even explored by several travellers since the days of Baron van der Decken and the earlier discoveries of Dr. Krapf on the upper reaches in 1851. The first scientific map of its course was that of the brothers Denhardt, who in 1878 ascended the river in company with Dr. Fischer. In 1889 Mr. Pigott, now Acting Administrator of the Imperial British East Africa Company, made his way to a point some twenty-five miles above the Hargazo Falls, obtaining a distant observation of Mount Kenia, and then struck south for Kikuyu, passing considerably west of the route taken by Sir Gerald Portal and Colonel Rhodes. A map was also produced by Dr. Peters, who followed shortly afterwards, the accuracy of which, however, has received considerable criticism. To Count Teleki and Lieutenant von Höhnel belongs the credit of making the first ascent of Mount Kenia, which they explored in 1887.

In the enlarging of our knowledge of the Tana, however, the most important expedition of recent times was that conducted in 1891 by Captain F. G. Dundas, R.N., who, accompanied by Mr. Hobley the geologist, and Mr. Bird Thompson, ascended the river in the I.B.E.A. Company's stern-wheel steamer *Kenia* as far as Hameye, the highest point to which navigation was possible, and thence continued his journey overland to Mount Kenia, where he finally reached an elevation of nearly 9000 feet above the sea-level, on the slopes of the mountain chain. Returning thence, Captain Dundas successfully navigated the *Kenia* through the precarious journey from Hameye back to the coast.[1]

The portion of the Diary in which the daily experiences of the Commissioner between Kikuyu and the coast are recorded, is given unabridged in the following pages as a further contribution to our knowledge of the subject. There are certain points in which his observations differ from those of Captain Dundas and Mr. Hobley, and it is therefore possible that they may be of value in rectifying previous cartology.

The circumstances under which the journey was performed rendered it an exceptionally arduous one,

[1] See *Proceedings of the Royal Geographical Society*, August 1892.

and Sir Gerald was of opinion that the result of his experiences went to prove that, owing to the inhospitable nature of the intervening country, and the actual difficulties encountered upon the river itself, the idea of establishing any alternative route to Kikuyu and Uganda by the Tana was an impracticable one.

Besides the entries in the Diary, the eventful story of the voyage is summed up in a full and very interesting letter, begun upon the 14th of September, and concluded at Zanzibar on the 22nd of October, when his long march had at length been brought to a successful termination. This was the last paper from his hand written in Africa, and with it the eventful story of his Mission closes.

26th August, Saturday. — Kikuyu. Took headman Wadi Banduki, who knows road, as guide; strongly recommended by Purkiss and Martin.

Had to shorten up tent loads a little to make room for three new chop boxes, champagne load, seven food loads, Banduki's porter, load of flour for selves, etc., the two last being shot on me at last minute.

Marched along very good and well-cut straight road to outside forest, not more than seven miles in all. Camped between forest and stream. Grass fires all round threatened camp; turned out men and extinguished it with branches.

Afternoon, shot three bull wildebeest and one Thomson. F. Rhodes, three Thomson; Hutchisson, one wildebeest.

27th August, Sunday. — Meruba R. outside Kikuyu forest. Start at 6. Crossed river S.E., then turned E. and N.E. across grass, not very thick, following right bank of river. Halted at 8.15, and there met some forty Wanderobbo going to hunt game, especially wildebeest. Saw many hundreds of wildebeest, at one time some 300 in one herd, also many hartebeest and *Thomsoni*, latter not nearly so wild. At 9.30 (two hours from leaving road) arrived opposite junction of Ngong river, and one mile later arrived at end of scattered trees. No more firewood visible for many miles, so camped 9.45.

Saw near camp waterbuck, mpallah, and hartebeest of mouse colour, all hind-quarters *white*. Hutchisson saw bush-buck. Saw Wanderobbo having drive of immense herd of wildebeest past archers with poisoned arrows posted behind ant-heaps.

Afternoon, skinned yesterday's heads. Shot two waterbuck, right and left shots, after long crawl.

28th August, Monday.—Started 6.10. Had to make small bridge over the Ngong, eight feet wide, but six feet deep. Took till 7 to get all caravan across. Pony of course went in. At 8 (2½ miles) crossed swamp of 300 yards running water going S.E. to join Ngong. Halt 9 (five miles from Ngong crossing). Marched again 9.45, and at 10 began to cross another swamp river running S.S.E. and S. to Ngong. Could not see how wide, as it was high papyrus, deep swamp, and then *very* thick papyrus, through which had to cut path inch by inch; could not see a yard in front: slightly east direction. Did not get clear till 2.30 P.M. (4½ hours in water and cutting thick papyrus); then on, 3.30, across bare plain N.N.E. (70°) for 1¼ hours, 3¼ miles, and crossed rapid and strong river twenty yards wide at 4.30 and camped. This river runs also S.S.E. Altogether in 10½ hours covered about 7½ miles.

No shooting. Saw hundreds of wildebeest and two rhinos within 200 yards of camping-place, who took no notice of us. Shot one guinea-fowl.

29th August, Tuesday.—Plains. Started 6.15. At 7.30 (2¾ miles) came to river running S.E. to Ngong. Crossed on fallen tree; took one hour for all. At 8.20 marched again, heading just north of north shoulder of Chianzabi. At 10 reached another river eight yards wide, but deep; found a ford only four feet deep, and camped 10.15 on E. side, about seven miles.

From camp Mt. Chianzabi's highest point bears 105°, *i.e.* 10′ S. of E. Distant about fifteen miles.

No shooting on road, but saw three rhino and lots of zebra, hartebeest, and wildebeest.

Afternoon, shot two hartebeest; saw waterbuck and rhino and mpallah. Aneroid, 7 P.M., 5800.

30th August, Wednesday.—On fifth river after Ngong.

BRIDGE OVER THE MALANGA RIVER.

Marched 6, direction 45° for two hours; then halt on banks of deep strong river running W. and E.; found ford, but did not cross, as I thought it probable this river goes into Tana. After consultation with F. R. and Mabruki decided to follow along south bank. Marched nearly due E. and a little inclined to N. for two hours till 11.30, and camped near old Wanderobbo boma, by river, near pool full of hippo. River swarming with hippo all along, largest river yet seen in East Africa.

Wounded a giraffe (one of six) on road, but did not get him; shot at 200 yards. Shot one hippo at camp. F. R. a very large crocodile of enormous girth, and quite twelve feet long.

In afternoon men secured my dead hippo with ropes and cut her up. I followed river down for three miles, still going due E.; could not well see its course; afterwards thought it appears to turn S. towards Athi, though according to maps it ought to go to Tana. Chianzabi bears 165°.

Shot one mpallah buck, and wounded giraffe badly, but lost her in dark.

Hutchisson, fever, temp. 4 P.M. 102·8´, gave Dover, 10 gr.
    Do.   8.30 P.M. 103·6°, sweating.
    Do.   11 P.M. 102·6´, 18 grs. quinine.
Aneroid, 7 P.M., 5700.

31st August, Thursday.—Large river, sixth from Ngong. River averages ninety feet wide and eight to ten deep; full of rapids and falls.

6 A.M. started, and followed right bank of river, at first E. and E.N.E., hoping it would prove to be Malanga tributary of Tana, as from its size and volume it seemed much too big for Athi or Sabaki. After 1½ hours it turned S.E. and S.S.E., between high steep hills which prevented our seeing its course ahead. At 8.15 halted (about 5½ miles), determined to cross, as it was evidently bearing towards Athi. Its width made bridging very difficult, even tall trees would not reach across. Half completed one very doubtful bridge by cutting tree, when F. R. discovered rapids and fall half a mile down, where river is in four branches; beautiful spot; traces of Wanderobbo bridge. Made four bridges over four branches of rapids. All across by 3.30. Camped on left bank. Hippos everywhere in shoals. My

Winchester rifle dropped in six feet of water, but recovered. Aneroid, 7 P.M., 5550.

1st Sept., Friday.—Left bank of sixth river. Started 6 over hills N.N.E. × N. for two hours; long grass, slow progress, skirting range of hills on our left running in N.N.W. × S.S.E. to river. At 8, turned N.E. over pass in hills; grass six feet high and very thick. After passing through gap between two hills found ourselves overlooking valley about 800 feet below us, but almost precipitous descent, impossible for loaded men. Had to keep along very steep sides of hills for two hours, N. by N.N.W., very slippery, steep, difficult going. At 11, descended into valley, and camp on far side of stream (nearly dry) running N.N.W. Valleys open before us on N.W. × N.E. side into apparently large plains with distant river, probably Tana?

Near camp, one askari sitting in grass attacked by small gazelle, and badly bruised just below left eye.

Hutchisson feeling bad, temp. on arrival 102°, but great pains in right side; gave 5 grs. calomel. Aneroid, 7 P.M., 5100.

2nd Sept., Saturday.—(?) Jigu Mts. in gorge. Started 6.15, after very bad night; sleepless; Hutchisson feeling very weak and ill. March N.N.E. for some three miles along a native track till it turned N.W., then over succession of low hills, and through long grass and stunted trees, always N.N.E.; crossed several dry torrent beds. After some six miles arrived at bigger stream bed with pools of water. Halted and camped to let Hutchisson have long day's rest (9.30).

Saw four rhino on road, but all took alarm and went off. In camp porter came at 11, and reported big river ahead N.N.E. At 2.30 walked three-quarters of an hour N.N.E., and came to Tana river at last. Fine river, some 100 to 150 feet wide, good strong stream and evidently deep, literally full of hippos in shoals and herds on every reach. Men caught good many fish of a Silurus kind. River running E. × S.E.

Shot three hippos dead, but they remained in mid-stream.

Went very little way up river; saw lots of small monkeys, and large herds of mpallah and waterbuck, and one bush-buck. Shot two mpallah and one partridge. Lost way back to camp; but when quite dark, some way beyond camp, going on in opposite direction, heard gun fired by F. R. and came back. Hutchis-

SWAHILI BRIDGE, OVER THE MALAGA RIVER.

son better in afternoon, but in pain again in evening. Can't lie down. Temp. 101½°. Aneroid, 7 P.M., 4600.

Both my hands bandaged and in bad state from thorns, etc., also intense irritation from innumerable ticks from long grass.

3rd Sept., Sunday.—In Jigu Mts., near Tana river. Started 6.15; arrived at bank of Tana N.E. at 6.45. Followed river E.S.E. × S.E. along well-worn path for some miles, passing many traces of native camps, probably Wanderobbo hunting hippos. At 8, path continued S.E. × S.S.E., leaving river and apparently going back to Jigu Mts.; but we stuck to it, and after six or seven miles it turned again E. across bare, burnt, ugly plain, with a few ostriches, hartebeest, and zebra. At 11.30 arrived suddenly on large river flowing S. to N. towards Tana, evidently the Malanga (Fischer), which we crossed with such difficulty on 31st. Found well-made bridge of big trees and poles tied with creepers, quite new, and which must have entailed much work: probably Swahili caravan, too good for natives. Camped on E. or right bank, near deserted village and boma. Six Wakikuyu came to camp in afternoon returning from Mumoni; say that is three days off and food scarce.

Shooting in afternoon, a rhino made unprovoked charge, but turned when he received a bullet from ·450 in chest; I had not got the ·577. Shot hartebeest on road, and waterbuck in evening; waiting for men till quite dark; very difficult and painful return to camp through darkness and thorns. Aneroid, 7 P.M., 4520.

4th Sept., Monday.—Started 6. Followed well-worn path going S.E. (145°); said to lead to Mumoni (Ukamba ya Mumoni). Natives in camp yesterday reported to have said it was our road. It led us continually about 145°, but very circuitous, across very long bleak and bare plain, river apparently leaving us. Crossed water in pools twice in early part, but later all watercourses dry, and everything burnt. At 10.15 passed Swahili camp near torrent bed now dry, then on through thornwood, no water, and still going S.E. At 12.15 reached dry torrent; halted; situation serious; dug for water, but no success. Sent on Wadi Bunduki, and found water *up* the hill, just below the sandy bed; plenty of it. This road evidently leaves river altogether. Wanted to turn N.E. at 11.15, but F. R. was for sticking to road.

Sent men out 4 P.M. N.E. to look for Tana, also others to follow porter ahead, and report if any cross track.

Saw giraffe, shot one rhino, F. R. one hartebeest. Aneroid, 7 P.M., 4900.

5th Sept., Tuesday.—Lanjora in Ukambi, E. of Mumoni and S. of Tiza. Men sent out returned 9 P.M. after much firing of guns and beating drums; report Tana about five hours. Started 5.30, having made all men fill their water-bottles. Marched N. by S. about 35°; hilly and long dry grass, very tiring. Halt 8.30. Three rhinos at different times came close up to head of caravan and frightened men. I sent them off by firing Winchester at them! one at fifteen yards. At 10.15 rose over high hill and saw what we thought was Tana N.E., about two hours down valley. Followed valley till 12.30; very bad going, very rough, innumerable dry, steep watercourses, long tangled grass, thick thorns and long grass, and millions of ticks. At 12.30 halted and had hot coffee and cold meat. Marched again 1.30 for one hour, and found water in hole in dry torrent bed, and camped.

Went on to look for river; it seemed at least ten miles farther, but F. R. thinks only seven. Krapf Kenzi hill bears N.E. We marched quite sixteen or seventeen miles, shows we went quite twenty-five miles wrong yesterday. About six men and one woman missing; lit large grass fire to guide them. Aneroid, 7 P.M. 4210.

6th Sept., Wednesday.—It appears that twenty-seven people are missing! *i.e.* twenty-one Zanzibar askari, four of the Kikuyu askari (mail men), my tent askari, and one woman. Set fire to grass in camp on leaving to give them a sign, and marched at 6, steering N. by E. about 25° for Mt. Albert, down ravine. After 2¼ hours through rather rough grass, rock, and thick thorn, arrived at river Tana, in strong cataract; three distinct branches of river; cataracts extend long way up stream, and some way down. Mt. Albert bears 24° from camp.

Camped here at 8.30 to give lost men a chance. Sent out Captain Hamed and Captain Amani[1] at 10 o'clock to look up and down river; they returned in two hours, saying that they had seen nothing. Told Hamed this was disgraceful, that I would cut all his pay from Kikuyu, and put him on half rations to

---

[1] Native officers of Zanzibar troops.

THE SEVEN FORKS TANA RIVER.

coast. F. R. and I spent all afternoon shooting hippos, several killed, but unattainable. Food badly wanted; gave out one bag grain, i.e. one kibaba to every three men.

Porter reports food about two hours off, and native path. Saw baobab trees. Aneroid, 7 P.M., 3850.

7th Sept., Thursday.—Tana river,—seven forks; Mt. Albert 24˚. 5.30, sent men to look for dead hippo, but all had floated away. At 6, was informed that Hamed had gone off on his own account with *all* his remaining men, and offered to look out for the lost ones, without asking leave, and without even asking our route and intended camp. Marched 6.30. Cutting road through thick thorns for an hour, then arrived at so-called ford. Crossed one branch of river, thirty yards, up above waist, very stony bottom, full of holes, and very strong current; then a second river, about the same; then across a quarter mile island to third branch. It was a roaring fall, slippery rocks, and falling water ten feet below; had to bridge about fifteen feet, and then awful scramble; noise of water terrific. This appeared to be last branch, but eventually in next half mile there were three more branches to cross, all cataracts, all above waist, and very strong stream. Immense difficulty with cattle, donkey and one calf saved, though nearly drowned, but had to kill two cows at number three, and one cow drowned.

Dealt out meat for three days. Not all over till 3. Marched down left bank; thick thorn bush till 5. Camped in old native camp; lit big fires to guide lost men. No signs of Hamed or others. Lots of bee-hives in trees. Aneroid, 3620.

8th Sept., Friday.—Captain Hamed and soldiers did not appear all night, but big fire kept up on hill. Started 6. Crossed a stream, and immediately afterwards saw three dead hippo in river. Halted, and with great difficulty man swam out in rapids and secured rope to one, which was hauled in and cut up. This took till 10.30.

At 8, Hamed and soldiers appeared on opposite bank, tried to ford, but failed; sent them back to our ford one hour up river. Marched 10.30 to 12.30, and 1 to 2.45, i.e. for $3\frac{3}{4}$ hours, about eight miles; general direction N.E., but river very winding; twice it went due south, and I left it and bore N.E., meeting it again. Thick bush everywhere; hard work. In camp one man reported missing, carrying 2 heads and 25 kibs. grain (our last grain); had been seen close to camp; sent out men and fired guns, but no result; had big fire lit on hill behind us.

New camp in bush about half a mile from river; met huge hippo walking about, fired four bullets from Martini into his head and shoulder; twice he tried to charge, but was stopped by bullet. He just reached the river, leaving great mess of blood on track. lay like a log, and then sank. Mt. Albert bears 350°. Aneroid, 3500.

9th Sept., Saturday.—Tana, Mt. Albert 350°. March 6. No signs of missing men. Three men in front with axes and bayonets; hard work cutting path through endless thick thorn, bare of leaves; desolate and altogether hideous and miserable country. River bore E. and then S.E. and S.; cut off a corner, and steered N.E. Marched till 8 (two hours, did about three miles only); halted half an hour, and then on till 10.45; rather clearer. Did about seven miles in the 4¼ hours' marching. At 10.45 arrived at quite recent Swahili camp, with good boma for many goats and donkeys, and strong bridge over part of river; but it does not appear certain that they crossed whole river, as their tracks appear along a good path towards Mt. Albert. River here flowing nearly N.E. F. R. went on in afternoon down stream, climbed a hill, and got clear view for miles all round; nothing but this interminable brown thorn bush.

I went straight inland and saw only the same. Mt. Albert bears 325°, so that Hobley's map is deceptive about the food district. His map and Dundas's also disagree very greatly as to course of river, and both are very different in every way from Mr. Ravenstein's.

Men still have plenty of hippo meat, and catch great quantities of fish. Bau caught eel about four feet long, like a conger, dark green sprinkled with black. In afternoon put up five buffalo from thicket not six yards from me. Shot a partridge; F. R. a guinea-fowl. No other meat in kitchen, no grain, and only a small tin of wheat flour given me by Martin. Aneroid, 3400.

10th Sept., Sunday.—Tana. Swahili camp in bush. Marched 6. Thick thorn; hard work cutting road; river went N.E. with many bends, once turning quite S.S.W. for ¾ of a mile. Kept usually close to river, but once lost road and went in circle, striking our old track again: this was my fault. Marched 6 to 8.30, and 9.10 to 1.15, and camp on river where it runs N.E. Men have no food left: we had one guinea-fowl only: no corn or flour.

Mt. Albert bears about 285° from here, and solitary mountain on right bank (evidently Krapf's "Kenze") in 83°, therefore by Hobley's map we should be in food country.

In afternoon I pushed on to where I got Mt. Kenze at 104°, and Albert 283°, i.e. in straight line on each side, but still same thorn bush all round. Hobley's and Dundas's maps misleading. Situation getting serious. Men have finished all meat and were hunting for berries, but good many fish caught. F. R. went to shoot hippos above camp, where he got two guinea-fowl; I got goose, but it fell into river. Aneroid, 3300.

11*th Sept., Monday.*—Tana, Mt. Albert 285° and Kenze 83°. Many men had nothing to eat last night, having finished two cows and a hippo in two days. Marched 6. Cutting as usual through thick thorn N.E. for two hours; there found three natives by river; made them come as guides, seizing their bows and arrows to prevent escape, and tying one round the waist to a headman. They led us 2½ hours (five miles) through thorn bush most of the way by native path, E.N.E., gradually away from river, till at 11.30 we emerged over high range on cultivated valleys. Harvest just gathered, and whole country very dry, but good lot of corn apparently been grown. Lots of natives came up, all well fed, all with bows three feet long and poisoned arrows, most wearing red and blue beads, some with brick-coloured dyed cloth on shoulder like Wakamba. On a very long and trying walk for water, which we didn't reach till 2 P.M., having been marching some six hours. Water under sand in dry river bed.

Natives want presents before they bring food; gave three hands cloth to four elders. Food in plenty, but natives don't seem to care for beads, want cloth and empty tins.

12*th Sept., Tuesday.*—Mbé. Halt all day. Issued two days' posho (two strings pink beads) to all men, and bought also 180 kibabas to carry on. Great numbers of natives in camp all day with mahindi, beans, flour, and honey for sale, but prices not cheap. Men over-eating themselves, and some sick. Bought some honey for selves, and flour. Porter lost on 8th appeared: had been four days in bush; luckily was carrying corn, which he opened and ate; said he lost caravan by following hippo track.

F. R.'s donkey stung by "Drobo" fly; seems very bad. Remained in tent all day, to give chance of healing to sore feet, and also because no boots. Hutchisson mending one pair.

Only one guinea-fowl between three of us all day. Aneroid, 3450.

13*th Sept., Wednesday.*—Mbé. Three guides appeared 6. Started 6.15, over steep and rocky hills and precipitous gorges, some cutting of thorn to be done, but not much. At 10.50 arrived at tributary from north, good water and cold, about 20 yards wide by 2½ feet deep, flowing over rocks in deep gorge. Crossed this river and camped at its junction with Tana river, about eight miles.

Man carrying all beads missing. Sent back askaris, and offered reward to Washenzi, but nothing heard or seen of him till night. Can't well move without beads, so decided to stay here tomorrow and send out search parties, both of my men and natives, to offer rewards.

At 4 P.M. F. R. went out shooting, and after a shot, heard it answered from opposite bank, and directly after two of our missing soldiers appeared. Report all the lost party safe and well in Wakemba (Mamoni) village close by; had crossed river, met Swahili caravan, and then recrossed. Told them to meet us at ford lower down to-morrow. Very hot, 94° in tents; aneroid, 2840. No meat at all; killed calf, then F. R. shot seven guinea-fowl.

14*th Sept., Thursday.*—Tana; junction of Abaziba river; Mbé country. Halted all day and sent search parties after man with beads; they found him and brought him in at about 12: the natives had offered to bring him before, but he refused!

Two hippos shot by F. R. yesterday found dead; one brought to this side by natives with some difficulty, and cut up.

Good many fish caught by men, chiefly scaled.

Local natives seized bows and arrows of our guides, and demanded compensation for bringing us to their country. Gave chief guide three hands cloth to redeem them.

15*th Sept., Friday.*—Tana; junction of Abaziba river; Mbé.

Started 6. One man deserted in early morning. Difficulty with guides, who wanted to strike for prepayment, but on my going on without them they came on. Guides quite useless, knew no path. For 2½ hours fairly open country, but numberless very steep ravines to cross; very hard for porters. Halted 8.30, opposite tall, conical, conspicuous hill. Marched again 9.15, now into very thick thorn bush, endless cutting, very slow progress, guides leading us in most erratic way. Arrived at river; not till 1.30 (? Guaso Nagur, Dundas), reached it half a mile from junction with Tana, thirty yards wide, and deep and strong. Guides wanted to take us far west to ford; eventually found ford at junction itself, waist deep, but very strong current; camped on opposite hill at 4.30 P.M. Cook lit grass fire; some danger and trouble. Aneroid, 2750.

16th Sept., Saturday.—Tana; junction of? Guaso Nagur? Started 6. Very slow cutting through thorn bush; reached top of lava cap at 8. Mbé guides refused to come on from camp, saying they were on bad terms with Wathaka. On top of cap met a lot of Wathaka, all friendly, led us (8.30) down hill on W. side, and for 2½ hours N. by N.E. by good roads, and camped by Tana at 11. Good deal of cultivation, harvest just gathered. Country very dry; marks of many goats and cattle.

Wathaka finer and bigger men than Mbé people; armed with bows, arrows, and a few spears and painted shields; wear beads of all sorts, especially pink; iron chain, and ivory rings in ears. Split ears very wide. Wathaka saw our big bush fire of last night; thought it was war, and were all on the watch,—cattle all driven up to hills.

Very hot, 97° in tents.

Natives very slow in bringing food, only a few came into camp late in the afternoon, could only buy one bag full (50 kibs.).

One Mkamba man here; says he saw me at Machakos on the way up to Uganda; tried to engage him as guide to Korokoro country.

Mt. Krupp bears about 37°, fine bold mountain. "Pelly range" visible due north. The Wathaka mountains bold volcanic formation, but not so high as Mumoni's, opposite river, and now S.E. of us. Apparently more cultivation on right bank of river.

Many natives crossed just below camp, but had to swim part of way, no canoes at all.

Men caught plenty of good fish, both scaled and silurus. Aneroid, 2630.

17th Sept., Sunday.—Tana. Wathaka country. Guide refused to accompany; said he was afraid. Marched 6. Following river, clear path, lots of cultivation, crops all in. Did not see a single native. Camped 9, about half a mile short of junction of "Guaso Niro," or "Mt. Tsombiso" (Dundas), just opposite Grand Falls of Tana. Falls about sixty feet in four branches, over rocks, and overhanging shady trees, very picturesque and striking. Found good new bridge over "Guaso Niro"; followed fair path for two miles beyond, then it ceased.

No natives came near camp all day; can't understand why they won't bring food for sale. At 10 A.M. sent on Bunduki and Mfaume, each with six men and guns, and beads, and bags, to go to villages and buy.

7 P.M. Headmen returned; Mfaume with $2\frac{1}{4}$ full loads, and Bunduki with less than a quarter load! Both report natives all run away, frightened by European. Aneroid, 2620.

18th Sept., Monday.—Tana. Wathaka; Grand Falls. Sent out Bau and Mfaume at 6 A.M. with men to buy food. He went far and to many villages, and succeeded in buying about eight or nine loads of mahindi, metamma, and kunde. Natives still refuse to come near camp; say they are afraid, as they were ill-treated by a European before. Can't find out when or by whom.

Gave three days' rations to men in beads, and told them to go and buy in villages.

We have by the evening three days' rations bought by men themselves, and three days' given out in grain, and ten bags = five days = in all eleven days.

In morning went forward for some two or three miles, path for $1\frac{1}{2}$ miles, a lot of clearing, then path ceased; thorn bush, but not so dense as above Mbé. River goes E. nearly in deep gorge.

On right bank all open and cultivated as far ahead as we can see. Tried to find ford or place for bridge below falls, but failed; decided to stick to left bank and cut through. Saw waterbuck and small antelope. Shot ten guinea-fowl near camp. F. R. got two. Plenty of fish caught by men.

18th Sept., Tuesday.—Tana. Grand Falls. Started 6. Crossed "? Guaso Niro" by fair native bridge of branches from rock to rock across rapids, then turned right to bank of Tana. Followed fair native path for nearly two hours, all through pretty thick bush, though fairly extensive clearings in first half hour. Path had evidently been cut either by natives or by a previous caravan. Halt 8.30 to 9. At 9 marched again; no path except few game tracks, very thick bush and steep hills, and very slow progress, about one mile between 9.30 and 11! From 11 to 12 found clear room alongside of water in river bed, but deep sand and often bad rock work. At 12.15 found good open place and camped, about nine miles. Lot of natives on opposite bank with many goats and cattle, tried to buy milk goats, but neither our men nor natives would swim across.

Water in Tana seems very much less than above falls, although it has taken in three big rivers! Very hot, thermometer 99° in tents 4 P.M. One man missing, carrying mess box, sent back to halting-place, no signs. Men caught many fish. Aneroid, 2550.

20th Sept., Wednesday.—Tana. Nine miles from Grand Falls. Missing man did not appear; he was a professional deserter, started in chain gang from Mombasa, deserted in Usoga, and was brought back by natives. He has all our flour for mess, and a box containing looking-glasses, butcher-knives, and some small beads and a lot of matches; the latter a serious loss.

Marched 6. Along river bed, alternately deep sand and scrambling over huge rocks; went fairly well to 8.45—about five miles. Halt opposite high conical peak on right bank, very conspicuous.

Marched again 9.30; for some way in river bed, then had to leave it and cut through dense thorn, very slow, but from 11 to 12 got on better. Halt 12, near river opposite rapids, just S. and close to two conical high rock hills about half a mile back from left bank; about ten miles in $5\frac{1}{2}$ hours' actual marching.

Very hot marching; thermometer 95° in tents 4 P.M.

Shot two geese on road, and ten blue vulturine guinea-fowl,

afternoon; beautiful birds, with bare head, no tuft, and blue breast. Aneroid, 2490.

21st Sept., Thursday.—Tana. Gneiss conical hill. Started 5.40 and marched to 8.20. A good deal of bush cutting, bad thorns, and climbing rocky hills, with occasional comparatively open places near river, about five miles in two hours forty minutes. On again 9 to 12.15. At first clear going, and got ahead well, then more bush cutting and rock work. At 11.10 crossed Swahili caravan road, marks of camps at ford.

Ford just below small rapids on and off island; found no "*falls forty feet*" as stated by Dundas, fall of perhaps four feet in all! After ford river goes S. one mile, and then nearly due N. for about three miles. Bush and rocky hills for half an hour, then clear path near river. Camped at 12.15; actual marching six hours (excluding halt).

Hobley's map marks none of the chief hills and landmarks, nor any of the important river bends. Distance actually walked at least thirteen miles.

Afternoon F. R. walked on some distance, but saw no sign of the tributary stream marked by Hobley as falling into Tana three miles from road.

Lovely moonlight night by river, hippos snorting, baboons barking, and two lions grunting, all close to camp. Aneroid, 2400.

22nd Sept., Friday.—Started 5.30. Fairly clear of thorn, and made good progress; reached tributary from N. at 6.40, about twenty yards wide, but only two deep. This makes it quite five miles (or six by river) from Swahili road. River running pretty steadily N.E. and N.N.E.; big bend south shown by Dundas doesn't exist.

Halt 8.15 to 9; then along fairly open ground in bush country to series of rocky hills, where river runs very narrow and quick. At 11.30 reached second tributary from N., 20 yards wide, 1½ feet deep; 3½ hours' good walking, or at least nine miles from first tributary. Just before junction Tana gets very wide again, and after junction turns E. by S.E. Camped just beyond mouth of tributary, 11.45.

Afternoon, went ahead some three miles, found river goes S.E. by S.S.E. for two miles, and then sharp turn N.E. Can cut off big corner. Flat country, much more open. Saw big fire N.E. about three miles off, probably Wanderobbo.

Country full of little Kirk gazelle; shot three; saw a *Clarkii*, also two waterbuck, and red antelope as big as a *Grantii*. Aneroid, 2250.

23rd Sept., Saturday.—Tana, second tributary after great falls. Started 5.50. Marched E. on rising sun; fairly open, but certain amount of bush cutting; river went away several miles south. After three hours' good marching due E., and at the end a little S. of E., struck river again at 9; halt to 9.40. Getting hot, and men all very thirsty. By this cut saved several miles of walking.

9.40.—Marched again along river N.N.E. and N.E. by E.N.E., over flat country with comparatively open glades. At 10.15 country became rocky, with small steep hills, and river runs between steep banks and very narrow. At 10.30 river divided, small island, and falls some ten to twenty feet in series of small falls and rapids.

At 11 came suddenly on Mackenzie river running in from N.W. between steep banks, and falls of some thirty feet, but at mouth easy ford only two feet deep. Camped 200 yards beyond mouth of Mackenzie river. Shot on road three *Kirkii*, two partridges. Afternoon, two *Kirkii*.

Afternoon, went on, found river goes S. of E., then nearly N. for two miles, then sharp turn due E. Got good view ahead over large plain covered with bush, and two bare hills prominent about twenty miles off, bearing 140° (S.E.).

First willow-tree on river bank opposite my tent. Hippos in shoals during march, sometimes quite out of water, also many baboons. Aneroid, 2090.

24th Sept., Sunday.—Mackenzie river. Started 5.50. Marched E. Cut off good corner of river, struck it again after two miles of rough rock and thorn bush, good deal of cutting; then river makes very sharp turn from N. to S.E. Rough, rocky, and thorny going for three miles, then get to depression about one mile wide and two miles long, semicircular, enclosed by cliffs, filled with very thick green bush and jungle, but clear at edges. I went on shooting round edge, perfectly clear, but F. R. led caravan through thickest part. Halt 8.30 to 9; then fairly clear plain with scattered thorns for five miles, and halt at 12.15, thick belt of dóm palms along river. Shot on road two *Kirkii*, one hog. Saw giraffe. F. R. saw rhino.

Afternoon, went straight inland, fairly open country, with scattered bush; shot three impallah and one big partridge. Aneroid, 2060.

25th Sept., Monday.—Tana plain, five miles from bushy depression. Started 5.50. For a mile or two good going and clear, then long succession of small, steep, rocky hills with deep gullies, all covered with thick thorn and broken gneiss and quartz, and lava.

At 8.30, river turns very sharp from N. to E. Halted till 9. From that corner river very broad and fine, willows in many places on banks, and dóm palms. At 9.45 arrived at Salt river, about eight yards wide, clear sweet water! then more small hills and stones till 11.15. Camped in dry river bed, about three miles from Salt river. Shot at Salt river one impallah.

Afternoon, went long way in bush; saw four rhinos together and one giraffe, did not get a shot; got two partridges. Aneroid, 2050.

26th Sept., Tuesday.—Tana, three miles below Salt river, in torrent bed. Started 5.40. Marched through bushy country, but along clear path at good three miles an hour till 8.20, first going S.E. for some four miles, then N. and N.N.E. for three miles. Did good seven miles before halt.

Started again 8.50. Still good path, marks of cutting by Chanler or other caravan; marched S.S.E. past long rapids (marked "no falls" by Hobley), then S.E. for three miles, good pace up till 11.15; camped in clear place. Pink prominent gneiss peaks just opposite, bearing about 176°. Marched at least fifteen miles, but by map only nine.

Afternoon, walked long way through thorn bush, seeing nothing; returned along broad bed of a river; saw three giraffes (shot at one), a *Walleri*, and some waterbuck, but all in bush; only got one *Kirkii*. Aneroid, 1900.

27th Sept., Wednesday.—Tana, opposite pink gneiss hills, near dry river. Full moon. Having ordered drum to sound early, they woke me at 3.15 to ask if it was time!

Started 5.30. Marched fast and well for three hours along fair path by river. Halt 8.30 to 9.10 at falls (Princess Louise, according to Dundas; Hoffman, Falls of Peters, and Hargazo of natives); not really falls at all, only succession of rapids for about three miles, full of wooded islands. On again 9.10 to 11.10; general direction S.E. Camped just beyond dry river. Shot one blue guinea-fowl; saw two *Walleri*.

Afternoon, went shooting, got into dry swamp, very thick green bush, beyond that open country, small gravel hills. No game whatever, but a few *Kirkii* (shot two) and sand grouse. Native Korokoro came into camp, could get nothing out of him, seemed rather off his head. Aneroid, 1780.

28th Sept., Thursday.—Tana. Started 5.25. Marched well away from river, over clear, rolling gravel; small hills. At 8 wanted to get to water for halt, but had to struggle through high grass of dry swamp. Halt 8.15 to 8.45; then Wadi Bunduki said he knew road, led us long way inland, and after two hours confessed he must have passed Hameye! Went straight to river and camped; sent Bunduki back to Hameye for food, canoes, and natives; saw many native game traps.

Afternoon, went out 3 to 6 P.M.; walked long way, saw hardly anything. F. R. saw no game at all. I shot two francolin.

Sent out Wadi Bunduki to find Hameye. He returned sunset, reporting Hameye deserted; saw only two small shambas on opposite bank. Aneroid, 1750.

29th Sept., Friday.—Started 5.45, and marched chiefly S.E. through rather thick bush; had to cut our way often. After two and a half hours (six miles) halted to 9, and at 9.30 came on Company's deserted station of Balarti; good boma, and good house, which we occupied. No signs of natives, but people (probably our canoe men) had been recently living here.

Passed many game traps made of nooses of good strong rope fixed to a bent bough, which springs back; also many native tracks. Sent Bau off at 10 down river with thirty men; returned 1.30, reporting no natives, nor shambas, but many game snares and bee-hives, and fresh native tracks.

Sent Capt. Mahomed and all soldiers on with Wadi Bunduki down river to look for natives, and seize canoes, and meet us tomorrow. This place delightful situation on river.

Afternoon shooting 3 to 6.30 ; very hot at first, bushy country with open glades ; walked many miles, saw only two very distant *Walleri ;* coming home shot waterbuck doe ; very useful, as men's posho all finished. Aneroid, 1700.

30th Sept., Saturday.—Balarti. Started 5.30, rather dark. After some searching found good human path leading E. and then N.E. ; followed it till 7.30, when we met our askaris and Banduki (sent on yesterday), who reported having found an island full of ripe mahindi, but no huts, nor canoes, nor inhabitants. Marched to bank opposite this island and camped, sending all men over to pick mahindi. Lots of sand grouse in flocks. Shot two. Men collected six days' food each in mahindi from island. W. Banduki discovered small dug-out canoe ; in this Bau and he visited larger island ; found cultivation (mahindi), but no inhabitants or canoes ; sent men up and down river for considerable distance ; they found one or two huts deserted some three weeks or month ago, but not a sign of man or canoes.

During day we came upon several more noose rope game traps, which seem to show near presence of people. We took all the ropes, which are really good and well made.

Men all in good spirits to-day, and all over-eating themselves. Hutchisson sick, complains again of pain in side, says he had another cold bath yesterday, although I and F. R. had especially told him that this was extreme folly.

Went shooting at 4, so did Frank ; hopeless country, not a sign of game, except few very wild *Walleri*, never seen within 200 yards, and always off like wind. Thin thorn bush, and dry, bare ground everywhere, bleak, ugly, desolate, inhospitable, with fringe of bush and willows and dried swamp near river. Fresh elephant tracks everywhere, and fair number of giraffe tracks. No signs of buffalo here, though about Hargazo Falls their tracks were numerous. Cooler day, cloudy.

1st Oct., Sunday.—Tana, about 4½ miles below Balarti, above Bokore. Hutchisson complains of being very tired and feeling pain ; offered him choice, and he elected to go in canoe with Wadi Baraka ; told them to start late and drift slowly down, keeping near left bank, that we should not go more than eight miles, and that they were to try and get hold of natives and canoes.

OBTAINING CANOES

We started 6. Had very difficult march over very rough ground, cutting through thick bush, and struggling through dried swamps, cut up everywhere by deep elephant track, sometimes three feet deep. In avoiding swamps we had to go some three miles from river, and at 10.30 began to cut our way back to it, very thick and hard work. At last struck river 11.30.

With much difficulty got into communication with some natives in a canoe, and soon afterwards others came (Wa-korokoro). Sent them off to get canoes. Shot on road one harnessed bush-buck.

Mzee Bonair, Galla chief, and some men came to camp; long shauri about canoes, etc. They say Gallas have no canoes, but at last undertook to send to all Korokoro people to bring canoes here for us to buy. They say our canoes from coast waited two months at Balarti, and only went twenty days ago. Our missing men three days ahead of us. Aneroid, 1650.

2*nd* Oct., *Monday.*—Tana, on sand-bank above Bokore. Plenty mosquitoes at night; waiting all day for promised canoes, but none came. A few came with food for sale.

Mzee Bonair sent to say he would send canoes by evening, but none arrived; said to be because the old man has fever.

Another very windy and dusty night on this beastly sand-bank, only six inches above the water, and impenetrable jungle all round.

3*rd* Oct., *Tuesday.*—Tana. Sand-bank. Captured a canoe at 6.30 A.M., and sent M. Bau to see Mzee Bonair, with message that unless all thirty canoes appeared by mid-day I should have to take them by force.

At 11 A.M. Mzee B. appeared, ill with fever, with eleven canoes, of which seven very small. Gave him one jora (7½ dotis) of amerikani and five rings of copper wire. Tied canoes side by side in pairs; got all tent loads and mess loads, selves, boys, and tent askaris into them, with two natives in each to punt. Started 1 P.M. (only two hours after first arrival of canoes), and went quickly down stream for about one mile, landed on left or south bank, at Chanler's camp; nice open camp on good clear ground, well above river, just opposite Mzee Bonair's place on island. Sent canoes back for second half of caravan, who all arrived by 3. Shooting afternoon, promising-looking country, but absolutely no game seen, except *Kickii*, etc. Lost road back to camp.

4th Oct., Wednesday.—Left Rhodes in charge of canoes; put all loads in canoes and Hutchisson, all sick, and about three men in each pair; sent Mahomed Bau with F. R.'s party.

Started myself with all rest of men by land to walk and try to effect a junction at camp. Impossible to keep near river, so struck in, found fairly open thorn bush and bare country; steered S.E. and then E., back to river, which we struck at 11.30; fired many guns, no signs of boat party.

At 2.30 started back with five men to look for others. After two hours' very bad going near river, signal gun answered up stream, and soon after Bau appeared in canoe. Reports F. R. in camp very long way back, so we got in his canoes and came back to our men; arrived 6. Secured five canoes on way down.

Bivouacked on bed of palm leaves, but mosquitoes bad. On march saw no game at all, all day!

5th October, Thursday.—Tana. Bivouac above Sandi's. Rather bad night, and mosquitoes, but plenty to eat with beef sent by F. R., and beans and mahindi from the men. During morning we secured eight more canoes, bringing total up to thirty in all. Tied all two and two together. At 10.30 Rhodes and party appeared.

He says he sent Ramadan out with one porter, both with guns (Ramadan with my Martini), to look for me; neither has appeared. Wadi Bunduki also lost one of his men, and returned, saying he can't find him. Started again 11, and went down stream till 1, and camped. On arrival Bau reported seven men refused to come in canoes, and started to walk; now they have disappeared!

Body of one porter found close to island opposite camp, with throat cut and mutilated, evidently killed while looting. Sent out search parties, but no signs of any of missing men. This is too disheartening. We must stay here to-morrow to give Ramadan a chance, and send canoes up and down stream.

6th October, Friday.—Tana, below Baboia. Sent canoes up and down river to look for Ramadan and other men. The disobedient porters were found a mile back, surrounded by natives and in a blue funk, and brought back to camp, when I ordered them to have their hands tied and kept so all day, till I should pronounce their punishment. No signs of Ramadan, though a shot heard inland, answered by me 11.30, and men at once sent in to fire two more shots, but there was no further answer.

Two natives came in; complained of their canoes having been taken this morning; on inquiring found it true, so gave them their canoes back, and promised big reward if they found Ramadan. They said he had passed Sadi Ramatha's, but undertook to go and bring him to see me, also to bring food, etc., for sale, but they did nothing of the sort.

In afternoon punished deserters, cut pay from Uganda, and to be bound from reaching camp to sunset every day for a week. Apportioned all men to their canoes. No meat left, nothing shot, hard up!

7th October, Saturday.—Same camp, below Baboia. No signs of missing men, no use waiting longer, so started in canoes at 6, and went down stream till 2 P.M. Only two accidents, and nothing lost; stream very tortuous, and very full of sunken snags and trees; banks lined with trees and forest all the way. At 2 camped on sand-bank on right bank. Went to shoot at 4; struggled for an hour through dense bush; gave it up and came back.

Shot on road two large waders of the stork kind; one of them not at all bad to eat, especially as we had nothing else!

8th October, Sunday.—Tana. Forest between Wapokomo and Korokoro. Started 5.45, all together; then a very difficult piece of navigation; sharp bends in river; quite full of countless half-sunk trees and snags, and strong current; many canoes got foul of trees. Rhodes and Hutchisson both got foul of trees, and had to land and mend canoes.

Thick forest on both banks all the way, and many very difficult and dangerous parts. Passed a few huts and small patches of rice at various intervals. Saw three Gallas, who said, "Kimabombe in three days' journey"; probably untrue.

After seven hours' good paddling camped at 1 on sand-bank, north bank. Pitched tents in small clearing in forest. Caravan all in by 3.30. Shot four-guinea fowl drinking by water.

9th October, Monday.—Started 5.50. River became more open; fewer trees and snags, and broader and longer reaches. At 9.30 in a clear part of the river ; Tembo and Wadi Baraka in charge of canoes with all my luggage ; ran into a large conspicuous tree trunk standing quite by itself in mid-stream, with heaps of room all round it ! canoes capsized, and all my things went into river and sank ; had to camp there, and by diving recovered all boxes, but all heads, skins, ·577 rifle, and bed were lost ! Gross carelessness on part of both Tembo and Baraka ; told them I cut all their pay to pay for losses. Would sooner have lost almost anything than this rifle and heads and skins. Only did about ten miles in consequence.

All afternoon drying things, as every box was full of water.

10th October, Tuesday.—(?) Manyole district. Slept on ground, bed being lost ; good many insects crawling over me. Started 5.45, river broader, clearer, straighter, but current getting pretty slow.

Passed a few patches of cultivation on either side, and a larger one at 12.30 on left bank, when some Gallas told me we were one day from Malululu, and that this was Manyole. The two statements hardly reconcile themselves. Thick wood both sides nearly all the way. Camped at 2 on sand-bank.

Went out at 4, to see if I could reach open country, but only found dense bush and dry swamp and elephant paths. Heavy rain came on, and I got soaked through. Shot on road three pelicans.

11th October, Wednesday.— Between Manyole and Kidori. Started 5.45. River very winding ; went N.E., E., W., and N.W. on its way south, but not many snags. At 11.45 passed Kidori, a collection of small shambas and villages all along left bank.

At 2 reached Tuni, on right bank, and camped. Hutchisson's canoe swamped ; he lost boots, bedding, and horns and shields. Good deal of cultivation on both banks, chiefly Indian corn and bananas.

12th October, Thursday.—Tuni. Started 5.45. River winding ; for an hour still in Tuni district. Then from 7.30 to 10 in Bura. From 10 to 12.15 in Massa. At 12.30 entered Malululu ; camped on right bank in fairly open grass and scrub at 1.30 ; canoes not all in till 2.30. Plenty of natives. Villages passed to-day a good deal larger than farther up.

Went out shooting; in a quarter of an hour got to dry and fairly open thorn scrub, hopelessly barren and dry; saw two waterbuck and shot two *Kickii*. No tracks or signs of much game anywhere.

13*th October, Friday.*—Above Malabati, in Malululu. Started 5.30. Found we were much farther back than had thought; progress slow, river very winding, and one or two difficult places with many sunken trees. Strong head wind blowing from S. At 8 passed Malabati. At 10.20 Sisini. Camped at 1 on right bank, above Marumbini, which natives say is close — how far that means is doubtful.

Self very seedy; in great pain in canoes and most of afternoon from internal chill, probably from sleeping on ground. Natives full of praise of Chanler and Höhnel. Natives say no game near; have to go day's march in for it.

14*th October, Saturday.* — Wachakoni, above Marumbini. Started 5.30. Passed Namoni (R.) 7.45. Passed Gallo (right bank) 8; Gorami 8.30; Korori 8.45, all left bank. Villages on right bank mostly deserted. Ndura, large village on right bank, 10.30; saw here one or two Arabs (Kiroboto).

Camped in Kinakombe district in open place on left bank at 2.15; most of caravan not in till 3 and 3.30. Natives friendly and confident; spoke well of Chanler.

Went shooting; open dry thorn country, and farther in very thick; saw nothing but some waterbuck late in evening. Shot buck who fell on his back, then suddenly recovered, went into bush, and was lost; getting too late and dark to follow.

Hutchisson sick and in pain from stomach.

Sultan of Kinakombe— *Gulu.*

Saw several Borassus palms on either bank, getting more plentiful as we go down.

15*th October, Sunday.*—Kinakombe. Started 5.30. Made good progress for four hours; passed Guano at 10; river straighter and broader. Saw one cocoa-nut tree, young one— looked ill. Also some pineapples, and, near Ndura, mango-trees. From 10 to 1 strong head wind; got very wet and shipped a lot of water; delayed progress badly. At 2 reached large village of Ndura, right bank; full of Gallas. High wind all afternoon. Heard here of severe fighting at Witu, one English officer said to be killed. Witu people all run out into Barra, and Witu now occupied by "Nubians" from Zanzibar, with Sultan of Zanzibar's flag.[1]

Sultan of Ndura—*Comoraludu*, or *Nife*.

Much bothered here by people crowding round my tent, mostly drunk!

4 P.M. Sultan sent to say he was drunk; would come later to see me! Didn't come.

16th Oct., Monday.—Ndura. Under weigh by 5.30, so Sultan had no chance of coming for his presents to-day. At 10.30 and 11.10 passed two villages, both on right bank, both calling themselves Mwina, both fairly large. Then numerous very sharp bends in river to N., S.E., and W. Strong wind from S. delayed us much, and wetted everything; went on till 2.15, making slow progress, and seeing no villages or people for the last two hours. Camped 2.15, under trees in deserted village on left bank, probably above Gaylwa. Saw shamba of cocoa-nuts, young trees not looking healthy. Native in canoe came in, said this had been Mitobe, and a big village, but all people bolted from this and neighbouring villages on account of Witu people's raids.

17th Oct., Tuesday.—Mitobe. Woke camp 4.30, and under weigh by 5.20, in order to get through as much work as possible before high S. wind which gets up at 11 every day. Made good progress past several deserted villages, including Mgatana. Lot of cultivation (chiefly plantains) up to there, then but little on to Merifano. At 11.30 river became very rough in places from high S. wind; one canoe of Zanzibar soldiers swamped, and Uganda boy drowned.

Very difficult to find camping-place, but eventually camped in dried swamp on left bank above Yunda. Sent on W. Baraka in canoe with letter to missionary at Golbanti to announce arrival to-morrow. Gave out posho, one hand amerikani for two days.

Mosquitoes simply awful, in thousands.

---

[1] The second Witu expedition, July and August 1893, against the brigand forest population in Witu, in which the Naval Brigade and the Sultan of Zanzibar's troops took part. No English officer was killed, but two were wounded at Punwani.

CANOES ON THE BEREZOVI CANAL.

8.30 P.M. W. Baraka returned with note from Mr. Bird Thompson,[1] who had opened my letter to Golbanti; sent us tea, beer, etc., and mails.

18th Oct., Wednesday.—Yunda. Started 5.25, and reading mails in canoe. Mosquitoes in thousands all round us. At 6.15 met Bird Thompson coming to meet us in canoe. Got into his, a very good large one, with three Wapokomo men; went great pace down stream past Ngao, where is German Mission on right bank, past Golbanti, to village 1½ hours below, where camping place prepared. Village, Fitina.

Thompson greeted everywhere by Wapokomo, who all seem to know and like him very much. Many fine muscular men came into camp. We arrived about 11.30, the caravan at 1.

Reading letters, etc., all afternoon. Heard Rodd very ill, and about fighting at Witu, etc.

19th Oct., Thursday.— Fitina, on Tana. Started with Thompson to go ahead to Witu, 1½ hours by canoe to mouth of Beledzoni Canal,[2] then 1½ hours' walk along bad and slippery path alongside canal while canoes are poled through. Canal very winding and not more than four to six feet wide, high grass on both sides. Then ¾ hour down Ozi river, and 1½ hours' walk across island of Kau to village of Kau, where Akida received us; crossed ferry and walked about seven miles across hot plain to Witu.

Station is open, undefended collection of huts and sheds and stores. Twelve Soudanese there and some fifty Swahilis.

Wali Omar Amadi seems good fellow, said to be trustworthy.

Caravan arrived at 5 P.M.

Talked through telephone to Rogers[3] and Hatch[4] at Lamu; sent telegrams by telephone to Rodd and J.

20th Oct., Friday.—Up at 4; gave over all spare stores to Thompson; got his receipt. Started at 5.30, marched to 8.15, halt at Pumwani, a collection of sheds built for blue-jackets

---

[1] Assistant Administrator in the British Protectorate embracing the Witu district.
[2] Connecting the rivers Tana and Ozi.
[3] Administrator of the British Protectorate N. of the Tana.
[4] Brigadier-General Hatch is in command of the Sultan of Zanzibar's troops.

in late row;[1] on to Mkinmumbe, arrived 2 P.M.—twenty-one miles.

Met by Rogers and Hatch. Lunch and dinner in small shed built for them. Embarked all men on three dhows at 8 P.M. Selves in steam-launch; tide out, could not start till 12 midnight. Slept well on board, and few mosquitoes. Embarkation of men done quickly, and no trouble. Much talk with Hatch and Rogers about whole Witu business.

21st Oct., Saturday.—Embarked on H.M.S. *Swallow* from launch 6 A.M. Told they could not get up steam and start till 11, and could not reach Zanzibar till Monday. Said I wanted particularly to reach Sunday evening. Captain Sampson promised to try, went full speed trial for four hours, shook and rolled a fair amount; F. R. and self both rather uneasy and delicate. Calmer in evening.

22nd Oct., Sunday.—H.M.S. *Swallow* at sea, calmer and well. Heavy current against us. Could not save the daylight, but arrived in Zanzibar at 8.30 P.M.

The staff of the Agency and the members of the Zanzibar Government came to meet us.

Went ashore 9. Saw Rodd for a moment, in bed, looked dreadfully weak and ill. Saw Doctor O'Sullivan, who strongly urged getting him away at first possible moment.

LETTER FROM SIR GERALD PORTAL TO LADY ALICE PORTAL

14th September 1893,
MBÉ COUNTRY ON TANA RIVER,
S.W. OF MT. KENIA.

. . . . . . I don't suppose you will get this much before we ourselves arrive in England, but as I have got a blank day to-day, I may as well write a few lines which may tell you some things which will be forgotten before we reach the coast. We left Kikuyu on the 26th of August, so that this is our twentieth day out, and we have had decidedly a rough time of it.

---

[1] This is a mistake; Pumwani was the chief town of the rebel Fumo Omazi, and was taken and destroyed in the second Witu expedition. What Sir Gerald saw was the temporary bivouac erected by the Expedition in a clearing some five or six miles from Pumwani.

The first day from Kikuyu we descended into the grassy plains of the Athi R., as if we were going to Machakos, but on arriving at a little river called the "Mgong" we turned sharply northwards, following this stream. There was no path, and the grass was usually about three feet high, very dry and tangled, which made marching in front of the caravan very tiring work; for those behind it was easier, as the front ones beat down a smooth path. The grass was also full of millions of ticks, which drove Rhodes and myself almost to desperation. They got into our clothes and on to our legs by dozens, and caused more irritation than double their number of fleas or other crawlers—in fact, we became really anxious lest we should be laid up with bad legs, or given fever by being kept awake at night by the irritation.

Our party consisted of about eighty porters, servants, and headmen, and thirty of the Zanzibar askaris. On these plains we had excellent shooting, and regretted that we had not more mouths to feed, as we only shot what was wanted for food. We could have got any number of hartebeest, zebra, wildebeest, gnu, and so forth, and could also have shot at least eight or ten rhino if we had wished. After three days of this we came across the very worst swamp that I have ever seen even in this journey. It was all full of tall papyrus twelve or sixteen feet high, and so thick and tangled that we couldn't see three yards ahead of us, while the mud and water was usually up to our middles. Every step of the way through this had to be cut by knives and choppers; and occasionally in the middle, where we couldn't see dry land or anything, we had to cut a long way out of our direction in order to avoid deep water and bottomless mud. We entered this swamp at 9 A.M., and didn't reach the other side till 3 P.M., the men not being all out till 4. In this beastly place we lost our pony, who stuck in the mud and was drowned, and two calves which belonged to cows on which we relied for milk. The calves being dead, the mothers at once ceased to give any more milk. After the swamp I pushed on, and at 5 the same evening we crossed a torrent boiling over great rocks, in which the water came up nearly to my shoulders. Here again we very nearly had some of the men carried off their legs and drowned—but not quite.

Still going northwards towards Mt. Kenia, we crossed five rivers in five days, and the 31st came suddenly on a sixth, ninety feet wide and twelve feet deep, running like a torrent. This was rather a thumper. It seemed impossible that it should be the Tana, though it might be a big tributary; so for a day and a half I marched along its right bank, hoping it would turn northwards to join the Tana, but the obstinate beast went S.E., and finally due south or even south-west, heading straight for the Athi river, so we decided that somehow we must cross it. After much hunting we found a place where it divided into four branches, forming islands; here it foamed, or boiled, or tumbled in a series of cataracts with a deafening noise. With tremendous work and difficulty we at last made four bridges, and got across and camped.

Next day we had to cross a mountain range, and all day were clambering and slipping on hills like the sides of houses, through long grass and huge boulders. This was a very tiring, long march, and awfully hard on the loaded men coming down on the northern side into deep valleys. We had some difficulty in finding any water—having had far too much of it before. Also Hutchisson was seriously ill—had got a chill in the liver crossing the big swamp; was in very great pain, and with a good deal of fever. We couldn't stop for any sick men, as our food supply was getting short, and there was now hardly any game to be seen in the stony, hilly, rocky country which we had entered.

At last, on the 2nd of September, we really struck the Tana itself flowing east, a fine swift river, 120 feet wide, and literally full of hippos, whose heads were popping up and snorting every five or ten yards in the smooth reaches. There were no signs of any sort of inhabitants, and, unfortunately, the banks were fringed with a belt several miles thick of dense, almost impenetrable thorn bush, while the mountainous nature of the country and the innumerable gorges in every direction made it impossible to tell with certainty the course of the river if we kept outside the skirts of the bush. However, having come across a fairly good native path, apparently following the course of the stream, we determined to follow it, with the result that after a long march of fifteen miles, on rising a hill after emerging from gullies, we found to our horror that while we had been complacently tramping S.E., thinking we were going parallel with the river, the Tana, hidden behind mountains, had suddenly turned due north, and was about fifteen miles away from us, while we could see absolutely no signs of water anywhere. All stream beds were dry and dusty, the whole country parched and baked, the men exhausted, and not a drop of water in the caravan. The situation was serious, but, providentially, at 2 P.M. we found some green plants growing in a dry torrent bed, and by digging a little came upon beautiful water. This was a most merciful escape from a very awkward predicament. Next day we tramped back to the Tana, cutting our way through hideous and obstinate thorns, torn to ribbons, scratched and bleeding, halting every moment as the men in front with knives and choppers were stopped by a tangled thicket, so that our progress was dismal and wearisome.

After some days of this terrible thorn work, we arrived at a place where we decided to cross to the north side in hopes of finding people and food. Luckily we had shot some hippos, but all the grain and flour was finished, and the porters cannot go on for long on meat alone, with nothing to help it. On the 7th we set to work on the crossing, at a place where the Tana had divided into six branches, all of them roaring cataracts.

The first was up to our waists, and the men had to cling two or three together to prevent themselves from being carried away. The second branch was about the same—each some twenty-five yards wide. The third was a narrow but sheer fall between two high precipitous rocks, where the water rushed with a noise that made it almost impossible to hear one's neighbour shouting at the top of his voice.

Over this very jumpy place we at last made a fairly strong bridge of poles tied together, and over this the men passed safely, but very slowly. We tried to get the cattle across, but one cow fell over and was at once smashed against rocks and drowned, so we killed the other on the spot. By extraordinary luck, and almost carrying the beast, Rhodes's donkey came safely over.

We then all thought we were safely across, but to our horror we found three more branches of the river in front of us, all cataracts, or foaming over huge boulders. At last, however, we all got safely across, and on the other side found more interminable thorn forests and dense bush. About this time, too, we were made very anxious as a party of twenty-one of the Zanzibar soldiers (who were always doing the wrong thing) didn't turn up. We lit fires, fired guns, sent out scouting parties, but to no purpose; for five days they were lost!—idiots! They have turned up again now, I am thankful to say.

To cut a long story short, we went on slowly carving our way through these hateful thorns till the 11th, occasionally seeing traces of where natives *had* been, and at last on that morning I suddenly came across three natives sitting by the river. They were frightened out of their wits, but we soon reassured them, and got them to guide us by some paths which we should never have found ourselves out of the thorn forest to some big clearings where we are now, and where there is abundance of Indian corn, beans, and sweet potatoes. Most of the men had had nothing to eat for twenty-four hours, and have consequently now all over-eaten themselves, and are incapable of moving, with stomachs swollen out and as tight as drums! I meant to march forward to-day, but a most serious thing has happened: the man carrying our whole stock of beads —the currency of all these countries—has disappeared with his load. I have sent out search parties in every direction, and have offered rewards to the native chiefs if they will bring him in, so I trust he will be found, but if he is really lost it puts us in a serious hole,—300 miles from the coast and no means of buying food! It is true we have some cloth, but that we shall want for buying canoes 100 miles lower down, where the river becomes less full of rapids, and also cloth is not good for buying grain, which has to be bought up in very small quantities by different natives.

Hutchisson is better, but still suffers a great deal of pain in his right side, and, as a last misfortune, the Colonel's invaluable donkey, which has always carried the invalids, has been stung by a fly which the natives say is fatal,—the poor beast certainly looks like dying.

I sincerely hope that we are now through the worst part of the journey, and that the rest will be easier work. One good thing is that we have now reached the part to which Capt. Dundas

THE TANA RIVER: THE GRAND FALLS.

came in 1891, and of which he made a rough map, so that we have now something to guide us from Hameye (150 miles ahead of us) down to the coast. I hope to be able to get canoes, which will be a great relief, as, even if I can't get enough for the whole party, we shall be able to embark most of the loads and rest the men. All these casualties and misfortunes will make us a fortnight later on the coast than I had calculated.

2nd October 1893,
Near BALAKTI, a little below HAMEYE.

To continue from where I left off a fortnight ago: the Colonel's donkey died next day from the fly-bite, but the man with the beads turned up all right. From the Mbé country we came pretty easily in two days to the country of the Wathaka people, where we had to buy sufficient food to take us through the 120 miles of uninhabited country which lay between them and Korokoro. We had a good deal of trouble in getting this food, although there were plenty of signs of a good harvest having been gathered, because we could not get into touch with the people. They all ran away and would not come near the camp. I sent into their villages, but again they ran away. When at last we managed to inspire a little confidence, the people complained that they had been ill-treated by a white man who had been there before, who had beaten them and taken all their corn and cattle by force.

Our last day in Wathaka we camped in a beautiful spot on the river bank under giant trees, and just where the Tana goes over its "Grand Falls," about sixty feet high, with a tremendous roar and excitement, and boiling and foam. The falls are quite lovely, in four or five branches, each overhung by great trees and palms and huge rocks. At last I had managed, on the 19th September, to collect enough food for ten days for the party,— all Indian corn and small beans, and we left the Wathaka and started again down the north bank of the Tana through uninhabited, desolate country.

We had confidently hoped that now we should find it much easier travelling, but were bitterly and very completely disappointed to find ourselves at once again in thick, impenetrable sharp thorns, and rocky hills and gorges. For days we had to chop and cut every step of the way, and it is no joke to cut through such thorns as these, which tear the men's hands and faces as they work, and run into their feet. Sometimes it took us an hour to get over half a mile. Sometimes we scrambled over rocks and large boulders, or else deep soft sand in the river bed itself, as the water was fortunately low.

All this time, ever since we first struck the Tana, we had seen no game, and we were greatly exercised about getting meat for ourselves and the men. For the latter we shot hippos, and about one in every three got caught up in rocks or near the bank, where the men by swimming and wading could make them fast with a rope, or tow them ashore. For ourselves, we depended entirely on my shot gun; and, fortunately, I was able, by much struggling through thorns in the afternoons, to keep us supplied with guinea-fowl, of which there were a fair number in most places. Very good they were, too, so we lived on nothing but guinea-fowl and an occasional partridge for about three weeks. As we got nearer Hameye the country became less mountainous and a little less thorny, and sometimes we strode along for quite a mile at a time without having to stop and cut. This was really luxury; and here, too, there were a lot of little gazelle, about as big as hares, which were quite excellent, and a change from the old guinea-hen. If I had not brought a shot gun I don't know what we should have done, as Rhodes has only rifles for heavy game. To cut a long story short, we arrived at last on 29th September at Hameye, where thirty canoes had been sent from the coast to meet us (above Hameye the river is one long succession of rapids and cataracts, and no canoe could live in it).

We arrived with sighs of relief and hope, to find nothing—and nobody! The canoes had waited, and had all gone back to the coast just fifteen days ago! This was real bad luck; no inhabitants could be found, and the old food difficulty was beginning again! The men all wanted a rest, as they had had very hard work for many days, and were all getting knocked up, and Hutchisson was again really seedy.

Now the character of the river changed, and instead of forest of thorn, the banks were fringed with swamps and impenetrable green jungles, sometimes extending for several miles back. But we had to push on at all costs, and after three more heart-breaking marches through swamp and jungle, here we are camped on a sand-bank in the river-bed, but in an inhabited country, and with the camp now full of Indian corn and naked niggers. These people all live on islands, and as the only means of communication are by river and canoes, there are absolutely no paths inland.

I am making a halt here all to-day to try to buy canoes. Yesterday, by great difficulty, and by sweetly smiling and waving handkerchiefs, we at last induced a somewhat more enterprising native to come near us; he was soon followed by others, and they had promised to bring canoes for sale, and food, and all sorts of good things. We shall see the result by this evening, but, if I can get thirty of these little dug-out canoes, I shall lash them two and two alongside of each other, and we shall swing down the river at the rate of twenty miles a day.

6th October.—Korokoro country. When I ceased writing on our sand-bank on the 2nd, I was hopeful (moderately) of getting canoes, and of everything going on smoothly, but it is fated in this really dreadful journey nothing is to go smoothly for more than one day at a time. On that day we managed to induce the natives to sell eleven canoes only—we wanted thirty—and neither for love, money, cajolery, nor threats could we get any more. Accordingly, as the banks and the country for miles inland at that part are absolutely impassable, we had to make a very short journey on the 3rd, and send back the canoes to bring up the men and loads in relays; and it was no joke to have to punt and paddle these "dug-outs" back against the stream.

On the 3rd we camped on the south bank, where the country seemed drier and more open inland, so we arranged that on the 4th Frank Rhodes should take all the loads into the canoes, and just enough men to guide them down stream, while I made my way across country with all the unloaded men, and we were to try to meet after about five hours' march. This sounded very well, and we had arranged for signal guns to be fired at certain fixed hours by two parties, but when it came to practice it was a dismal failure. I found after a few miles' march that it was quite impossible to keep near the river, which became fringed with an impenetrable belt of swamp and tropical jungle several miles wide. I had to push on till at last I found a thinner place, and by cutting and tunnelling our way through the tangled green wall for half a mile, arrived at the river bank to find no signs of Rhodes and the canoes. Guns were fired, but no answer came. It was awfully hot; we had had a long and tiring march of some eighteen miles over very rough country, and I felt sure Rhodes must have camped farther up stream; so after a short rest I left all the men by the river, and started with three men to struggle up stream again through the jungle. For 2½ hours I panted, and crept, and crawled, and ploughed my way through the most horrible tangle that ever was seen, till at 4.30 P.M., to my immense relief, one of my signal shots was answered a long way up the river, and shortly afterwards the headman with Rhodes's party appeared in a canoe, and reported that they had been delayed by swampings and accidents, and were camped a long way back, and that it would be quite impossible to get back to Frank Rhodes before dark. I therefore jumped into the canoe, and came down by river to where I had left my men, and bivouacked there for the night. I had no tent, no food, no clothes, no nothing, and the mosquitoes were awful. However, the men had lots of rations of Indian corn and beans, and there was plenty of good water in the river, so I was pretty comfortable as far as food was concerned, and by cutting and spreading a few fan-palm leaves on the ground, managed to get a moderate night in spite of mosquitoes; but I would not advise Europeans, as a rule, to sleep on the ground in Central Africa just under the Equator on the bank of a river which overflows periodically. Next morning Frank and the canoes appeared at 10.30, and meanwhile both he and I had succeeded in collecting several more canoes and plenty of food, and were now able to embark the whole party.

So far so good; but as nothing could go quite right, it appeared that the day before, Frank had sent out my "boy" (my chief gun-bearer), who had gone with the canoes in charge of all my baggage to look for our party, and that he had not returned! He had taken one of my rifles with him, by Frank's order. Frank had naturally thought that Ramadan (the "boy") had found me and stayed with me, and so had come on to us.

Now we had to wait and send out search parties for Ramadan in all directions, but it was hopeless work in the jungle. We searched right back to Rhodes's camp, but found no sign. Meanwhile a porter was reported missing as well. At last it was decided to be useless to wait, and that the missing men having lost us would certainly follow the river down. So we all embarked again, and came on down stream. Yesterday the body of the missing porter was found floating down the stream, with his throat cut and gashed all over with spear wounds. The man had evidently been looking for food, etc., in the native plantations, and being alone and unarmed had been murdered. This made us more anxious about Ramadan, who, though not a particularly plucky one (especially if face to face with a rhino, when he invariably bolts up a tree with my second gun), is a good fellow, and has worked well for me ever since we left the coast.

So to-day once more we have waited all day, and sent canoes up and down stream, and search parties everywhere, but with no success! It is useless to wait longer, and to-morrow morning we must go on. There is still a slight chance that he may have pushed right past us on land, and that we may see him sitting on the bank to-morrow waiting for us to pass. If he is sensible that is what he will have done, but it is, I fear, a very slight chance. He has one of the porters with him, and also my rifle, so I don't think the natives will have harmed him unless he tries to loot for food. This is a lovely camp by the river, under giant shady trees, but we are really prisoners, with a dense wall of impenetrable jungle between us and the open country miles back.

This river is by no means easy navigation for canoes. It is literally full of snags, sand-banks, and great trees which have been swept down by the floods, and whose bare branches can be seen just above the water at frequent intervals—sometimes as many as twenty of these sunken trees in half a mile, and with the water foaming over their branches. The most dangerous are those that barely show above the surface, and whose branches are perhaps a few inches below the surface of the water.

Ndura, 15th Oct.—I am very sorry to say we have heard and seen nothing of Ramadan, or of the porter who was with him, and can only hope that they are all right, and have got to some friendly natives, but one can't help feeling that they may have come to grief in spite of his having my rifle and plenty of cartridges.

The natives of Korokoro are not by any means a trustworthy or good lot. I can't quite understand Ramadan, who has been so many caravan journeys as servant and gun-bearer, being quite such a duffer as to lose us altogether, and can't help fearing he may have come to harm.

From daybreak on the 7th till now we have pushed ahead well in the canoes, and have paddled hard from about 5.30 A.M. till 2 P.M. every day. Fearfully dull and monotonous work it is, too, and uncomfortable beyond words, to sit for eight and a half hours at a stretch in a narrow "dug-out" canoe. Some of the navigation has been really difficult with the river-bed quite full of sunken trees (carried up and left by big floods) over which the water boils and roars in an alarming manner. There have been several swampings, but I myself have been by far the greatest sufferer. The canoe, or rather the two canoes, containing all my worldly goods, tent, clothes, guns, bed, everything, were in charge of Tembo, who succeeded a few days ago in running them against a very visible tree trunk sticking right out of the water. The canoes were capsized, and everything at once went to the bottom.

Unfortunately just there the river was about twelve feet deep and very swift. We halted at once, and all the afternoon made men go on diving, I having offered a high reward for every box recovered. By this means most of the boxes were recovered, but all full of water and in a dreadful state. But, alas! the things irretrievably lost were just those I valued most. They were (1st) Mathews' rifle, which he lent me—a very excellent and valuable one. (2nd) My bed, so that now I have always to sleep on the ground. Luckily some blankets were saved and the mosquito net! (3rd) All my shooting trophies—heads, horns, skins, etc.—shot since we left Kikuyu. These I regret as much or more than anything. I had some very good and rare heads and skins, including those of what I believe to be two brand-new sorts of antelopes, hitherto never been shot by any one. It is too annoying for words.

Hutchisson has also been swamped; has lost his bed and all his boots, but we shall not have to walk much more.

There has been absolutely no shooting since we got the canoes, though Frank and I go out religiously every afternoon and struggle through swamps and thorns. We have seen just nothing. It is most fortunate I had a shot-gun, as nearly every day I have been able to shoot a goose or two, or a water-bird of some sort, from the canoes, so that we have not been quite reduced to a diet of beans yet.

Zanzibar, 22nd Oct. — Arrived all safe and well. We were met by Mr. Thompson at the mouth of the Tana, where for two nights we were simply devoured by mosquitoes in millions, which made dinner, sleep, and early breakfast periods of utter horror. Then we marched to Witu, and from thence a twenty-two mile walk to the head of the long creek, where three dhows and a steam-launch were waiting to take us to Lamu.

In Witu we met Captain Rogers and General Hatch, and at last we had a moment of supreme happiness, as we drank off a bottle of beer apiece (the first for ten months) and ate real fresh fruit.

At Lamu the *Swallow* was waiting, and brought us slowly down here, where I am horrified to see how terribly ill Rodd looks. He has been dreadfully bad, and the doctor is most anxious to get him out of the country at once, so he comes with us by French mail.

Sir Gerald Portal left Zanzibar for England on the 4th of November.

PART III

CAPTAIN RAYMOND PORTAL.

DIARY OF CAPTAIN RAYMOND PORTAL.

INTRODUCTION

ALTHOUGH the present book only purports to contain Sir Gerald Portal's own account of his mission to Uganda, it has been necessarily supplemented with matter from another hand; and therefore, when the Diary of his brother, the late Captain Portal, was submitted to me, I felt that nothing could be more appropriate than to include in what has now become a memorial volume a document which appeared so fresh, simple, and manly, and to add a few more words in introduction about one who, in the narrow circle of his friends, has been so deeply regretted, and who only needed, as Sir Gerald has said himself, an opportunity to show the stuff which all his contemporaries knew was in him. And if I seem to some to speak almost with an excess of warmth of one whose name was perhaps scarcely known to the public until the news of his untimely death reached home, I trust that the sincerity of this appreciation will excuse the form; and I feel certain that it will find an echo in the hearts of all his friends.

Captain Raymond Melville Portal, the eldest son

of Mr. Melville Portal of Laverstoke, was born on the 9th of October 1856. He was educated at Eton and at Balliol, but he left the former early without having made any particular mark there, and spent the interval between school and college acquiring a knowledge of foreign languages in France and Germany. In these early days, while at Havre, he was awarded a medal for saving the life of a man from drowning, a recognition which he always modestly deprecated as out of proportion to the service rendered. At Balliol he became distinguished as the finest athlete of his year, during that brilliant period between 1870 and 1880 when the college had as great a reputation on the cricket field and river as in the schools, and he twice represented Oxford on the running path in the annual competition with the sister university for the hundred yards and quarter-mile races. He also contributed with Grenfell, Mulholland, Wickens, and other famous oars, to bring the Balliol Eight to the head of the river on the last occasion on which it occupied that proud position.

His inclinations had always been for a military career, but by the time he had taken his university degree he had already passed the prescribed limit of age, and was only eligible for a commission in a West India regiment. He entered Sandhurst after a very creditable examination, and while there renewed his Oxford laurels in the athletic contests with Woolwich at Lillie Bridge in 1880. Passing out of the college with honours, he was gazetted a second lieutenant in the 1st West India Regiment in 1881, and, after a course of instruction with the 52nd at Chatham and in Ireland, joined the former in Sierra Leone. He subsequently served in the West Indies and in Demerara, and after suffering severely from the consequences of fevers contracted on the West Coast, exchanged into the 81st Foot. Then for some four years he acted as A.D.C. to Sir George Willis at Portsmouth, and was eventually appointed adjutant to the mounted infantry at Aldershot, an appointment which he still held when Sir Gerald was enabled to offer him a place on his Uganda staff. This offer he unhesitatingly accepted, and after barely a week in which to make the most necessary preparations, he sailed in company with Major Owen and myself for Zanzibar, not without grave misgivings on the part of friends, when they learned that one whose constitution had already been severely tried by African fever was embarking on an enterprise inevitably fraught with many risks and hardships.

An interval of nearly fifteen years had passed since he had left me behind at Balliol before we met on board the s.s. *Aca* at Marseilles, once more to spend three weeks in close and daily companionship. These years had changed him little. He was still the glorious type of physical manhood we remembered on the Iffley path; he still had all the old commanding sunny charm, his honest, kindly nature beaming through the eyes. Grave on occasion, reserved, almost shy with strangers, he was full of a light-hearted humour among his intimates, and his smile went straight to the heart—a man whom men would follow anywhere,

and who only needed opportunity to lead. He was
the type and pattern of an English gentleman at the
best, calm, sensible and just, generous, simple and
sincere, and his head was as good as his heart.

It was not long before that irresistible charm
which his contemporaries had always recognised in
him made itself felt among his companions on the
Uganda Expedition. No one was so well able to
manage the refractory porter as he was, no one
more patient in the thankless task of keeping the
rearguard up to the mark. All who have returned
hitherto bear common testimony to this; as in fact
his brother has written, "he was the best of them
all," and there is not one that will grudge him this
simple praise.

It was just as he was preparing to return from
Toru, where he had gone under the circumstances
already narrated, that the fever overpowered him,
and to those who read the following pages it must
appear to have been the inevitable result of the life
he was there doomed to lead. Sick as he was, however, he started for Kampala with the enlisted
Soudanese whom he had been instructed to bring
down. It was a fortnight's march for a man in
vigorous health, and he, growing daily weaker and
weaker, almost without supplies and medical stores,
absolutely alone as far as human sympathy was
concerned, with his motley crowd of half-drilled
irregulars, his porters, and his native servant almost
a stranger to him, pressed forward with indomitable
pluck day after weary day, until at last he could go

no longer, and the men carried him in a hammock, right willingly, and doing their honest best for him as they were able.

A messenger despatched to Kampala brought news of his critical condition, and Lieutenant Villiers at once volunteered to go out and meet him, taking all such comforts and drugs as could be collected. The rest of the story has been already told. That last march back to camp had worn him to a shadow. His strength had ebbed away, and the gallant life was not to be saved. It was a dark day for that little band of Englishmen in the heart of Equatorial Africa. It was a day of sadness for many of us when the news reached the coast, and up in the Witu forest, where we were at that time, men who had known him but slightly during the short period of his passage through Zanzibar, spoke reverently of his name, and seemed touched with the shadow of a personal loss. If he was known to comparatively few, at least it may be said of him no man died more beloved by his friends and contemporaries, and many a tender thought has gone out since over the thousands of intervening miles towards the green hill in Kampala, where, before long, an iron cross will mark the distant grave of one of the finest fellows who ever died in his country's service, for the Greater England's sake.

R. R.

Left England, Sunday, 11th December 1892.
Left Marseilles, Monday, 12th December 1892.
Arrived Zanzibar, Thursday, 29th December 1892.

1893.

1st Jan., Sunday.—Left Zanzibar 5 A.M. in H.M.S. *Philomel*, after big dinner night before given us by British residents. Much speaking, eating, and drinking. Rough sea for two or three hours, and several distinguished people invisible. Arrived Mombasa about 4. Went on shore and did a walk with Roddy. Dinner given by skipper in the evening, also very big thing. Nice harbour, but didn't see town.

In the last two days everybody has eaten and drunk a very great deal too much for good walking.

2nd Jan., Monday.—On shore about 11; Gerry rowed by captain and officers of *Philomel*; salute of guns and cheers of crew. By tramway about six miles, then four-mile walk to camp at Mazeras. Everything prepared with greatest comfort and luxury by Gen. Mathews. Also there, Rogers and Wilson, of I.B.E.A. Co.; was rather seedy.

3rd Jan., Tuesday.—Left about 7. Went with rearguard; porters rather weak and lazy. Very short march of about five miles to camp at Muachi. Waste of a day, as we might have come on here yesterday. Mathews sent on more luxuries—champagne, beer, fruit, etc. Water plenty, but beastly. Head-man seems a fool. He has brought a smart harem of six.

4th Jan., Wednesday.—Marched 6.30, minus harem. No sleep at all for mosquitoes; thick scrub; no food or water till 11.30, where water, undrinkable. In rear with Frank and Berkeley, who is rather ill. Porters very bad; stoppages every five minutes; some of them clean done up. Met parties of Wa-Nyika; no houses. Camp at 2.30; rather cooked; more than an hour after the head. Got a wetting.

5th Jan., Thursday.—Left 6.15. Short march to Samburu, arrived 11.45; just got tents up before heavy storm. Put out all baths and basins, and got lots of clean water. Berkeley and Moffat both seedy. Afternoon Villiers arrived from Muachi with nine porters and pony. Porters good; pony poor. Went shooting; got one guinea-fowl; saw deer, quail, and pigeon.

6th Jan., Friday.—Left 6.20. Got blisters from wet socks. Did last two hours bare feet. Got through last of good water. Arrived Toru noon; rain-water holes. Stopped mail down from Unyoro.

7th Jan., Saturday.—Started at 12. Feet rather bad. Rode Villiers' pony to first halt, afterwards got on boots and walked. Got to Butzuma about 6.30. No water; went on two miles farther, and halted four hours. Did nice sleep. The Company seem to have done nothing to collect water on this plain; have cut wide path for twelve miles from Butzuma.

8th Jan., Sunday.—Started just before midnight; long and tiring march. Halted about 6.30. Villiers produced some much-needed Liebig. Horrible winding path; men sewn up. Head of caravan got to Maungu about 9, tail not till after 2; the last bit very tiring. On getting to top of ridge the finest view I ever saw. Unfortunately water one hour up the mountain, so got very little and no bath. Rather seedy, slight fever. Hamilton[1] came in with homeward caravan. This march more than thirty-four miles, without water and very little food.

9th Jan., Monday.—Felt bad. Started 6.30. Walked two hours, then rode. Marago ya Kanga about 12.30; lovely camp under mountain. Looks fine game country; saw lots of quail, and tracks of lion, giraffe, hartebeest, etc. Laid up for feet. They got a few quail.

10th Jan., Tuesday.—Rest here to-day; stayed in bed; others went out early to get meat for men. Two zebra, one Clarke's gazelle. Feet better. Villiers brought sugar-cane, not very good, and a goat; excellent.

11th Jan., Wednesday.—Started 6.30. Rode; beautiful country. Crossed River Voi on foot; long swamp, long rushes. Camped far side. Lots of tracks of all sorts, but saw no game.

12th Jan., Thursday.—Started 6.30. Rode again; sick of it. Pretty country. Gerry and Villiers on ahead; got shots at zebra and hartebeest, no result; halted 11-2. Four men absent starting; got three apiece. Roddy, Frank, and G. ahead. Roddy one *Kirkii* antelope. Ngorungo M'Buyuni about 5.

13th Jan., Friday.—Off at 6. Rode. Halt 11-1. Very hot

---

[1] Of the I.B.E.A. Co.'s service—killed by Somalis and mutinous garrison at Tuzki Hill Fort, near Kismayu, August 1893.

afternoon. Tsavo 4.30. They got a few pigeons. Wretched place—one mud hut, with feeble stockade; nice river, no cultivation whatever; a little bit of widened path, the only sign of improvement by Company except the bit of road over Toru plain.

14th Jan., Saturday.—Left noon. Rode. Two porters deserted at Tsavo. Uninteresting country—low, thick scrub, quartz and granite. More food at Tsavo, making loads heavier. Much struggling and very slow. Arrived two hours after the head, at 5.30, at Ngorini; nasty, dirty place, full of creeping things.

15th Jan., Sunday.—Left 6.10. Rode; very thick scrub and jungle; path nearly grown over. Rear of caravan *very* bad, all lame or sick. Camp noon, Kinani; good big water hole. Got good view of Kilimanjaro, due west.

16th Jan., Monday.—Left 6. Walked two hours, then rode. Camp about 11.30, Mto Ndei; got on new road about 10. Moffat still got fever. M'Donald coming down, is camped here—dined with us; gave awful accounts of Uganda. They went out shooting, but of course got nothing. M'Donald says he got one mail in nine months.

17th Jan., Tuesday.—Left at 6. Passed M'Donald at start; walked to-day about fourteen miles. Still on road, fast being grown over. Very thick stifling jungle part of the way, then open plains, good timber and long grass, rather park-like. Camp Masongole about 12.30. Too much inhabited by Wakamba to go shooting. Heard leopard.

18th Jan., Wednesday.—Left 6.10. Walked about ten miles to Kibwezi, pretty park-like country; good road, cleared for the last two miles. Nice tidy place, and a good deal seems to have been done, in a short time. Mr. Watson gave us milk and butter on arrival—great treats. Afternoon had trial shots with rifles, and filled a few hollow bullets; result to be seen. Roddy not well, with tummy ache. Strike among men, headed by Sudi, about going on. Lots of Wakamba about; amused them with burning glass, telescope, etc. Great dinner with Mr. Watson—champagne, and all kinds of things.

19th Jan., Thursday.—Walked on at 7 with Gerry and Frank. Caravan followed at 12. Six miles to Mbwinzao; bad, rocky road. Knocked over guinea-fowl with ·450, but couldn't find him. F.

had a stalk at hartebeest, but missed. Walked miles, had shot at hartebeest galloping hard, but didn't get him. Large herd, saw nothing else, no tracks.

20th Jan., Friday.—Left 5.45. In front with Villiers; he had a shot at hartebeest; missed. At lunch saw herd of quite 100. Sudi and Moffat each got one. Had two stalks and one long shot, missed. Saw tremendous lot, also ostriches. Gerry got one *Kirkii* antelope. Big open plains, full of hartebeest. Tracks of giraffe. Villiers got one lesser bustard. Long day, about seventeen miles; camp 5.15, Kiboko river.

21st Jan., Saturday.—5.50, about 10 miles to near Ngurungani: did nothing in afternoon. Roddy got a rhino, men all squabbling over meat. They only brought away half, but enough for all.

22nd Jan., Sunday.—6 A.M. Long march, about seventeen miles to Nzoi, 3000 feet. Pretty mountain country. Improved tribe of Wakamba, very smart, but ugly, much brass ornament and red ochre. Great traffic going on. We got hens, milk, native flour, sugar cane, etc. They will only take one very particular shade of blue bead, which rather checks business.

We passed one nice river 2½ hours from here, the Ndange. Saw a herd of waterbuck or mpallah, and one of hartebeest. Roddy went out early to look for lions at the remains of rhino, found only fresh tracks.

23rd Jan., Monday.—Very nearly frozen to death last night. Off at 6.15, like an October morning. Mountain country, beautiful strong air, shambas all the way, but very poor soil except valleys. About fourteen miles to Kilungu, shallow river; burst my water-bottle by carrying fresh milk, but produced some butter. Dosed my boy with chlorodyne—doctor says it ought to have been the other thing.

24th Jan., Tuesday.—Started 8. Awful cold night, had all my clothes on, and don't know what to do when it's colder. Deputation of Wakamba. Presented a goat. Tiring march, porters bad; first half up and down hill; second up the middle of river. Camp about ten miles, on river, crowds of Wakamba, butter, milk, and vegetables. Have got nothing to buy with except empty cartridge cases, and nearly spent them all. Lovely country, much cultivation.

25th Jan., Wednesday.—6.30. Cold, half-way up river, remainder over spurs of hills; met runners with mails, bringing also two sheep and fresh vegetables for us from Machakos. Camp about 1, eight miles from Machakos. Came about ten miles. Lovely air, but rather bare country; good deal of cultivation, lots of milk and butter. Went out at 4 with some Wakamba after guinea-fowl. Got five, horned—might have got lots more, but they pumped me out. Whole tribe joined in beating, much excited. One covey of fourteen.

26th Jan., Thursday.—6.15. Short march. Machakos 9.30. Nice station among the hills. Great luncheon with Ainsworth: fresh vegetables, milk, etc. Found 200 of Foaker's men here sent down from Kikuyu to get food. Can't get any there because of rows with the people. Gerry, Frank, and Moffat go on to-morrow with them and all ours, loaded: Roddy, Villiers, Berkeley, and I stay here shooting, I think, till porters return. Beastly wind, and tent full of dust and muck.

27th Jan., Friday.—They went off at 9; Moffat with Wakamba porters at 2. I went after guinea-fowl, with two tame Wakamba, but only saw one. Got three partridges and a duck after very long walk. Afternoon filled a few hollow bullets. Villiers and Berkeley rather seedy. Blows here like blazes.

28th Jan., Saturday.—Roddy and I started at 9, with twenty-nine Wakamba and a few others. Villiers too seedy to go; went about eight miles and camped. Huge undulating plain, simply swarming with huge herds of all sorts. Roddy went on and had shot at rhino. I went out after putting camp right. Saw several rhino, had long shot at hartebeest. Hard to get near them, no cover. Nineteen Wakamba are volunteers, who have come in hopes of meat.

29th Jan., Sunday.—Out early. Stalked ostriches; couldn't get shot. Then a long stalk, one hour, at a rhino in the open and moving. At last he lay down; got within fifty yards and plugged in two shots, which he didn't mind, but bolted away. Saw another a mile away. Walked up to eighty yards, put a shot behind his shoulders, didn't mind a bit, and went off. No more rhino with these bullets; heard all three hit.

This morning I saw ten rhino. Roddy got another shot at cow with calf—no good. Got small antelope. We got near nothing else. Villiers came out afternoon. Lovely air, nice breeze, like Switzerland.

30th Jan., Monday.—Three in a tent rather tight. Out at 6. Tried a drive; failure. Villiers got long shot at hartebeest. He and I came back disgusted at 11. Had lunch and went to sleep. At 2 saw two rhino three miles off. Shortly after Roddy returned, he had shot both and wounded them. Gave it up and returned to Machakos at 4, arriving 6.30. Quite impossible to stalk anything but rhino: ought to have had some of them with proper bullets. Roddy also wounded lion. Heard that Gerry shot lioness two days from here.

31st Jan., Tuesday.—Stayed at station. Went out with Roddy for an hour, afternoon, to get partridges. Having only shotguns saw a buck and a leopard; of course got neither.

1st Feb., Wednesday.—Went out about 9 with Roddy to camp at Lanyoro, nine miles out. Afternoon tried to get at beasts, without success. Roddy got small antelope. Afterwards he saw some lions go into a bush; went at them; I, like an ass, with only two solid bullets. They faced us about ten yards. He fired, result unknown, confused flash of four lions, all disappearing into ravine; one lioness appeared far side, about eighty yards. I got her. Afterwards I saw one crouching in grass, facing him, fired and killed her. Doubtful whether wounded one of his. About six miles home in dark. Skinning took long time with blunt knives. On our way out met Wakamba porters returning from Kikuyu.

2nd Feb., Thursday.—Very tired; out latish, about 9. Went back to lion place, found nothing. Home to lunch about 3—twelve miles. Afternoon, went out; I got long shot at hartebeest; broke hind leg—long chase; he was caught by the leg by a porter running out from camp. We both ate too much as usual. Did about twenty-five miles walking to-day, very fit. Morning, met porters returning from Kikuyu, opened letter, we to start to-morrow.

3rd Feb., Friday.—Packed things, started at 9. Wasted hours over attempting drive with Wakamba and Machakos porters, who understood not one word of what they were to do. Swarms of game; of course didn't get a shot. Then I viewed three rhino. Having Berkeley's 8-bore we stalked two, put in four bullets at fifty yards, and both went away smiling. Another cow and calf were 200 yards away all the time. Another long stalk; I put a bullet under ear, seventy yards—off she went three miles. Another stood up 300 yards away; walked straight at him. Roddy shot at 100 yards, same thing; sickening. On way to new camp Roddy killed hartebeest; had only his boy, Wakamba having gone, also Machakos men. Cut off head and haunch, and started, I carrying two 8-bores and ·450, boy the meat. Boy is played out in a mile, darkness coming on. When dark and no signs of camp I fired 8-bore, nearly stunned, but answered by shot not far. Soon met four soldiers, sent them back for Roddy and boy, whom they never found, and reached camp beyond Lanyoro Point about 8.

4th Feb., Saturday.—Started nominal 6, really 7.15. Tried shooting on the way, but no good. Villiers had many shots at about half a mile, and at last got a Thomson at 250 yards. Swarms of game, but too long a march to shoot much. About twenty miles, I think, to edge of Kikuyu forest, near nice running stream. Party of soldiers from Kikuyu to meet us. We are a day later than expected. Two lions seen to-day, also buffalo and wildebeest.

5th Feb., Sunday.—Start 7; cold drizzle and mist. Great precautions taken going through forest belt, but saw nobody. Caravan for once closed right up, partly from funk of natives, partly because of 100 porters sent from fort last night to help our needy lot. Arrived about 11.45; strongish fort, and need be, apparently. Natives have been murdering a bit, but peace now, they think. Seem treacherous lot. We are not to go on to-morrow, as Moffat has been taken worse. Glad of a day here; very cold brick huts, kitchen garden, best of food, and Purkiss providing all sorts of needed things.

6th Feb., Monday.—Wind all night; my tent pole broken again; new one supplied by Purkiss. Nelson's grave here. 117 donkeys started off mid-day to next camp. Moffat very bad. I am staying here to bring him on if he can travel in four days. Cast ·577 bullets; tried a few shots. Lots of repairs being done in fort.

7th Feb., Tuesday.—Cold; rats running over my bed, fleas in it. Caravan started 2.30, leaving me twenty-five porters and twenty-five soldiers. Moffat slightly better. Moved into room in fort, which seems great comfort. Purkiss says he has a fire every day in the year; lat. 1° 35'!!

Delighted to have the opportunity of leaving behind my miserable yellow Abdullah. He has been sick for the last fortnight. Am taking on the blackest boy I can find, with the pretty name of Sali Boko, or Sally, for short.

8th Feb., Wednesday.—Much more comfortable in fort. My tent has been enlarged, the bath-room part. Rigged camera and took six photos to send back, to see if they will do. Moffat up and eating a little. We may perhaps get away Saturday. Hyænas kick up an awful row all night here, walking all round fort. Caravan left us no headman, no guide or any one who knows road, no interpreter, and no port wine for Moffat, no tarpaulin, spades, axes, filter, or rug for pony.

9th Feb., Thursday.—Moffat better, talk of getting away to-morrow; will see. Took photos of station askaris and natives, and made a lot of things with skins. Mail arrived from coast. One man killed by Masai near Nzoi, and two parcels, for Villiers and Rhodes, stolen.

Orders received here to make roads both ways; looks like decision to keep Uganda. Nearly murdered by fleas last night; captured six in morning, but missed about ten badly.

10th Feb., Friday.—Moffat a little better, but I think not strong enough to start, though very anxious to. Bowled over ten fleas in my bed, and boy afterwards bagged eleven, so there seems a fair stock. Am nearly eaten up. Purkiss sent off a special mail to coast, fearing that Martin might exaggerate state of things here. Busy all day with various repairs. Decided to start early to-morrow, Purkiss sending on our loads eighteen miles. One man died.

11th Feb., Saturday.—Off at 8, caught P.'s porters, also a runaway, about five miles. Our men, without loads, awful lot of weedy cripples. Very long march, twenty-two miles. Purkiss said fifteen, or would not have tried it. Burnt, barren plains, traces of elephants, rhinos, etc. Down a precipice to Keedong Valley. Camp about three miles farther. Moffat not so done as I expected. Camp at 6.15; just getting dark. Tents up, mine at least, too late to do anything but eat in a hurry, and to bed, filthy, dirty. Blowing a regular hurricane.

12th Feb., Sunday.—Tents nearly blown away. One sheep taken by hyæna. Off 6.30. Porters not so bad as I feared, but want the needle a bit. One man died. Dusty, dry, barren valley, zigzag roundabout road, to the upper camp, where lunch about 11.30. On at 1, filled up with water. Met Leith's caravan returning (without him) with letters from our people. They seem to be two marches ahead. Went on till end of firewood, about 4.15, and camped. Shall get no water till mid-day to-morrow, and am very thirsty. Moffat rather done, and no wonder, about fourteen miles.

13th Feb., Monday.—6.30; marched over dry plains down to Naivasha. Met a party of Masai on war-path, going to touch up the Wa-Kikuyu. Afterwards met several other parties, very friendly. Fine, strong-looking men; got to a camp about 2.15, both rather done and dirty. Went out about 4 and got a duck. Swarms of wild-fowl, but didn't get very near them. Mosquitoes awful, and my curtains have gone on.

14th Feb., Tuesday.—No sleep, bad headache, bitten to pieces. Started at 6.30. Nobody knows the road, but somehow we fetched up at Gilgil river about 11.30. Moffat got a *Grantii*. Saw good many antelope, and several parties of Masai, one lot on war-path, with jingling knee bracelets, very effective as they stepped together. All asked for presents, but didn't much mind not getting them. Found fires still burning in camp.

Went out about 3, Moffat three florican, I one florican, one guinea-fowl, and one goose on the way. Had long shots at wild antelope. Sun to-day wonderfully hot.

15th Feb., Wednesday.—Still trying to catch them. Luncheon at Karia Ndouss. Their fires still burning. Afternoon through seven miles of burning bush. Country seems alight all round; must have bothered them rather. Walked on alone to camp at Mbaruk. Boy and I both saw tents of large caravan when about 500 yards away, and hurried on, to find nothing. Must have been effect of smoke, and rather a blow. Along Lake Elmenteita to-day, bitter water and barren shores. Sun very hot on these dry plains. Moffat and I both knocked over at noon.

Got a marabout stork with rifle at 200 yards. Shall probably be burnt out to-night; fire all round.

16th Feb., Thursday.—Got off about 6.30, but nobody knew the road, and we were delayed by starting on wrong one. Shot Moffat's donkey as he wouldn't move. Moffat shot a good deal on the way, and got two *Thomsonii*. Hot march to Nakuru. Salt lake; arrived 12. Went out at 3, and got one *Thomsonii*, and Moffat two. Saw *Grantii* and zebra; also the caravan, camped ten miles away. Ought to catch them by twenty-mile march to-morrow. Saw nobody to-day; deserted country; bush still burning in front and behind.

17th Feb., Friday.—Started 6.30. Went to their camp; off the road and off direction, lost two hours finding it. Lunched there. Found an old man nearly dead; brought him on, on moke. Great difficulty in finding road; rather anxious about it, as we were clean off my map. When found, started off ahead, and walked in in three hours thirty-five minutes, fifteen miles at least. Sent thirty men back to help, brought them in after dark. Long day. We did twenty-three miles at least. Found Roddy with bad leg.

18th Feb., Saturday.—Got up too early—at 3; such a row was going on. Very seedy and sick. About fourteen miles to Equator camp; through pleasant bits of dark forest, icy cold streams. Lay down all afternoon, and went to bed at 6. Lucky I didn't knock up two days earlier, also lucky we caught them up yesterday. Should never have found road. Lots of elephant tracks, not very new.

19th Feb., Sunday.—Woke up at night by cold, put on clothes and went to bed again. Don't think much of Equator for warmth. Still rather weak, so rode. Gerry and Villiers killed five zebra on march. Roddy still with bad leg, in a hammock. Went about twelve miles to camp at Big Ravine; patches of forest and open land, very up and down.

Two sick men died, one of them the old man we brought on two days ago. Did not feel like shooting, and I suppose it's nearly the last chance. This cold at nights is the devil. Got no more clothes, and it's as hot as fury from 9 to 3.

20th Feb., Monday.—Started 7. Crossed ravine and camped other side, about 300 yards. Bush all that side, so no good trying to shoot. Gerry stayed on other side and got three hartebeest.

21st Feb., Tuesday.—Very cold night; 42° inside tents, so probably 32° outside. Came on behind. Very trying march, all up and down mountain, through dense forest, dark and cool. In parts very tall cedars, quite 200 feet. We are 8200 feet up, which accounts for cold and hot sun. Many men ill from cold; two died.

22nd Feb., Wednesday.—Met real hoar frost at bottom of hill we camped on. Within an hour the heat must have been at least 75°, time 7.30 A.M. Very hilly march, about ten miles, bare downs, just like English ones, except for roughness of grass and ground. Many English wild-flowers and plants and grasses. Height to-day about 8700 feet. Saw a few hartebeest at a distance.

Saw nettles, thistles, blue scabious, mignonette, forget-me-nots, kind of dandelion, and many others whose names I don't know.

23rd Feb., Thursday. — About eleven miles; open, hilly country; a few hartebeest. Frank got two. Began to rain 8 P.M.

24th Feb., Friday. — Rain soon after starting, down hill gently about seven miles, then six more on plain. No firewood except along river. Went out with G. and Berkeley; five partridges. Went after rhino, which walked up to eight yards of me, then fled—result, two hits, but didn't get him. Another man died.

25th Feb., Saturday.—Beautiful morning; marched about twelve miles. Moffat got a waterbuck; while his boy left it for five minutes it was bagged entirely by natives. We have seen none about. They would certainly have cut his head off if he had been there. One man died.

26th Feb., Sunday.—About eleven miles over plain. A rhino ran straight at head of caravan, and received about fourteen shots, which eventually proved fatal. Wonderful scene of worrying the meat. Met a party of Wanderobbo near camp, going on to a fight with some chief three days' march off; rather like Masai, but not so gaudy. Shook hands, every one, first picking grass and pressing it into palm of your hand. Tried to get hartebeest, but only one hit. G. and F. R. each got one.

27th Feb., Monday.—About thirteen or fourteen miles—very hot indeed. The Guaso Masai stream has become a formidable river. Got to camp about 12, and did nothing. Gerry got a small antelope, but we are out of game country. One man died.

28th Feb., Tuesday.—Across the Kabras mountains and river; also other streams, about fourteen miles. Not a sign of animal life. A few natives came into camp. Very hot. Box containing all our lime juice dropped and smashed. Several other loads dropped into river by these weeds of porters.

1st March, Wednesday.—Horrible day. Behind with Moffat. Was six hours before sick and donkeys had got six miles. One sick man nearly dead when we came across him; quite dead about half an hour after. Scratched ground and covered him with leaves. Lots of muddy, swampy gullies. Passed through great number of native villages, all surrounded by well-made mud walls, loopholed, and ditch. Ugly people, next to no clothes: seem good farmers, but crops looking dried up. Did not get in till 3, fifteen miles, rather beat. Donkeys, etc., in at 8—fifteen hours.

2nd March, Thursday.—Through ugly, cultivated country to Mumia's, fourteen miles. Mumia brought goat, etc. Smart-looking person. Village not great at supplies. Williams is waiting in Uganda for us.

3rd March, Friday.—Stayed here for a day's rest. Tried to catch fish in river, but didn't. Got some honey, bananas, and milk, very little else to be got. Took a few photos to send home, cleaned guns and put them away. No hippos within miles of here, they say. Mumia himself came down prepared to go after them with me: nice-looking man, rather dressy.

4th March, Saturday.—Started 6. Great business crossing the Nzoia. Gerry out of his depth; I mostly undressed, well over waist, took over an hour; lost my burning glass and tinder, which is a great nuisance. We left all the donkeys and thirty-five sick behind, also letters, etc., to go down with Leith. Orders for stores for six months also went. Hot march of thirteen miles through ugly country. Villages, but no cultivation. So much for the promised land of plenty.

5th March, Sunday.—Past Mtindi's, curious Druidical-looking stones, about one mile from camp. Marched about fifteen miles through ugly hot country and swamps; very well-made fish-pots and dam on one stream. Quails in baskets hanging on poles. Thunderstorm after luncheon. Distance to Wakoli's discovered to be sixteen miles more than we were first told. There seems to be next to no attempt at cultivation, though any amount of villages. People all look half-starved, many villages deserted.

6th March, Monday.—Started at 5 A.M. Country still bare and villages deserted. At 11 came among cultivated ground and flourishing villages, and a much improved tribe—Wasoga or Kavirondo. Fine, tall, well-made men. Camp, about 1.30, a mile from head of Sio Bay of Victoria Nyanza. Beastly water from swamp; crowds of natives, and much trade, milk, eggs, etc. Only pink beads here. The people wear absolutely nothing. Distance about sixteen miles.

7th March, Tuesday.—About eleven miles, through better country; wonderful extent of banana plantations for miles. Camped near one of Mramba's villages. Very nice-mannered youth. Brought, besides goats and hens, about half a ton of steamed bananas; good, like mashed potatoes, and steaming hot, and about fourteen gallons of fresh pombe; better than the water, but mawkish; fermented. It is rather bitter, and not very nasty. Did some trade, and got long knob-kerries and many bananas for a few cartridge cases.

8th March, Wednesday.—About fifteen miles to Wakoli's, or now Mtanda's village. Banana groves most of the way; remainder very pretty mountain pass. Small station of Company. A German in charge; quite a boy, but seems smart. Mtanda in Uganda, but prime minister and chiefs came in state; also another party, Mtanda's mother, sister, etc. Former an ugly old hag, who asked for baccy. Gave presents, brass wire and handkerchiefs. They brought four goats. Bananas still our main food and drink; wonder how long before they sicken us. Heavy thunderstorm in afternoon.

9th March, Thursday.—Fire last night while at dinner. Grass hut inside enclosure blazing; marvellous that whole place not burnt down; huts almost touching. Pulled grass and thatch off nearest, and it soon burnt itself out. March about ten miles. Still bananas. People here shy and wouldn't bring food for some time. Thunderstorms afternoon and evening. Camp in middle of banana grove.

10th *March, Friday.*—Rain and thunder all night; steamy morning. Moffat's boy bolted in night with two rifles—luckily not his express. Very hot and damp walking; still bananas. Guides took us all wrong, and we went about fifteen miles instead of ten. Chief came into camp; not very enthusiastic; apparently had lately been attacked.

11th *March, Saturday.*—Wandered about winding paths; nobody seems to know the way. Camped about 1; twelve or thirteen miles. Within sight of Speke Gulf; nice pool of water. Straight road wanted badly. Went out and got guinea-fowl. Shot others, but bush too thick to pick them up.

12th *March, Sunday.*—About thirteen miles to the Nile. Began crossing about 1, finished about 7. Took photos while they were crossing, and walked about half a mile down to see Ripon Falls. Lovely scenery. Afternoon went with Gerry in canoe. Got three king cranes, two guinea-fowl, one hippopotamus. Swarms of hippo. We killed probably one other; shall see in morning. Cranes excellent eating; the best bird I have eaten in Africa.

Arrived in Uganda on G.'s birthday. Nice-looking, intelligent people, very civil.

13th *March, Monday.*—Stayed with G. and went to Ripon Falls with Sudi and Hutchisson to fish. Got none; tried spinning and bottom fishing. Swarms of big fish jumping the Falls like salmon. Tried cupful of euphorbia juice, but too deep. Had lunch, and came on about ten miles to camp, arriving 5.30. Camp in village surrounded by bananas. People most hospitable and civil. Country looks very rich for dry season.

14th *March, Tuesday.*—Went on alone with ten men up to Kampala, forty-six miles, Thursday, to get ready for their arrival. Camped where Foaker told me. He said nineteen miles, but I think fifteen or sixteen. Very civilised country, wide roads, bridges, tidy villages, and very nice-mannered people. Passed missionary Baskerville building new station. Chief here, Nansambo, very civil, but gave me a lot of his company. Wanted pens, can read and write; mosquitoes bad

z

—bore having no cook, shall do without dinner, except bananas and biscuits.

15th *March, Wednesday.*—Tremendous road-making going on. Gangs of young and old women, separated mostly. Got a wetting in morning; after, just like vapour bath or greenhouse. Bits of forests very steamy, also the elephant grass. Had a lot of talk with many chiefs, all of them rippers. Met Mwanga's Katikiro going in state to meet caravan. Did about twenty-one miles, and got to horrid place near Salu Salu's; sure it can't be the right place. Mosquitoes deadly and as big as partridges. Killed to-day the only two snakes I have seen in Africa: one, a pretty green one, two feet long, evidently poisonous, the other black, doubtful, but wouldn't trust him.

16th *March, Thursday.*—Got to Kampala about 9.30. Tidy town, great broad streets. Found only Smith and Wilson, others away, not known where or for how long. Looked out camping grounds, etc., and went to give Bishop his letters. Comfortable house his. Afterwards went to see Katikiro. Fine-looking youngish man, with excellent two-storied house. It is like getting back to civilisation, but I am told this is only first impression. Squared headman with three hands cloth. Turned up in old 52nd tunic.

They are wonderfully neat builders, these Ugandese. All their fences, and the linings of the better houses, are made of elephant grass canes (they are not really canes, but look like it) bound and woven together beautifully neatly with bark. It seems hard to believe that some of these buildings are run up without a single nail, and with no tool of any sort except a rough, native-made hatchet; the English church, for instance, that would hold about 3000 people.

17th *March, Friday.*—Went out with Bishop to meet caravan. Awful howling, shouting crowd, full of excitement. They were all looking clean and shaved. In course of the day various visitors, head Mohammedan, Bishop and missionaries, French priests, Katikiros, etc. Made an oven for bread. Heavy rain, dinner-time, lasting two hours. Bad camp for us; cramped, and full of fleas.

18th *March, Saturday.*—Got ready to go and see king at 9. The military gents in curious masquerading dresses, some red serges, breeches mostly brownish. Hats, terai, and various coloured helmets, gaiters, putties, field boots and button boots. Rained very hard, and visit put off. Went on raining till nearly 4. Macdonald came in, looking very well, and Wolf, very ill. There are only two months' stores here, and German route blocked. What will happen goodness only knows. One soldier died.

19th March, Sunday.—Dined with Pilkington of the Mission last night; gorgeous repast. Wish we could get any fresh food. Wet morning, tent beastly and smelling, won't be long before fever appears, everything damp. Fine afternoon. All went to church; English service; sermon by Bishop on standing fast to principles—never mind being called bigoted or narrow-minded, and don't give and take to secure peace or better results. Probably good religion, but policy doubtful. Fine church, room for 2000 people. One young elephant brought into fort by the Kangan for Williams.

20th March, Monday.—Masquerade again at 9 to visit king. Nubian army in front, Zanzibar army behind. Mwanga very cheerful; weak-looking man; when he says anything funny gives his hand to the nearest toady to be clasped.

King returned visit 4 P.M., but no state, and no masquerade for us. Heavy storm, afternoon, everything wetted again. Got into new mess shed, thank goodness.

21st March, Tuesday.—Wet all morning; copied maps, etc. Afternoon went to tea with Pilkington, and after to see Mtesa's tomb. Visit from several parties of king's wives, touting for presents. Discovered that my last six photos were taken *without* plates—great pity. The masquerade group would have been valuable.

22nd March, Wednesday.—Not so much rain; messed about in fort all day. Baby elephant said to be dying; given a pill size of walnut by Moffat, which ought to do him. Williams came in late.

23rd March, Thursday.—Carpenter's work all day, without proper tools. Rain all night. Smith packing his ivory—about £1400 worth. Williams has some good heads, from Buddu, etc. Roddy and I are to go to Toru in four days. Elephant dead and skinned.

24th March, Friday.—Studied Maxim guns, and fired them at target, to the admiration of large crowd. Bought ·450 express from Smith £45, only fifty solid cartridges. Filed fore-sight of ·577, and tried three shots; not quite right.

No rain to-day, for a wonder. Tried to sell bay pony; asked eight frasilas, offered five. think we shall deal at seven.

25th March, Saturday.—Headache from sun yesterday: did nothing all morning. Afternoon, short walk with Villiers; no more heard from chief about pony. News from Grant that he will be at last Toru Fort before end of month, so we shall probably stay here till his report is in. No rain.

26th March, Sunday.—No rain again. Six of them went to the Lake to look at site for proposed new station; I didn't go, but spent very lazy day, and slept mostly.

27th March, Monday.—Walked to Lake, eight miles, with Villiers. Saw nothing there. G. went to see king about making roads to Toru. He says the Roman Catholics and Mohammedans won't do their share. He certainly can't make them. Chief came to say he won't buy our bay pony; wants the gray, but Frank has taken him for £130; must be mad.

28th March, Tuesday.—Great mess in fort, taking over, etc. They have a lot of useless things, and antiquated ammunition. We expect to be off day after to-morrow or Friday. Gedge sat in my tent an hour. Roddy all over the place. One man died.

29th March, Wednesday.—Fearful fuss all day, as if a huge expedition was starting for an unknown country. We start to-morrow with about 130 loads, about one-third utterly useless. Smith starts for coast following day. Took on Nubian boy of Williams at Rs. 20 a month. Doubt if he's worth it; looks a fool, but speaks a little Swahili.

30th March, Thursday.—Start nominally 8.30, really 11. Never seen such fuss or such a mess. Sat down to look on. After start, guides sent by Kangan apparently went home. Came on with none. Long swamp half-way, nearly 400 yards long. Tried to carry Roddy, but took a fall over a root, up to waist. Pouring rain, wet to bone. Camp after three hours in nasty shamba. Mosquitoes awful. About seven miles.

31st March, Friday.—No sleep at all for mosquitoes, swarming inside curtains. A poorish performance to-day, very bad road, nearly grown over; one very bad swamp, up to chest, and 400 yards. Tried Berthon boat, but not enough water. Several other swamps, steep hills, and forest. Marched six hours, about fourteen miles. Men very late and tired; two deserted to-day, probably many more to follow. Difficulty about food, but got enough. Bed broken, sleeping on wet floor. Camp believed to be Kaima.

1st April, Saturday.—Roddy had drum beaten and woke everybody at 11.15 P.M. Pouring wet; bed wet and mosquitoes awful. Cheerful life. Started in rain rather late, went about ten miles to Katumbala's village. Several nasty swamps. Believe we are on wrong road, but impossible to find out from these people. Curious that road from Kampala to nearest fort should be practically unknown after several years of occupation, but so it is.

2nd April, Sunday.—Nice night, and nice, fine day, for a wonder. Three or four swamps. Walked about $2\frac{1}{2}$ hours and stopped at Kibibi, where we purpose to put small station. Superior-looking Mohammedan chief; name difficult to find out as they told us at least four; had useful afternoon cleaning guns, all smothered in rust—some spoilt, I'm afraid.

3rd April, Monday.—The country is looking better, not so many swamps and elephant grass, and better air; looks like game, but saw no tracks. Very little inhabited. Passed Kitunzi and came on to Bujigu; shambas nearly deserted, and not much food. Effects of late war. The patches of forest in the hollows very thick, and path nearly grown over. Lots of glittering stuff on paths over hills, looks like mica, but was transparent like talc. Got a king crane on getting into camp about 1. Two heavy storms and wettings. About fifteen miles; a lake about four miles to north.

4th April, Tuesday.—About $12\frac{1}{2}$ miles to shambas, believed to be Kisiba. Very bad papyrus swamp, stinking like fun. Passed two shambas or small villages, Mugema (?) $1\frac{1}{2}$ hours, and Mosika (?) three hours. Country more open, no game. Camp about two miles south of west end of lake. Went out to try to get birds, but saw none. Party of Swahilis camped here, the late garrison of Salt Lake Fort, just relieved by Soudanese, I suppose.

5th April, Wednesday.—Caravan went on; we went shooting. Saw a lot of zebra and some hartebeest. I got two zebra. Left two Nubians with the meat and went on to camp—Matongo; arrived 3.30, after three hours' hard walking, too late to send back for meat and Nubians left. Caravan only did 3¾ hours; can't make it out. Camp in banana grove; water beastly; chief not very willing; two more porters deserted. Carry three days' food from here.

6th April, Thursday.—Roddy got one zebra soon after starting. After three hours saw herd of elephants. Foaker and I both counted them twice, and made them well over 250; thought it too far from camp to go after them, with no spare men. Soon after saw two near road; went after them, into patch of bush, and found myself between two lots of about 20 each. One lot moved towards main lot. As the second was following I got a shot at one, about 100 yards, hit, I think, somewhere near temple, but did not fall, and went in among another large herd in the open. They formed a sort of square, but did not move away. Had only three cartridges, so turned away. Urged by Shukri [1] to go after single one, gone opposite way into bush; when within eighty yards he came smack at us, and we ran like the devil different ways; luckily he gave it up. Nice park country, no swamps. Fourteen miles.

7th April, Friday.—Same country, very foggy and hot; saw a few hartebeest. Long and tiring march, about sixteen miles. Camp about 1.30; loads an hour behind. Roddy had shot at hartebeest, didn't get him. I went out for an hour and got two partridges, only could find one. Swarms of them, but can't get them to get up; more like French partridges than any I have seen yet. Elephants seem to have flattened out every bit of wood we have passed through, trees all torn up. Bimbashi Shukri got two hartebeest. One man deserted. Mosquitoes, if possible, more awful than yesterday.

8th April, Saturday.—About fifteen miles. Two bad swamps and one other. Camp about 2. Lots of banana plantations, but only lately taken into cultivation again, so no bananas. Plenty

---

[1] Bimbashi Shukri Effendi was the chief officer of the Soudanese after Selim Bey. He was subsequently killed in a skirmish with some of Kabarega's people.

of potatoes. Went out for an hour and got two king cranes and one pigeon. Going on early to-morrow to the fort. Caravan to do it in twice.

9th April, Sunday.—Went twelve miles to deserted shamba, with twenty porters. Stopped there for lunch, where rest of caravan overtook us. Came on again, 6½ miles to Fort de Winton. Wild country, but very picturesque. Great masses of rock, granite; swamps at bottom, but not deep, and clear-running streams, sources of river Katonga. Has been a good deal of cultivation apparently, potatoes and bananas, but deserted. Fort a square mud bank and ditch, full of Soudanese huts mixed up anyhow, flying Turkish flag! Grant living 100 yards outside, surrounded by grass huts of Soudanese, Swahilis, and slaves. Very piggish. The garrison paraded and made a hideous noise with four bugles in different keys. After, reception of about six native officers, queer-looking old savages.

10th April, Monday.—Had up the garrison and read Selim Bey's letter, also manifest of Roddy's. Enlisted about sixty, rejected about fifteen. Picked out worst half to go to Kampala, with the last ones, slaves and women, etc. Not so many as we expected. Afternoon took over a lot of rusty guns of all sorts, and ammunition. The fort is a smelly place, and would do nicely for an outbreak of small-pox. Chose site for a hut for us, and hope to get it begun to-morrow, if not too rocky. Caravan came in about 10. Got three presents of bread from Nubians; curious-looking, like leather, but one sort not bad, rather like sour crumpet. Native chiefs came in, and apparently willing to cultivate and sell grain, on having things explained. Potatoes seem plenty, grain very scarce.

11th April, Tuesday.—Taking over things, Grant having a stiff time of it. Very heavy storm mid-day, tents flooded. Nothing done towards building house by 100 porters except collection of very small pile of crooked bits of wood.

12th April, Wednesday.—Roddy and Grant left for No. 3 Fort about 7.30, after a good deal of preparation. Tried without success to get ground cleared for house, and got about ten square yards done. Had a drill of Nubian savages, apparently their first, but they did very nicely. Went out with Foaker in afternoon after guinea-fowl; saw none, but got one king crane.

Everybody, without exception, drunk to-night, from headman to tent-boy. Bimbashi Shukri is being married, which may account for some free liquor. Begged forty rounds of ammunition on the ground of its being the invariable custom. They are being rapidly expended, probably without removing the bullets.

13th April, Thursday.—Uneventful day; no rain: drilled Nubians, and learnt their Arabic words of command. Building of house progressing. Got two poles up. Afternoon despatch from Roddy altering all previous arrangements. All the inhabitants of this place to go in, instead of half, on Saturday. This place getting horribly filthy, and stench awful.

14th April, Friday.—Roddy arrived 3 P.M., about ninety useless people and slaves from No. 3. Another muster of the population, for no particular purpose, except to see if slaves would engage as porters. About twenty out of a hundred responded.

One of our cows killed by lion last night; didn't know there were any.

15th April, Saturday.—Got off a crowd of about 1000 people about 8 o'clock. Then assembled the remainder; found that at least fifty more had to go. Many deserted caravan and came back. Had a house-to-house search, found a few slaves, and some horrible sick people. Lots of food left behind. Collected nearly fifty bushels of wimbe. Got rid of my Nubian idiot of a boy, the worst bargain I ever had; wants a whole load carried for him; scored off him by giving him 8-bore and ·577 to carry.

16th April, Sunday.—House progressing very slowly. Roddy and Grant off again to-morrow to forts. I shall be left with only fifteen porters and twenty-five Nubian soldiers. Unyoro chiefs came in for a talk. Reported large force of Kabarega's people two days from here, said to be going to attack us. Another later account makes us doubt this. They promised to give us all information about this, also about contraband caravan returning with ivory from K.'s country. Also promised to form a market here. One of Foaker's porters died.

17th April, Monday.—R. and G. off at 6.30. Wanyoro very prompt about market. Sent in twenty loads of potatoes, which nobody was likely to buy with all this spare food about, so I bought it for one doti, to keep up delusion. House progressing well, at last. Had a drill of new lot of Nubians in afternoon, and tried to find guinea-fowl, but didn't. Doctored a lot of diseases. One goat died, leaves thirteen. Killed sixty-four mosquitoes on my hands and arms while at a hurried solitary dinner. Such a bag is worth recording.

18th April, Tuesday.—Mohammedan Christmas, so they say, whatever that may mean, but no work to be done. Woke last night by shots; after three or four made sure we were being attacked, and went out; found sentries firing at or near hyæna with goat; ten rounds, they loosed off. Crossed swamp and plunged about in bush with pyjamas on, got bitten to death; went in afternoon with one of the same men to find the hyæna; found his hole under big rocks, impossible to get him out, man very keen to fire down hole. Later went climbing up mountains to north-west to choose spot for look-out picket. A motherless calf died; we killed a sickly goat. Another goat died, ten left. Fifteen soldiers in from Roddy at No. 3.

19th April, Wednesday.—Drilled natives morning and afternoon. After lunch, alarm of leopard having carried off goat close by. Went after him with two Nubians, who tracked him wonderfully well, to the same den I visited yesterday; doubts as to hyæna, this certainly leopard; must do something to the place, as it's getting serious. A lot of rain to-day. Natives brought present of bananas and four loads of potatoes to sell; gave sixty shells. Killed *one* mosquito at dinner last night, two fires each side of table. Think I'm going to have fever at last.

20th April, Thursday.—Wrong about fever, but feel uncomfortable, everything damp and more than filthy. Got in two more loads of potatoes for twenty shells. Also present of bananas and large jar of pombe, which gave to porters. Going to No. 3 to-morrow with three Nubians and ten porters, leaving Shukri boss here. Went round cultivation with old Yuzbashi. If looked after, quite enough to keep population. Letters from Roddy.

21st April, Friday.—Two of our goats and five inside fort killed by leopard in night, leaves us eight. Shall not kill another, as I can't eat one before meat rots. Started about 7, got ill with violent pains in head half-way, which partly passed off in an hour. Had to stop and lie down. Big swamp roughly bridged over by natives and Nubians, also one smaller one; arrived about 3. More prosperous-looking place, but a regular labyrinth inside. Good hut to live in, so tent not needed. Fine wild country; remains of many shambas; natives living in caves, not funking Nubians quite so much.

22nd April, Saturday.—Sent back four porters, gave out seeds for planting. Had two drills of these stupid people, who are assembled with some difficulty. I like this little beehive of a house, and shall improve it, as somebody will live here off and on. Went out with Nubian to try for guinea-fowl. He walked me to death nearly. Saw three, only got one shot, bird towered and fell, but couldn't pick him.

Second day without meat, but don't mind a bit, get lots of presents of vegetables, bread (excellent), and milk. Brought one cow besides. Had talk with ten or twelve Unyoro chiefs. Gave one doti to the six principal ones.

23rd April, Sunday.—Two crown cranes reported about 9.30; went out and got both, luckily, long way off; one not much hurt, and now walking about round the house. Rained hard all afternoon. Sorted a bagful of seeds we brought from Kampala. All very mouldy, and none labelled except some green peas. Planted some of them, and a few of what may possibly turn out to be onions. Am provided with the best of food by the Yugbashis. Vegetable diet not unpleasant. Made puddings, at least the useful Tom did, of wimbe and mehinde. Latter very good.

The people from Kampala, from No. 2 Fort, ought to have arrived to-day, but didn't. Got seven loads potatoes for them from Wanyoro chiefs.

24th April, Monday.—Still no people from No. 2. Busy with these savage soldiers all the morning. Rain began at twelve, and went on till five, so nothing much done. Askari from Roddy arrived afternoon, no letter or message, but says No. 2 people hadn't started yesterday, and were not expecting to start. Roddy having gone through in a hurry on hearing report that Wanyamwesi had kidnapped six of Salt Lake garrison. Shall wait another day for news, and then go back to No. 4 for a day or two.

25th April, Tuesday.—No people arrived, spent day much as

before. Planted garden seeds. Letters from Kampala. They start on 25th. I am expected by 15th. Doubtful at this rate. Going to No. 4 to-morrow.

26th April, Wednesday.—Started 7, arrived 1.30. Got guinea-fowl and a sort of curlew on the way. During the night more Wangamwesi have passed through to Kabarega's country. Wish we could catch them. Got rather bad again on the road; violent headache. Can't make it out. Went to sleep on arriving, and lay down all afternoon. House not much forwarder—two rooms done, however; very rough work.

Sending three Nubians off with the Kibibi mail men to-morrow; we are to have men there on 1st and 15th of each month. Letters for Roddy left early this morning.

27th April, Thursday.—Woke up at midnight by letter from Roddy, rather complicated one, to say refuse from Nos. 11 and 2 arrive at 3, 26th and 27th, total 700! also details of about six different moves of soldiers. Got off Kampala letters early. Bimbaka of 4 to be in charge, and Yuzbasha of 3 to go—rather short notice. Rushed over to 3 again. Awful afternoon with Yuzbasha's retinue, all wanting to stay for various reasons. Up to dark none of the leaders had come in, and only fifty people. Can't leave here to-morrow.

28th April, Friday.—People coming in; seen all the leaders. Letters from Roddy, from Kampala, arrived by native, who apparently has taken his time. Have decided to go on to Kampala with this mob. Sent letter to Salt Lake.

Evening.—Letters from Kampala, dated 22nd, saying, Don't bring this crowd in—nice mess. Sent on to Salt Lake. This will stop me here another fortnight, looking after this wild mob. Shall go back to No. 4 to-morrow with half the lot, and camp them there.

29th April, Saturday. — An awful day. Started at 7, after talk with natives, Yuzbasha and chief men from No. 1. The Nubians from No. 2, 220, also started. It rained very heavy all the way, the path at tops of hills four inches deep and a torrent elsewhere. Got chilled to the bone, though walking fast ahead. Found two children and a girl, all very nearly dead, deserted by some brutes of Nubian soldiers I sent on yesterday. Camped these wretched people about half a mile from the fort, in long wet grass. Went to bed on arriving, under four blankets, but could not get warm. New house leaking pleasantly, and very damp, muddy floors. Mail men from Kampala off to-morrow early.

30th April, Sunday.—Am very seedy, pains in head, but hardly any fever. Also am most uncomfortable in the new mansion; though unfurnished, it already swarms with rats and mice. Gave the owners of the two children forty each, and took children away—would have given them a hundred if I had known they stood it so well. Am quite wretched, and can only sit down and do nothing except record my woes; worse to-night, rather.

This marks the beginning of the serious attack of fever from which he was not to recover, and sickening thus he started on the march back to the capital. A short entry in the Diary on 7th May runs as follows:

Thank goodness my Shakespeare returned; no more setting myself impossible algebra sums.

And there is a singular pathos in the last two entries, somewhat wearily and weakly pencilled:

Kibibi, 17th May.—Found Villiers who had come out in about two days to meet me—rather upset me. Brand, eggs, champagne.

18th May.—Came a long way; hard on my six (carriers) to Kaima, seventeen miles. All drowsy, painless, and almost motionless.

Ten days later the Soudanese battalion fired the farewell volley over the soldier's grave at Namirembe.

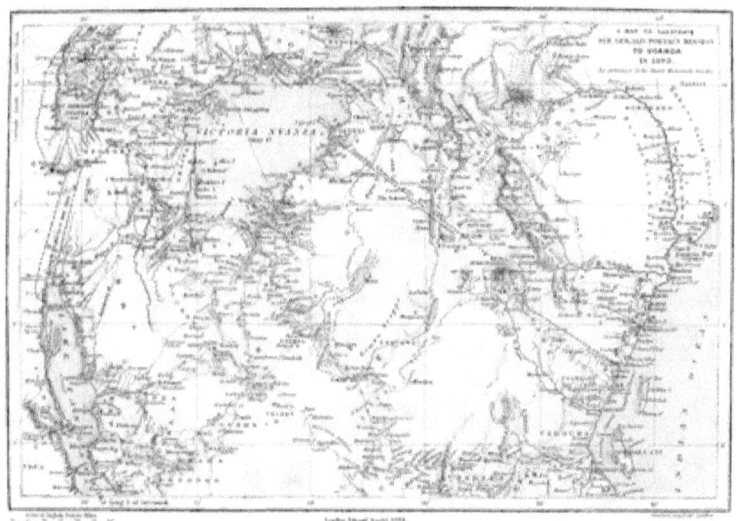

EPILOGUE

Britain has never failed to find among her sons the men that she has need of. Willingly they have always devoted their health and lives in her unsparing service, welcoming the jungle bed, the desert path, the mountain, or the wave, in the spirit of a summer holiday with the eager heart of the playing-fields of youth. And they will never fail her till she turns her back on empire, and forgets the sea. In her luxurious country palaces, as under the humbler cottage thatch, they are found, with the sea-born love of adventure in their veins, able to command and ready to obey, with the same earnest sense of duty, just, in the main, according to their lights, brave, strong, and merciful. And when that call of duty comes, there is no moment's hesitation, no ties however dear will hold them back; whether it be to tropic sands, or into the winter zone, it is enough that their country needs them, and round the world they go. Such was the brood which built our island Empire, and became of old knights-errant of the sea, founders of new nations and pillars of their own. Such there are still ready, as every year bears witness at all that Empire's outposts and round the

perilous coasts of a hundred treacherous seas. And
such were these two brothers; eagerly and with a
frolic welcome they accepted this hard service, and
leaving all that gladdens life, they gave their youth
and the promise of their years to their country.
Speech is vain, and sounding words seem out of
place, therefore we do not dwell on these things, but
we feel them none the less, and their country is proud
of them and will not forget them.

But it is not alone of those who died and now sleep
sound that we must think, and, ere we close the pages
in which we read their manly record, a tribute of silent
sympathy is justly due to those that are left behind,
who surrendered husband, son, or brother, in whose
homes are the vacant chairs and the sorrow that does
not pass. To these their country's love and honour
too, for theirs was the greater sacrifice.

What is hidden in the mists of the future we may
not tell; we dare not prophesy how soon the great
Dark Continent will enter into light and draw the
life-springs of the teeming Northern lands into her
ample heart. But slowly, after the night of centuries,
the dawn of a new sunrise is breaking into promise
over that God-forgotten world, and the message of the
pioneers is eagerly interpreted by hope.

If some day on those eastern ranges a new race
shall quicken into life, when peace and goodwill have
supplanted internecine feuds in the child-heart of the
savage, when the greed of the white has ceased to
seek for profit in the damnation of the black man's
body and soul, when the story of the slave-raider is

only a sullen page in the past, then one would wish to dream maybe that, as they reap the harvests that are still unsown, men will speak with an almost mythic reverence of the goodly man who came in the beginning from the white Queen to give the country peace, and that the first traditions of a land which has no memory yet, may gather round the grave on Namirembe hill.

THE END

Printed by R. & R. CLARK, *Edinburgh*

Catalogue of Works
of
General Literature
Published by
Mr. Edward Arnold

LONDON
EDWARD ARNOLD
37 BEDFORD STREET, STRAND, W.C.
Publisher to the India Office

Summary of Contents.

	PAGE		PAGE
Volumes of Reminiscences	5	History, Philosophy, etc.	13
Works by the Dean of Rochester	7	International Education Series	17
Works by Professor C. Lloyd Morgan	8	General Literature	19
		Oriental Literature	21
Works by Edward Brown	8	Books for the Young	23
Works by Rennell Rodd	9	Children's Favourite Series	26
Works of Fiction	9		
Gift Books	11	Periodicals	27

Mr. Edward Arnold's
LATEST PUBLICATIONS.

THE BRITISH MISSION TO UGANDA.

By

THE LATE SIR GERALD PORTAL, K.C.M.G., C.B.

Edited, with a Memoir, by RENNELL RODD. With over Forty Illustrations from photographs taken by Colonel Rhodes, engraved from sketches by E. WHYMPER, WARD R. CHESHIRE, and others.

Demy 8vo., cloth, 21s.

POLAR GLEAMS.

An Account of a Voyage in the yacht *Blencathra*.

By HELEN PEEL.

With a Preface by the Marquis of DUFFERIN and AVA, K.P., and Contributions by Captain JOSEPH WIGGINS and FREDERICK G. JACKSON.

With several Illustrations, demy 8vo., cloth, 15s.

ENGLAND IN EGYPT.

By ALFRED MILNER,

Formerly Under-Secretary for Finance in Egypt.

New and Cheaper Edition, with a prefatory chapter on Egypt in 1894 by the Author.

Large crown 8vo., with Map, cloth, 7s. 6d.

COMMON-SENSE COOKERY.

By COLONEL KENNEY HERBERT ('WYVERN'),

Author of 'Culinary Jottings,' 'Fifty Breakfasts,' etc.

A standard work on the management and economy of the kitchen, containing full directions as to the best methods of cooking and serving dinners, etc., with a great variety of recipes and menus.

Large crown 8vo., cloth, 7s. 6d.

MISTHER O'RYAN:

An Incident in the History of a Nation.

By EDWARD McNULTY.

A powerful story of Irish Life by a new Author.

Small 8vo., elegantly bound, 3s. 6d.

Uniform with 'Stephen Remarx.'

THE DRAUGHTS POCKET-MANUAL.

By J. GAVIN CUNNINGHAM,

Editor of 'Boys'" Chess and Draughts Corner,"' etc.

A complete handy guide to the rules and best methods of play for beginners and students. A large number of carefully-selected games are given; and the English, Italian, Spanish, Polish, and Turkish forms of the game of draughts are explained and illustrated.

A Companion Volume to the Chess Pocket-Manual.

Small 8vo., cloth, 2s. 6d.

Catalogue of Works
OF
General Literature

PUBLISHED BY

Mr. EDWARD ARNOLD,

37 BEDFORD STREET, STRAND, LONDON,

Publisher to the India Office.

1894.

VOLUMES OF REMINISCENCES.

SEVENTY YEARS OF IRISH LIFE. Being the Recollections of W. R. LE FANU. Third Edition, one vol., demy 8vo., 16s. With Portraits of the Author and J. SHERIDAN LE FANU.

'It will delight all readers—English and Scotch no less than Irish, Nationalists no less than Unionists, Roman Catholics no less than Orangemen.'—*Times*.

RECOLLECTIONS OF LIFE AND WORK. Being the Autobiography of LOUISA TWINING. One vol., 8vo., cloth, 15s. With Two Portraits of the Author.

'There is much to interest our readers in this autobiography. Miss Twining looks back over her work and the changes that have passed over society with the calm reflection won by long experience.'—*Guardian*.

RIDING RECOLLECTIONS AND TURF STORIES. By HENRY CUSTANCE, Thrice Winner of the Derby. Second Edition, one vol., 8vo., cloth, 15s. With a photogravure frontispiece, and eight other full-page illustrations.

*** Also a large-paper edition, 21s. net.

'An admirable sketch of turf history during a very interesting period, well and humorously written.'—*Sporting Life*.

ECHOES OF OLD COUNTY LIFE. Recollections of Sport, Society, Politics, and Farming in the Good Old Times. By J. K. FOWLER, of Aylesbury. Second Edition, with numerous illustrations, 8vo., 10s. 6d.

*** Also a large-paper edition, of 200 copies only, 21s. net.

'A very entertaining volume of reminiscences, full of good stories.'—*Truth*.

THE MEMORIES OF DEAN HOLE. With the original illustrations from sketches by LEECH and THACKERAY. New Edition, one vol., crown 8vo., 6s.

'One of the most delightful collections of reminiscences that this generation has seen.'—*Daily Chronicle*.

STUDENT AND SINGER. The Reminiscences of CHARLES SANTLEY. New Edition, crown 8vo., cloth, 6s.

'A treasury of delightful anecdote about artists, as well as of valuable pronouncements upon art.'—*Globe*.

WORKS BY CANON BELL, D.D.,

Rector of Cheltenham and Honorary Canon of Carlisle.

POEMS OLD AND NEW. Crown 8vo., cloth, 7s. 6d.

'Canon Bell's place among the poets will, we feel sure, be finally settled by this volume. In the amount of his workmanship, in the variety of it, and in the excellence of it, he makes a claim which will hardly be disputed for a place, not simply among occasional writers of poetry, but distinctly for a place among the poets.'—*The Record*.

THE NAME ABOVE EVERY NAME, and Other Sermons. Crown 8vo., cloth, 5s.

'A series of sermons which will prove a model of excellence in preaching.'—*The Rock.*

WORKS by the DEAN OF ROCHESTER

(The Very Rev. S. REYNOLDS HOLE).

A LITTLE TOUR IN IRELAND. By AN OXONIAN. With nearly forty illustrations by JOHN LEECH, including the famous steel frontispiece of the 'Claddagh.' Large imperial 16mo., handsomely bound, gilt top, 10s. 6d.

'Leech's drawings comprise some of that artist's happiest work as a book illustrator.'—*Saturday Review.*

ADDRESSES TO WORKING MEN FROM PULPIT AND PLATFORM. One vol., crown 8vo., 6s.

'The orator is a happy combination of the divine and the man of the world—thoroughly in earnest, but looking at everything with the eyes of one who knows what men are and what life is.'—*The Globe.*

THE MEMORIES OF DEAN HOLE. With the original illustrations from sketches by LEECH and THACKERAY. Twelfth Thousand, one vol., crown 8vo., 6s.

'One of the most delightful books of the season.'—*Athenæum.*

A BOOK ABOUT THE GARDEN AND THE GARDENER. With steel plate frontispiece by JOHN LEECH. Second Edition, crown 8vo., 6s.

'A delightful volume, full, not merely of information, but of humour and entertainment.'—*World.*

A BOOK ABOUT ROSES. Twentieth Thousand. Crown 8vo., cloth, 2s. 6d.

'A perfectly charming book.'—*Daily Telegraph.*

WORKS BY PROFESSOR C. LLOYD MORGAN, F.G.S.,

Principal of University College, Bristol.

ANIMAL LIFE AND INTELLIGENCE. With forty illustrations and a photo-etched frontispiece. Second Edition. Demy 8vo., cloth, 16s.

'The work will prove a boon to all who desire to gain a general knowledge of the more interesting problems of modern biology and psychology by the perusal of a single compact, luminous, and very readable volume.'—Dr. A. R. WALLACE, in *Nature*.

ANIMAL SKETCHES. With nearly forty illustrations. New Edition, one vol., crown 8vo., cloth, 3s. 6d.

'One of the most delightful books about natural history that has come under our notice since the days of Frank Buckland.'—*The Guardian*.

THE SPRINGS OF CONDUCT. Large crown 8vo., 3s. 6d.

'The material is so well arranged, and the views so lucidly expressed, that the work constitutes a most interesting epitome of modern thought upon psychology and ethics.'—Dr. G. J. ROMANES, F.R.S., in *Nature*.

WORKS BY EDWARD BROWN,

Lecturer to the County Councils of Northumberland, Cumberland, Hampshire, Kent, etc.

POULTRY KEEPING AS AN INDUSTRY FOR FARMERS AND COTTAGERS. With fourteen full-page plates by LUDLOW, and nearly fifty other illustrations. One vol., demy 4to., cloth, 6s.

'The most useful book of the kind ever published.'—*Farming World*.

PLEASURABLE POULTRY KEEPING. One vol., crown 8vo., cloth, 2s. 6d.

'This handbook is as useful as it is comprehensive.'—*Scotsman*.

INDUSTRIAL POULTRY KEEPING. Paper boards, 1s.

A small handbook chiefly intended for cottagers and allotment holders.

'The book is one of very easy reference, and ought to be in the hands of not only every farmer, but also of all cottagers throughout the country.'—*Newcastle Journal*.

WORKS BY RENNELL RODD.

POEMS IN MANY LANDS. Crown 8vo., cloth, 5s.

'It is hardly rash to say that of the younger poets none exhibit a truer love of Nature, or a more intimate knowledge of her phenomena.'—*Academy*.

FEDA, with other Poems, chiefly Lyrical. With an etching by HARPER PENNINGTON. Crown 8vo., cloth, 6s.

'The descriptive passages possess the delicacy of vision that springs only from intimate and reverent communing with nature. Few readers of Mr. Rodd's poems can fail to be touched by its purity and grace.'—*Saturday Review*.

THE UNKNOWN MADONNA, and Other Poems. With a frontispiece by W. B. RICHMOND, A.R.A. Crown 8vo., cloth, 5s.

THE VIOLET CROWN, AND SONGS OF ENGLAND. With a frontispiece by the Marchioness of Granby. Crown 8vo., cloth, 5s.

THE CUSTOMS AND LORE OF MODERN GREECE. With seven full-page illustrations by TRISTRAM ELLIS. 8vo., cloth, 8s. 6d.

WORKS OF FICTION.

THIS TROUBLESOME WORLD. A Novel. By the Authors of 'The Medicine Lady,' 'Leaves from a Doctor's Diary,' etc. In three vols., crown 8vo., 31s. 6d.

'An extremely vigorous, well-constructed, and readable story. It abounds from first to last in clever contrivance and thrilling interest.'—*Daily Telegraph*.

DAVE'S SWEETHEART. By MARY GAUNT. A Story of the Australian Goldfields. In two vols., crown 8vo., 21s.

'From the opening scene in the tin store at Deadman's Flat to the closing page we have no hesitation in predicting that not a word will be skipped, even by the most *blasé* of novel-readers.'—*Spectator*.

THE TUTOR'S SECRET. (Le Secret du Précepteur.) Translated from the French of VICTOR CHERBULIEZ. One vol., crown 8vo., cloth, 6s.

'An admirable translation of a delightful novel. Those who have not read it in French must hasten to read it in English.'—*Manchester Guardian*.

HARTMANN THE ANARCHIST; or, the Doom of the Great City. By E. DOUGLAS FAWCETT. With sixteen full-page and numerous smaller illustrations by F. T. JANE. One vol., crown 8vo., cloth, 3s. 6d.

'A very remarkable story, which is supplemented by really excellent illustrations by Mr. F. T. Jane.'—*World*.

LOVE LETTERS OF A WORLDLY WOMAN. By Mrs. W. K. CLIFFORD, Author of 'Aunt Anne,' 'Mrs. Keith's Crime,' etc. One vol., crown 8vo., cloth, 2s. 6d.

'One of the cleverest books that ever a woman wrote.'—*Queen*.

THAT FIDDLER FELLOW: A Tale of St. Andrew's. By HORACE G. HUTCHINSON, Author of 'My Wife's Politics,' 'Golf,' 'Creatures of Circumstance,' etc. Crown 8vo., cloth, 2s. 6d.

'A strange history of hypnotism and crime, which will delight any lover of the grim and terrible.'—*Guardian*.

STEPHEN REMARX. The Story of a Venture in Ethics. By the Hon. and Rev. JAMES ADDERLEY, formerly Head of the Oxford House, and Christ Church Mission, Bethnal Green. Small 8vo., paper cover, 1s.; elegantly bound, 3s. 6d.

'It is brilliant, humorous, pathetic, trenchantly severe, sound in intention, grand in idea and ideal.'—*Manchester Courier.*

GIFT BOOKS.

WINCHESTER COLLEGE, 1393—1893. Illustrated by HERBERT MARSHALL. With Contributions in Prose and Verse by OLD WYKEHAMISTS. Demy 4to., cloth, 25s. net. A few copies of the first edition, limited to 1,000 copies, are still to be had.

'A noble volume, compiled by old Wykehamists, and illustrated by Herbert Marshall in commemoration of the 500th anniversary of the foundation of the oldest public school in England. Lord Selborne discourses eloquently on Wykeham's place in history.... "Wykeham's Conception of a Public School," by Dr. Fearon is most interesting; the Dean of Winchester writes of Wykeham's work in the cathedral; old traditions and customs are treated of by T. F. Kirby, the Rev. W. P. Smith, A. K. Cook, and others, while the Bishop of Salisbury contributes "Hymnus Wiccamicus," and the Bishop of Southwell, Canon Moberley and other writers supply appropriate poetry, all the verses being inspired with that intense love of his old public school which distinguishes a true Englishman.'—*Daily Telegraph.*

GREAT PUBLIC SCHOOLS. ETON — HARROW — WINCHESTER — RUGBY — WESTMINSTER — MARLBOROUGH — CHELTENHAM — HAILEYBURY — CLIFTON — CHARTERHOUSE. With nearly a hundred illustrations by the best artists. One vol., large imperial 16mo., handsomely bound, 6s. Among the contributors to this volume are Mr. Maxwell Lyte, C.B.; the Hon. Alfred Lyttleton, Dr. Montagu Butler, Mr. P. Thornton, M.P.; Mr. Lees Knowles, M.P.; his Honour Judge Thomas Hughes, Q.C.; the Earl of Selborne, Mr. H. Lee Warner, Mr. G. R. Parker, Mr. A. G. Bradley, Mr. E. Scot Skirving, Rev. L. S. Milford, Mr. E. M. Oakley, Mr. Leonard Huxley, and Mr. Mowbray Morris.

'No one who has been, is, or expects to be at a public school should be happy till he gets it.'—*Westmorland Gazette.*

ROUND THE WORKS OF OUR GREAT RAILWAYS.

London and North-Western Works at Crewe. Midland Railway Works at Derby. Great-Northern Railway Works at Doncaster. Great-Western Railway Works at Swindon. Great-Eastern Railway Works at Stratford. North-Eastern Railway and its Engines. North British Railway Works. With over one hundred Illustrations. The papers are in nearly every case contributed by officials of the Companies, and the illustrations from official photographs. One vol., crown 8vo., 3s. 6d.

'Their authors are well-known men; the essays are well written and well illustrated from official photographs. This interesting little work will be read with pleasure by both railway men and the travelling public.'—*Railway Herald.*

Volume X. of THE ENGLISH ILLUSTRATED MAGAZINE.

October, 1892—September, 1893. With nearly one thousand pages, and one thousand illustrations. Super-royal 8vo., handsomely bound, 8s.

'Decidedly the best and most continuously readable of any volume of its class. . . . This volume is richer in its contents than any of those that went before, and is in the best way fitted to secure universal approval.'—*Irish Times.*

WILD FLOWERS IN ART AND NATURE.

An entirely new and beautifully illustrated work, to be completed in six parts. By J. C. L. SPARKES, Principal of the National Art Training School, South Kensington, and F. W. BURBIDGE, Curator of the University Botanical Gardens, Dublin. Each part contains three or four beautiful coloured plates of Flowers from water-colours specially drawn for the work by Mr. H. G. MOON. In order to do full justice to the plates and enable the Flowers to be represented in their full natural size, each part is printed on royal quarto paper, and enclosed in a stout wrapper. Price of each part, 2s. 6d. Subscription to the six parts, 15s. post free. It is intended to publish the complete series in one volume, handsomely bound for presentation, in cloth gilt, price One Guinea.

'The lithographic representations of these flowers (in Part I.) in colour are very successful, and the work promises to be an attractive as well as useful one.'—*The Field.*

WINE GLASSES AND GOBLETS of the Sixteenth, Seventeenth, and Eighteenth Centuries. By ALBERT HARTSHORNE. With many full-page plates and smaller illustrations. In course of preparation.

THE CHESS POCKET-MANUAL. By G. H. D. Gossip, Author of 'Theory of the Chess Openings,' etc. A complete handy guide to the rules, openings, and best methods of play. Small 8vo., cloth, 2s. 6d.

'Combines brevity with fulness perhaps more successfully than any similar work to be had.'—*Pall Mall Gazette.*

FIFTY BREAKFASTS. Containing a great variety of new and simple Recipes for Breakfast Dishes. By Colonel Kenney Herbert ('Wyvern'), Author of 'Culinary Jottings,' etc. Small 8vo., 2s. 6d.

'Colonel Herbert's book is one of the best of its kind, for it is thoroughly practical from beginning to end.'—*Speaker.*

HISTORY, PHILOSOPHY, AND SCIENCE.

ENGLAND IN EGYPT. By Alfred Milner, formerly Under-Secretary for Finance in Egypt. New Edition, crown 8vo., with map, 7s. 6d.

'An admirable book which should be read by those who have at heart the honour of England.'—*Times.*

MY MISSION TO ABYSSINIA. By the late Sir Gerald H. Portal, K.C.M.G., C.B., Her Majesty's Consul-General for British East Africa. With photogravure portrait, map, and numerous illustrations. Demy 8vo., 15s.

'The dangers to which the mission was constantly exposed, and the calmness and courage with which they were faced, are simply and modestly recorded, whilst we obtain also much light as to the habits and characteristics of the Abyssinians as a nation.'—*United Service Institution Journal.*

THE POLITICAL VALUE OF HISTORY. By W. E. H. Lecky, D.C.L., LL.D. An Address delivered at the Midland Institute, reprinted with additions. Crown 8vo., cloth, 2s. 6d.

'It should be read by all students of history and political science.'—*Cambridge Review.*

THE CULTIVATION AND USE OF IMAGINATION. By the Right Hon. GEORGE JOACHIM GOSCHEN. Crown 8vo., cloth, 2s. 6d.

'The book is full of excellent advice attractively put.'—*Speaker.*

THE RIDDLE OF THE UNIVERSE. Being an Attempt to determine the First Principles of Metaphysics considered as an Inquiry into the Conditions and Import of Consciousness. By EDWARD DOUGLAS FAWCETT. One vol., demy 8vo., 14s.

'We are agreeably impressed with the intellectual power and philosophical grasp of the author, as well as with the evidence of his high literary attainments. . . . The first part of the work is critical, and lucidly sets forth the landmarks in the history of modern philosophy; this is exceedingly well done. . . . One of the best parts of the book is that devoted to the criticism of materialism.'—*Westminster Gazette.*

LOTZE'S PHILOSOPHICAL OUTLINES. Dictated Portions of the Latest Lectures (at Göttingen and Berlin) of Hermann Lotze. Translated and edited by GEORGE T. LADD, Professor of Philosophy in Yale College. About 180 pages in each volume. Crown 8vo., cloth, 4s. each. Vol. I. Metaphysics. Vol. II. Philosophy of Religion. Vol. III. Practical Philosophy. Vol. IV. Psychology. Vol. V. Æsthetics. Vol. VI. Logic.

'No man of letters, no specialist in science, no philosopher, no theologian but would derive incalculable benefit from the thorough study of Lotze's system of philosophy.'—*Spectator.*

THE SOUL OF MAN. An Investigation of the Facts of Physiological and Experimental Psychology. By Dr. PAUL CARUS. With 150 illustrative cuts and diagrams. Large crown 8vo., cloth, 12s. 6d.

'A most interesting book, subtle and thoughtful, charged with lofty aspirations.'—*Literary World.*

HOMILIES OF SCIENCE. By Dr. PAUL CARUS, Editor of *The Open Court*, Author of 'The Soul of Man.' Large crown 8vo., cloth, 6s. 6d.

'This book may be read with intellectual and moral profit.'—*Manchester Guardian.*

POLITICAL SCIENCE AND COMPARATIVE CONSTITUTIONAL LAW. By JOHN W. BURGESS, Ph.D., LL.D., Dean of the University Faculty of Political Science in Columbia College, U.S.A. In two volumes. Demy 8vo., cloth, 25s.

'The work is full of keen analysis and suggestive comment, and may be confidently recommended to all serious students of comparative politics and jurisprudence.'—*Times.*

THE MARK IN EUROPE AND AMERICA. A Review of the Discussion on Early Land Tenure. By ENOCH A. BRYAN, A.M., President of Vincennes University, Indiana. Crown 8vo., cloth, 4s. 6d.

HARVARD HISTORICAL MONOGRAPHS. Vol. I. The Veto Power: Its Origin, Development, and Function in the Government of the United States. By EDWARD CAMPBELL MASON. Demy 8vo., paper, 5s. Vol. II. An Introduction to the Study of Federal Government. By ALBERT BUSHNELL HART, Ph.D. Demy 8vo., paper, 5s.

BETTERMENT. Being the Law of Special Assessment for Benefits in America, with some observations on its adoption by the London County Council. By ARTHUR A. BAUMANN, B.A., Barrister-at-Law, formerly Member of Parliament for Peckham. Crown 8vo., cloth, 2s. 6d.

'Should be read by every ratepayer of the Metropolis.'—*St. James's Gazette.*

THE LAW RELATING TO SCHOOLMASTERS. A Manual for the Use of Teachers, Parents, and Governors. By HENRY W. DISNEY, B.A., Barrister-at-Law of the Inner Temple. Crown 8vo., cloth, 2s. 6d.

'This manual should be in the hands of every schoolmaster.'—*Law Journal.*

SIX YEARS OF UNIONIST GOVERNMENT, 1886-1892. By C. A. WHITMORE, M.P. Post 8vo., cloth, 2s. 6d.

'Not only of ephemeral but of lasting interest.'—*Dublin Evening Mail.*

'MODERN MEN' FROM THE 'NATIONAL OBSERVER.' Literary Portraits of the most prominent men of the day. Two volumes in the series are now ready. Crown 8vo., paper, 1s. each.

'All of these sketches are good, admirable alike for the matter and the manner in which it is put, and show a faculty for judging men which is uncommon in these days.'—*Graphic.*

A GENERAL ASTRONOMY. By CHARLES A. YOUNG, Professor of Astronomy in the College of New Jersey, Associate of the Royal Astronomical Society, Author of *The Sun*, etc. In one vol., 550 pages, with 250 illustrations, and supplemented with the necessary tables. Royal 8vo., half morocco, 12s. 6d.

'A grand book by a grand man. The work should become a text-book wherever the English language is spoken, for no abler, no more trustworthy compilation of the kind has ever appeared for the advantage of students in any line of higher education.'—*Professor Piazzi Smyth.*

PLANT ORGANIZATION. By R. H. WARD, Professor of Botany in the Rensselaer Polytechnic Institute. 4to., flexible boards, 4s. This volume consists of a synoptical review of the general structure and morphology of plants, clearly drawn out according to biological principles, fully illustrated, and accompanied by a set of blank forms to be filled in as exercises by the pupils.

'The order of its arrangement, and the fulness and clearness of the printed hints and directions which introduce the main section of the book, render it a work of high value to a beginner in the study of botany, and of great use for classes.'—*Scotsman.*

A HISTORICAL GEOGRAPHY. By the late Dr. MORRISON, New edition, revised and largely rewritten by W. L. CARRIE, English Master at George Watson's College, Edinburgh. Crown 8vo., cloth, 3s. 6d.

'The style of the book is as good as its method, making it quite as interesting for mere reading as it is valuable for study and for school purposes.'—*School Board Chronicle.*

BY D. H. MONTGOMERY.

THE LEADING FACTS OF ENGLISH HISTORY. With Maps and Tables. Crown 8vo., cloth, 6s.

'A clear and intelligent idea of the main facts of English history in connection with the social and industrial development of the nation.'—*Professor Goldwin Smith.*

THE LEADING FACTS OF FRENCH HISTORY. With Maps and Tables. Crown 8vo., cloth, 6s.

'The right books have been consulted, the facts and views are well up to date, and the language itself is bright and attractive.'—*Educational Times.*

THE LEADING FACTS OF AMERICAN HISTORY. With numerous maps and illustrations. Crown 8vo., half morocco, 5s. 6d.

'Historical instruction is seldom so interesting in book form as it is in Mr. Montgomery's "Leading Facts of American History." It is as entertaining as a good story-book, yet faithful to the author's three chief objects, "accuracy of statement, simplicity of style, and impartiality of treatment." The numerous woodcuts and maps, some of which are from old and curious sources, are excellently illustrative of this capital compendium of American History.'—*Saturday Review.*

THE INTERNATIONAL EDUCATION SERIES.

THE INFANT MIND; or, Mental Development in the Child. Translated from the German of W. PREYER, Professor of Physiology in the University of Jena. Crown 8vo., cloth, 4s. 6d.

ENGLISH EDUCATION IN THE ELEMENTARY AND SECONDARY SCHOOLS. By ISAAC SHARPLESS, LL.D., President of Haverford College, U.S.A. Crown 8vo., cloth, 4s. 6d.

'The whole of the chapter "The Training of Teachers" is excellent. Excellent, too, is the chapter on the great public schools—full of keen observation and sound good sense. Indeed, the whole of the book is as refreshing as a draught of clear spring water.'—*Educational Times.*

EMILE; or, a Treatise on Education. By JEAN JACQUES ROUSSEAU. Translated and Edited by W. H. PAYNE, Ph.D., LL.D., President of the Peabody Normal College, U.S.A. Crown 8vo., cloth, 6s.

'The book is well translated and judiciously annotated.'—*Literary World.*

EDUCATION FROM A NATIONAL STANDPOINT. Translated from the French of ALFRED FOUILLÉE by W. J. GREENSTREET, M.A., Head Master of the Marling School, Stroud. Crown 8vo., cloth, 7s. 6d.

'The reader will rise from the study of this brilliant and stimulating book with a sense of gratitude to M. Fouillée for the forcible manner in which the difficulties we must all have felt are stated, and for his admirable endeavours to construct a workable scheme of secondary education.'—*Journal of Education.*

THE MORAL INSTRUCTION OF CHILDREN. By FELIX ADLER, President of the Ethical Society of New York. Crown 8vo., cloth, 6s.

'A work which should find a place on every educated parent's bookshelves.'—*Parent's Review.*

THE PHILOSOPHY OF EDUCATION. By JOHANN KARL ROSENKRANZ, Doctor of Theology and Professor of Philosophy at Königsberg. (Translated.) Crown 8vo., cloth, 6s.

A HISTORY OF EDUCATION. By Professor F. V. N. PAINTER. Crown 8vo., 6s.

THE VENTILATION AND WARMING OF SCHOOL BUILDINGS. With Plans and Diagrams. By GILBERT B. MORRISON. Crown 8vo., 3s. 6d.

FROEBEL'S 'EDUCATION OF MAN.' Translated by W. N. HAILMAN. Crown 8vo., 6s.

ELEMENTARY PSYCHOLOGY AND EDUCATION. By Dr. J. BALDWIN. Illustrated, crown 8vo., 6s.

THE SENSES AND THE WILL. Forming Part I. of 'The Mind of the Child.' By W. PREYER, Professor of Physiology in the University of Jena. (Translated.) Crown 8vo., 6s.

THE DEVELOPMENT OF THE INTELLECT. Forming Part II. of 'The Mind of the Child.' By Professor W. PREYER. (Translated.) Crown 8vo., 6s.

HOW TO STUDY GEOGRAPHY. By FRANCIS W. PARKER. Crown 8vo., 6s.

A HISTORY OF EDUCATION IN THE UNITED STATES. By RICHARD A. BOONE, Professor of Pedagogy in Indiana University. Crown 8vo., 6s.

EUROPEAN SCHOOLS; Or, What I Saw in the Schools of Germany, France, Austria, and Switzerland. By L. R. KLEMM, Ph.D. With numerous illustrations. Crown 8vo., 8s. 6d.

PRACTICAL HINTS FOR TEACHERS. By GEORGE HOWLAND, Superintendent of the Chicago Schools. Crown 8vo., 4s. 6d.

SCHOOL SUPERVISION. By J. L. PICKARD. 4s. 6d.

HIGHER EDUCATION OF WOMEN IN EUROPE. By HELENE LANGE. 4s. 6d.

HERBART'S TEXT-BOOK IN PSYCHOLOGY. By M. K. SMITH. 4s. 6d.

PSYCHOLOGY APPLIED TO THE ART OF TEACHING. By Dr. J. BALDWIN.

GENERAL LITERATURE.

THE LIFE, ART, AND CHARACTERS OF SHAKESPEARE. By HENRY N. HUDSON, LL.D., Editor of *The Harvard Shakespeare*, etc. 969 pages, in two vols., large crown 8vo., cloth, 21s.

'They deserve to find a place in every library devoted to Shakespeare, to editions of his works, to his biography, or to the works of commentators.'—*The Athenæum.*

THE HARVARD EDITION OF SHAKESPEARE'S COMPLETE WORKS. A fine Library Edition. By HENRY N. HUDSON, LL.D., Author of 'The Life, Art, and Characters of Shakespeare.' In twenty volumes, large crown 8vo., cloth, £6. Also in ten volumes, £5.

'An edition of Shakespeare to which Mr. Hudson's name is affixed does not need a line from anybody to commend it.'—*Oliver Wendell Holmes.*

THE BEST ELIZABETHAN PLAYS. Edited, with an Introduction, by WILLIAM R. THAYER. 612 pages, large crown 8vo., cloth, 7s. 6d.

'A useful edition, slightly expurgated.'—*Times.*

THE DEFENSE OF POESY, otherwise known as AN APOLOGY FOR POETRY. By Sir PHILIP SIDNEY. Edited by A. S. COOK, Professor of English Literature in Yale University. Crown 8vo., cloth, 4s. 6d.

'A more scholarly piece of workmanship could hardly have been produced. We have never seen a better student's manual.'—*Westminster Review.*

Leigh Hunt's 'WHAT IS POETRY?' An Answer to the Question, 'What is Poetry?' including Remarks on Versification. By LEIGH HUNT. Edited, with notes, by Professor A. S. COOK. Crown 8vo., cloth, 2s. 6d. This is the first essay in Leigh Hunt's 'Imagination and Fancy,' which is among the very best of his prose works.

A DEFENCE OF POETRY. By PERCY BYSSHE SHELLEY. Edited, with notes and introduction, by Professor A. S. COOK. Crown 8vo., cloth, 2s. 6d.

SELECTIONS IN ENGLISH PROSE FROM ELIZABETH TO VICTORIA. Chosen and arranged by JAMES M. GARNETT, M.A., LL.D. 700 pages, large crown 8vo., cloth, 7s. 6d.

'Mr. Garnett has made his selection for the most part with judgment and good taste.'—*National Observer.*

BEN JONSON'S TIMBER. Edited by Professor F. E. SCHELLING. Crown 8vo., cloth, 4s.

'For strength, sense, and learning, there are not many books in English literature that can beat this.'—*Saturday Review.*

THE PRACTICAL ELEMENTS OF RHETORIC. By JOHN F. GENUNG, Ph.D., Professor of Rhetoric in Amherst College. Crown 8vo., cloth, 7s.

'A useful and interesting book on a subject that ought to be especially useful and interesting to an age and nation like our own.'—*Professor J. E. Nixon, King's College, Cambridge.*

A HANDBOOK TO DANTE. By GIOVANNI A. SCARTAZZINI. Translated from the Italian, with notes and additions, by THOMAS DAVIDSON, M.A. Crown 8vo., cloth, 6s. The Handbook is divided into two parts, the first treating of Dante's Life; the second, of his Works. In neither is there omitted any really important fact. To every section is appended a valuable Bibliography.

'This handbook gives us just what we require—a faithful representation of the man—his life, his love, his history, and his work.'—*Perth Advertiser.*

DANTE'S ELEVEN LETTERS. Translated and Edited by the late C. S. LATHAM. With a Preface by Professor CHARLES ELIOT NORTON. Crown 8vo., cloth, 6s.

'An interesting and serviceable contribution to Dante literature.'—*Athenæum.*

SPANISH IDIOMS, WITH THEIR ENGLISH EQUIVALENTS. Embracing nearly 10,000 phrases. By SARAH CARY BECKER and Señor FEDERICO MORA. 8vo., cloth, 10s.

'This is a most useful combination of a phrase-book and a dictionary. It gives in tabular form the various usages of the verbs and other parts of speech most commonly employed in Spanish. Thus, while many of the phrases might be committed to memory by one learning the language for colloquial purposes, others will serve to explain the numerous idiomatic expressions found in Spanish literature.'—*E. Armstrong, Esq., M.A., Fellow and Lecturer of Queen's College, Oxford.*

ORIENTAL LITERATURE.

OMARAH'S HISTORY OF YAMAN. The Arabic Text, edited, with a translation, by HENRY CASSELS KAY, Member of the Royal Asiatic Society. Demy 8vo., cloth, 17s. 6d. net.

'Mr. Kay is to be heartily congratulated on the completion of a work of true scholarship and indubitable worth.'—*Athenæum.*

LANMAN'S SANSKRIT READER. New Edition, with Vocabulary and Notes. By CHARLES ROCKWELL LANMAN, Professor of Sanskrit in Harvard College. For use in colleges and for private study. Royal 8vo., cloth, 10s. 6d. For the convenience of those who possess the old edition, the Notes are also issued separately. 5s.

'The publication of the long-expected Notes to Professor Lanman's "Sanskrit Reader," completes a work for which every beginner of Sanskrit, and not less every teacher of it in America and England must be thankful.'—*Classical Review.*

HARVARD ORIENTAL SERIES. Edited, with the co-operation of various Scholars, by CHARLES ROCKWELL LANMAN, Professor of Sanskrit in the Harvard University. Vol. I.—The Jātaka-Mālā; or, Bodhisattvāvadāna-Mālā. By ARYA-CŪRA. Edited by Dr. HENDRIK KERN, Professor in the University of Leyden, with Preface, Text, and Various Readings. Royal 8vo., cloth, 6s. net.

'The names of Professor Lanman and of Dr. Kern are a sufficient guarantee for the sound and accurate scholarship of this edition of the "Jātaka-Mālā." The Sanskrit text leaves nothing to be desired; the type is clear and readable, the printing and paper excellent.'—*Asiatic Quarterly*.

Vol. II.—Kapila's Aphorisms of the Sāmkhya Philosophy, with the commentary of Vijñāna-bhiksu. Edited in the original Sanskrit by RICHARD GARBE, Professor in the University of Königsberg. [*In the press.*

A SANSKRIT PRIMER. Based on the *Leitfaden für den Elementarcursus des Sanskrit* of Professor Georg Bühler of Vienna. With Exercises and Vocabularies by EDWARD DELAVAN PERRY, Ph.D., of Columbia College, New York. 8vo., cloth, 8s.

'It ought to prove a very useful book to beginners of Sanskrit. With its aid students should be able to acquire a practical knowledge of Sanskrit in a shorter time than any other elementary Sanskrit book known to me could enable them to do.'—*A. A. Macdonell, Esq., Deputy Professor of Sanskrit, Oxford University*.

THE RIGVEDA. The oldest literature of the Indians. By ADOLF KAEGI, Professor in the University of Zürich. Authorised translation by R. ARROWSMITH, Ph.D. 8vo., cloth, 7s. 6d.

'Arrowsmith's translation of Kaegi's "Rigveda" I have found, on comparing two or three passages with the original German, to be perfectly trustworthy. It is a book that every student of the "Veda" should possess, as no other work gives so condensed an account of the "Rigveda," and of the literature bearing on it.'—*A. A. Macdonell, Esq., Deputy Professor of Sanskrit, Oxford University*.

PUBLICATIONS OF THE INDIA OFFICE AND OF THE GOVERNMENT OF INDIA. Mr. EDWARD ARNOLD, having been appointed Publisher to the Secretary of State for India in Council, has now on sale the above publications at 37 Bedford Street, Strand, and is prepared to supply full information concerning them on application.

INDIAN GOVERNMENT MAPS. Any of the Maps in this magnificent series can now be obtained at the shortest notice from Mr. EDWARD ARNOLD, Publisher to the India Office.

BOOKS FOR THE YOUNG.

MEN OF MIGHT. Studies of Great Characters. By A. C. BENSON, M.A., and H. F. W. TATHAM, M.A., Assistant Masters at Eton College. Crown 8vo., cloth, 3s. 6d.

CONTENTS:

Socrates.
Mahomet.
St. Bernard.
Savonarola.
Michael Angelo.

Carlo Borromeo.
Fénelon.
John Wesley.
George Washington.
Henry Martyn.

Dr. Arnold.
Livingstone.
General Gordon.
Father Damien.

'Models of what such compositions should be; full of incident and anecdote, with the right note of enthusiasm, where it justly comes in, with little if anything of direct sermonizing, though the moral for an intelligent lad is never far to seek. It is a long time since we have seen a better book for youngsters.'—*Guardian*.

THE BATTLES OF FREDERICK THE GREAT; Extracts from Carlyle's 'History of Frederick the Great.' Edited by CYRIL RANSOME, M.A., Professor of History in the Yorkshire College, Leeds. With a Map specially drawn for this work, Carlyle's original Battle-Plans, and Illustrations by ADOLPH MENZEL. Cloth, imperial 16mo., 3s.

'Carlyle's battle-pieces are models of care and of picturesque writing, and it was a happy thought to disinter them from the bulk of the "History of Frederick." The illustrations are very spirited.'—*Journal of Education*.

FRIENDS OF THE OLDEN TIME. By ALICE GARDNER, Lecturer in History at Newnham College, Cambridge. Illustrated, square 8vo., 2s. 6d.

A capital little book for children, whose interest in history it is desired to stimulate by lively and picturesque narratives of the lives of heroes, and the nobler aspects of heroic times. Leonidas and Pericles, Solon and Socrates, Camillus and Hannibal, the Gracchi and Alexander, form the subject of Miss Gardner's animated recitals, which possess all the charm of simplicity and clearness that should belong to stories told to children.'—*Saturday Review*.

LAMB'S ADVENTURES OF ULYSSES. With an Introduction by ANDREW LANG. Third and Fourth Thousand. Square 8vo., cloth, 1s. 6d. Also the Prize Edition, gilt edges, 2s.

'Boys in reading the story of the hero's wanderings find in it the same sort of charm that attracts them in "Robinson Crusoe."'—*Manchester Guardian.*

ETHICS FOR YOUNG PEOPLE. By C. C. EVERETT, Professor of Theology in Harvard University. Crown 8vo., cloth, 2s. 6d. OUTLINE OF CONTENTS : Chaps. 1-10, Morality in General ; Chaps. 11-20, Duties towards One's self ; Chaps. 21-29, Duties towards Others ; Chaps. 30-36, Helps and Hindrances.

'A series of essays on the generally-recognised virtues and the commoner faults to which the young are liable. It has a truly educative tendency, and is one of a type of book that we should be glad to see more frequently studied in our schools.'—*Guardian.*

A NEW SCHOOL HISTORY OF ENGLAND. By C. W. OMAN, M.A., All Soul's College, Oxford, Author of 'Warwick the Kingmaker,' etc. [*In preparation.*

RICHARD II. Edited by R. BRINSLEY JOHNSON. Small crown 8vo., cloth, 1s.

A MIDSUMMER NIGHT'S DREAM. Edited by BRINSLEY JOHNSON. Small crown 8vo., cloth, 1s.

These are the first volumes of *Arnold's School Shakespeare*, and will be followed immediately by *The Merchant of Venice*, *Julius Cæsar*, and other Plays. The text is that of the Globe Edition, through the kind permission of Messrs. Macmillan and Co.

This series is under the general editorship of Mr. J. Churton Collins.

TALES FROM HANS ANDERSEN. With nearly Forty original illustrations by E. A. LEMANN. One vol., foolscap 4to., handsomely bound in cloth gilt, 7s. 6d.

'The artist has entered into the spirit of these most delightful of fairy tales, and makes the book specially attractive by its dainty and descriptive illustrations.'—*Saturday Review.*

BARE ROCK; or, The Island of Pearls. A Book of Adventure for Boys. By HENRY NASH. With numerous full-page and other illustrations by LANCELOT SPEED. Large crown 8vo., over 400 pages, handsomely bound, gilt edges, 6s.

'A book vastly to our taste— a book to charm all boys, and renew the boy in all who have ever been boys. There are all kinds of delights—a shipwreck, a desert island, a Crusoe-like life enjoyed by two boys, a "surprise party" of savages, and a wonderful coil of exciting incidents among West African blacks.'—*Saturday Review.*

THE CHILDREN'S DICKENS. DAVID COPPERFIELD —THE OLD CURIOSITY SHOP—DOMBEY AND SON. Illustrated from the original plates, and abridged for the use of children by J. H. YOXALL. Square 8vo., cloth, 1s. 6d. each volume.

Also, specially bound for Prizes and Presents, with gilt edges, 2s. each.

'The books have been cut down to manageable length by the excision of passages unsuited to the comprehension of children, or unlikely to maintain their interest, the continuity of the story being preserved by the interpolation of short passages from the editor's pen, printed in italics. The work of compression is judiciously carried out, the type is bold and clear, and the illustrations are taken from the original plates.'—*Guardian.*

'The abridgments of Dickens seem to me excellent. It is the kind of thing that I have always longed for, and that I, in common with many other parents, probably have practically done by skipping while reading aloud. But it is delightful having it in this convenient form, in a book which one can put into the child's own hand.'—*Mrs. Hugh Bell.*

TWILIGHT THOUGHTS—CLAUDE'S POPULAR FAIRY STORIES. With a Preface by MATTHEW ARNOLD. Crown 8vo., cloth, 2s. 6d.

'There is nature and fable and pathos and morality in these stories, something for every taste.'—*From the Preface.*

THE NINE WORLDS. Stories from Norse Mythology. By MARY E. LITCHFIELD. Illustrated, crown 8vo., cloth, 3s.

'These short stories are intended for children, but the author hopes they will not be uninteresting to older persons. We suspect that the latter will enjoy them even more than the former.'—*Journal of Education.*

The Children's Favourite Series.

A charming Series of Juvenile Books, each plentifully illustrated, and written in simple language to please young readers. Special care is taken in the choice of thoroughly wholesome matter. Handsomely bound, and designed to form an attractive and entertaining Series of gift-books for presents and prizes.

PRICE TWO SHILLINGS EACH.

'A charming set of books, which will rejoice the hearts of mothers, teachers, and children.'—*Child Life.*

'Prettily bound, well illustrated, edited with much good sense, and are admirable for presents.'—*Tablet.*

MY BOOK OF FAIRY TALES.

'For children of seven or eight there could not be a better fairy-book.'—*British Weekly.*

MY BOOK OF BIBLE STORIES.

'Written so that the youngest child can understand them.'—*Saturday Review.*

MY BOOK OF HISTORY TALES.

'A splendid introduction to English history.'—*Methodist Times.*

DEEDS OF GOLD.

'A first-rate book for lads and lassies is this. Children cannot but be better for reading such splendid examples of the performance of duty as those illustrated in this book.'—*Schoolmistress.*

MY BOOK OF FABLES.

'A very good selection. The morals are rarely more than one line long, the type is large and clear, and the pictures are good.'—*Bookman.*

MY STORY-BOOK OF ANIMALS.

'This book will be found a favourite among the favourites.'—*The Lady.*

RHYMES FOR YOU AND ME.

'It is sometimes thought that slovenly verse is good enough for children, so long as the sentiment and intention are right. The compiler of this volume does not think so; his choice is seldom at fault.'—*Spectator.*

*** *Other Volumes of the Series are in course of preparation.*

EACH VOLUME CONTAINS ABOUT THIRTY ILLUSTRATIONS.

PRICE TWO SHILLINGS.

PERIODICALS.

THE FORUM. The great success of this Famous American Review, which holds a position in the United States equivalent to that of the *Nineteenth Century* in England, has justified the proprietors in carrying out a wish they have long entertained of reducing its price so as to render it the cheapest first-class Review in the world. With this year its price has been reduced to 1s. 3d. monthly; annual subscription, post free, 15s. A conspicuous feature in the Review is the prominence it gives to articles by European contributors, nearly every number containing articles by the best English writers. It is obtainable in England about the 10th of each month.

'Nothing that I could say would exaggerate my high opinion of the *Forum*, its scope, its management, the ability of its articles, and the importance of its influence.'—*Mrs. Lynn Linton.*

'There is scarcely a number which does not contain one or more striking papers.'—*Ven. Archdeacon Farrar, D.D.*

'In the rank of American periodical literature there can be no doubt that it takes a foremost position.'—*Professor Edmund Gosse.*

THE JOURNAL OF MORPHOLOGY : A Journal of Animal Morphology, devoted principally to Embryological, Anatomical, and Histological subjects. Edited by C. O. WHITMAN, Professor of Biology in Clark University, U.S.A. Three numbers in a volume, of 100 to 150 large 4to. pages, with numerous plates. Single numbers, 17s. 6d.; subscription to the volume of three numbers, 45s. Volumes I. to VII. can now be obtained, and the first number of Volume VIII. is ready.

'Everyone who is interested in the kind of work published in it knows it. It is taken by all the chief libraries of colleges, universities, etc., both in England and the Continent.'—*Professor Ray Lankester.*

THE PHILOSOPHICAL REVIEW. Edited by J. G. SCHURMAN, Professor of Philosophy in Cornell University, U.S.A. Six Numbers a year. Single Numbers, 3s. 6d.; Annual Subscription, 12s. 6d.

'Indispensable to the serious student of philosophy.'—*Leeds Mercury.*

AMERICAN PHILOLOGICAL ASSOCIATION, TRANSACTIONS OF THE.
Vols. I.—XXI. Containing Papers by Specialists on Ancient and Modern Languages and Literature. The price of the volumes is 10s. each, except Volumes XV. and XX., which are 12s. 6d. each. Volumes I. and II. are not sold separately. An Index of Authors and subjects to Vols. I.—XX. is issued, price 2s. 6d.

Mr. EDWARD ARNOLD'S *List of American Periodicals will be sent post free on application.*

L'AMARANTHE : Revue Littéraire, Artistique Illustrée.
Dédiée aux filles de France. A monthly Magazine containing original articles by the best French writers, specially intended for the perusal of young people. 1s. monthly; annual subscription, including postage, 14s.

Index to Authors.

	PAGE
ADDERLEY.—Stephen Remarx	11
ADLER.—Instruction of Children	18
AMARANTHE (L').	28
AMERICAN PHILOLOGICAL ASSOCIATION	28
ARROWSMITH.—Rigveda	22
BAUMANN.—Betterment	15
BELL.—Poems	6
,, Name above every Name	7
BENSON.—Men of Might	23
BROWN.— Pleasurable Poultry Keeping	8
,, Poultry Keeping as an Industry	8
,, Industrial Poultry Keeping	9
BURBIDGE.—Wild Flowers in Art and Nature	12
BURGESS.—Political Science	14
CARUS.—Soul of Man	14
,, Homilies of Science	14
CHERBULIEZ.—The Tutor's Secret	10
CHILDREN'S FAVOURITE SERIES	26
CLAUDE.—Twilight Thoughts	25
CLIFFORD.—Love Letters	10
COOK.—Sidney's Defense of Poesy	20
,, Shelley's Defence of Poetry	20
CUSTANCE.—Riding Recollections	6
DAVIDSON—Handbook to Dante	21

	PAGE
DICKENS, CHILDREN'S	25
DISNEY.—Law relating to Schoolmasters	15
ENGLISH ILLUSTRATED MAGAZINE	12
EVERETT.—Ethics for Young People	24
FAWCETT.—Hartmann the Anarchist	10
,, Riddle of the Universe	14
FORUM	27
FOWLER.—Old County Life	6
GARDNER.—Friends of Olden Time	23
GARBE—Kapila's Aphorisms	22
GARNETT.—English Prose Selections	20
GAUNT.—Dave's Sweetheart	10
GOSCHEN.—Use of Imagination	14
GOSSIP.—Chess Manual	13
GREAT PUBLIC SCHOOLS	11
GREENSTREET.—Fouillée's Education	17
HANS ANDERSEN.—Tales from	24
HARTSHORNE.— Glasses and Goblets	12

	PAGE
HARVARD.—Historical Monographs	15
„ Oriental Series	22
HERBERT,—Fifty Breakfasts	13
HOLE.—Little Tour in Ireland	7
„ Addresses to Working Men	7
„ Memories	7
„ Book about Garden	7
„ Book about Roses	7
HUDSON.—Characters of Shakespeare	19
„ Harvard Shakespeare	19
HUTCHINSON,—That Fiddler Fellow	10
INDIA OFFICE PUBLICATIONS	22
INTERNATIONAL EDUCATION SERIES	17
JOHNSON.—Richard II.	24
„ Midsummer Night's Dream	24
KAY.—Omarah's Yaman	21
KERN.—Jātaka Mālā	22
LAMB.—Adventures of Ulysses	24
LANMAN.—Sanskrit Reader	21
LATHAM,—Dante's Letters	21
LECKY.—Value of History	13
LE FANU,—Irish Life	5
LOTZE.—Philosophical Outlines	14
'MEDICINE LADY, THE,' authors of.—This Troublesome World	9
MILNER.—England in Egypt	13
Modern Men	15
MORGAN.—Animal Life	8
„ Animal Sketches	8
MORGAN.—Springs of Conduct	8
MORPHOLOGY, JOURNAL OF	27
MORRISON.—Historical Geography	16
NASH.—Bare Rock	25
OMAN.—History of England	24
PAYNE.—Rosseau's Emile	17
PERRY.—Sanskrit Primer	22
PHILOSOPHICAL REVIEW	27
PORTAL.—Mission to Abyssinia	13
PREYER.—Infant Mind	17
RANSOME.—Battles of Frederick the Great	23
RODD.—Poems	9
„ Feda	9
„ Unknown Madonna	9
„ Violet Crown	9
„ Customs of Modern Greece	9
Round the Works of our Railways	12
SANTLEY.—Student and Singer	6
SCARTAZZINI.—Handbook to Dante	21
SCHELLING.—Jonson's Timber	20
SHARPLESS.—English Education	17
SHELLEY.—Defence of Poetry	20
SIDNEY,—Defense of Poesy	20
SPARKES.—Wild Flowers in Art	12
TATHAM.—Men of Might	23
THAYER.—Elizabethan Plays	20
TWINING.—Recollections of a Social Worker	5
WHITMORE.—Unionist Government	15
Winchester College	11
YOUNG.—General Astronomy	16

www.ingramcontent.com/pod-product-compliance
Lightning Source LLC
Chambersburg PA
CBHW051737300426
44115CB00007B/605